Dave Mills' autobiography is as entertaining as it is inspiring. If you, or a parent or grandparent, grew up in the 1940s and '50s, came of age in the '60s, and lived a life of faith, family, service, and freedom, then this easy-to-read account of Dave's life will resonate with you. You will understand his devotion to family, his service to community and to the honorable defense of our country, as well as his enormous enjoyment of the great outdoors through hunting, fishing, and camping. This is a good read for anyone who shares Dave's great American values, both for those lucky to have known him through the years, and just as much, for those now making his acquaintance.

—Paul C. Kettler, friend, and shooting companion of the Bremerton Trap and Skeet Club

This is a very well written account of a young man's journey growing up in the 1940's, 50's and 60's. I highly recommend this book as excellent reading for people of all ages

—Mike Haugen, CK class of '63

"What Happened To The America I Grew Up In?" is a unique and refreshingly candid chronicle of David Mills' journey through life guided by the hand of God.

David has a conversational writing style that makes you feel you're sitting across from him while he tells you stories about his travels and hunting and fishing adventures.

Most any outdoorsman can spin a good yarn, but none better than David.

—Al Montinger, West High class of '63, Lifelong friend and skeet shooting partner.

David Conrad Mills and I met in 1957 at Coontz Middle School in Bremerton, WA. Along with Fred Kegel, we've bonded during unlimited fishing, hunting, crabbing, and geoduck trips ever since.

David has always impressed me with the details he can remember from every trip. He has a memory like a steel trap. While reading his book, my wife and I were both either laughing out loud or crying real tears. The book is full of hilarious adventures and tender stories of touching moments between David, his Savior Jesus Christ, family, and friends. This is a wonderful book for all ages.

—Jim & Kris Bennett

What Happened To The America I Grew Up In?
Updated Edition, published 2023

Written by David Conrad Mills
Edited by Jacquie Wagner
Cover art by Reprospace, LLC

Copyright © 2023

Paperback ISBN 13: 978-1-95-268554-5
Hardcover ISBN 13: 978-1-95-268557-6

The author has done his best to obtained permissions for the pictures and content contained herein.

All rights reserved. No part of this book may be reproduced or transmitted in any form or by any means, electronic or mechanical, including photocopying, recording or by any information storage and retrieval system, without written permission from the author, except for the inclusion of brief quotations in a review.

KITSAP PUBLISHING

Published by Kitsap Publishing
Poulsbo, WA 98370
www.KitsapPublishing.com

Dedication

I have dedicated this book to:

the memory of my grandparents
Conrad George & Myrtle Fairbanks Mills and John & Bessie Talich;

my parents Donald and Gail;

my two boys: Douglas, his wife Susie, and their son Conrad, and Derek, his wife Jennifer, and their daughter, Sophia, and son, Davis.

But most of all, to my loving wife, Dalene, who has been blessed with an extraordinary amount of unconditional love.

Dalene, I love you.

Table of Contents

Dedication
Foreword
Introduction
Prologue
- Vacations
- Boy Scouts!
- Cruisin'

Family Life 1
- **Parents** 1
- **Mother** 2
- **Grandparents** 9
- **Father** 14
- **Brother Jim** 20
  - For My Brother 23

Married Life 26
- **Our Wedding** 26
  - May 28th, 1966
  - Pastor John Sara First Covenant Church 28
- **Our Life Renewed** 33
  - My Near-Death Experience in Fall 1969 33
  - Renewal 34
- **God's Provision ~ 1st Hand** 36
- **A "Death" in Our Church Life** 36
- **Phil Linden** 37
- **And Now as Parents of Adult Children** 39
  - Derek and Jennifer Meet 39
  - Meeting Jennifer's Parents / The Courtship Continues 39
  - Rehearsal Dinner / The Wedding 40
  - Doug and Susie: The Engagement Party 41
  - Thanksgiving 2012 at the Damon Hunt Club 42
  - Doug and Susie's Wedding 44

My Two Sons — 45
- "Not Everything, Ol' Man" — 47
- Family Memories — 48

Let me leave you with the following: — 52
- Douglas: — 52
- Derek: — 52
- (For You Both) Listen: — 53
- Mikey (Mike Neimann): — 54
- To all of 3 of you: — 55
- And For All 3 Couples — 56
- Sophia, Davis, and Conrad: — 58
- Sophia: — 58
- Davis: — 60
- Conrad: — 62
- Final Thoughts For Y'all — 67

Kid Life, Scouting Life, Youth Life — 68

Kid Life — 68
- Kid Life at Home & On Vacation — 68
- Mrs. Bandy — 72
- Kite Flying
- (and more on community) — 73
- At School — 74
- Always Sumpthin' To Do — 77
- Fishin' — 78
- My Bike and A Paper Route — 78
- Baseball — 80

Scouting Life — 81

Youth Life — 85
- Church — 85
- I was no angel — 86
- Sword Drills and Bible Memory Verse — 87
- Youth For Christ — 90
- Legalism and Stupidity — 91
- Covenant Beach and Island Lake — 94
- Also, a couple of notes that should not be left out: — 97

Working Life/College Life — 99

Working Life — 99
- Summer of '61
- (A Hobo's Life & Legal Lessons) — 99
- Alaskan Fishing Life — 104
- Jr. College and Logging — 110
- Fall 1964 ~ Summer '65 — 115
- USMC — 118
- The Rifle Range ~ BRASS — 121

   Officiating — 122
   Working Life Epilogue — 125

Hunting & Fishing Life — 126
Hunting Life — 126
   Stormy Night at Camp 5 — 129
   The Good Ol' Days — 131
   Columbus Day Storm — 132
   The T's — 135
   The Pigeon Tree
     (and how Jim became a "claimer") — 137
   George and the Bottle — 137
   Point Defiance in Moses Lake? — 140
   A Confrontation, A Duck Call, and A Calling — 145
   Fred and Barb, David and Dalene — 151
   Crab Creek — 154

Fishing Life — 157
   Seven Lakes Basin — 157
   Captain Puget and Elling Simonsen — 159
   Hot Shots — 163
   Hood Canal Was Our Playground — 165
   Westport and Kelpers — 169
   Steelhead, Salmon, and Boldt — 170
   A personal diatribe: — 171
   One final vent — 173
   Northwest Outdoors
   (northwestoutdors.com) — 175
   Some Final Memories
   (maybe) — 179
   Summing It Up ~ Courtesy of Bill Nylund — 180

Other Outdoor Life — 182
   Trailer Life — 182
   Giltner, Nebraska and the Talich Life — 184
   Skiing Life — 188
   Outdoor Gear and Clothing Then vs. Now — 189

Dahlia Life — 191
   How I Got Started Into Dahlias — 191

Life on the Colorado — 193
   The "Rookie" aka… — 193
   That Ain't No Jet — 195
   Flora and Fauna — 196
   ABC — 197
   Lava Falls — 200
   Forever Eddy — 201
   Killer Fangs Falls Rapid — 202
   Summing It Up? — 204

My 9 Lives and Saving Lives — 206
My 9 Lives — 206
- Dahlia Shears — 206
- Gun Point at Fircrest — 207
- Halibut Fishing with Howard — 209
- Ski Vacation Alta, Utah — 209
- Upper Quinault River — 210
- Fall Off the Roof — 210
- Hospital Trips ~ By Request — 211

Saving Lives — 215
- On the Bogy — 215
- Frog's Mayday Call — 215
- Build A Wall, Save a Life — 217
- Another Hospital Visit (not mine) — 218
- Another Chance Meeting? — 220
- The Plot Thickens — 221

Jesus Is My Life — 223
- Christians, Hypocrisy, and Confession — 223

Epilogue — 231
Acknowledgments — 231
Addendum — 236
Appendix — 240
The Simple, Good Life — 240
- Cooking Life — 240
- Final Thoughts on Food — 248

Reading Life — 249
- Great Reads (In No Particular Order) — 249
- My Bucket List — 251

Foreword

What Happened to the America I Grew Up In? is very engaging! It's very easy to read, but hard to put down.

This book brought back so many memories from my childhood - from a world so much simpler than today's. I've never fished or hunted in the Northwest, but David creates such vivid pictures in my mind that I wish I had, and in some ways, I felt I was right there with him.

The stories are entertaining and I felt like I grew up with him. His descriptions of the people and their relationships were so relatable. I loved the inspirational passages and how they relate to real life. They are just as important, if not more so, today as they were in the America he grew up in.

I'm anxious to get my hands on the next book by this author. Thanks for the uplifting journey!

Dave Nowak

Introduction

Looking back at my high school days, book reports were an integral part of English class. Of course, I never read ANY of the books I reported on; I would simply read the flap on the cover and submit that. Do you think the teachers ever figured it out? Not sure I even cared; that's how "into it" I was.

It wasn't until college that I actually read a book cover to cover ~ The Adventures of Tom Sawyer and then The Adventures of Huckleberry Finn. I was so taken by the writings of Mark Twain I started reading as many of his books as I could find. I spent time in the library looking for the memorable quotes for which he was much noted. At first blush, some of his quips seem light and airy, but they are truth nonetheless:

"The secret of getting ahead is getting started."

"Kindness is the language which the deaf can hear and the blind can see."

"If you tell the truth, you don't have to remember anything."

Toward the end of Twain's life, on the verge of bankruptcy, he traveled the world giving speaking engagements for which he was paid quite handsomely. At the end of one speech, the words were so profound it's a shame we have strayed from such a simple principle:

"Men will always vary in nature, race, creed, and desire. There will always be the belligerent and oppressed among us, but in our country we can and must hold fast to our ideal of democracy, because we've made it a shimmering reality. Let us cherish our proud tradition of freedom and tolerance. Let us vow that our tolerance will not become indifference and our freedom become license. Let us respect each other's rights and defend, with the pen if possible, or the sword if need be, our inalienable privilege to be a free and united people."

Those words should be front and center of every classroom across this great land we call the UNITED States of America.

During the late '40s, maybe it was the early '50s, my dad took me to a revival tent meeting where the young Billy Graham spoke. Billy Graham, without a doubt, was the most respected evangelist this world has ever known. At the time, I had no idea what was going on; to me, it was just an outdoor church service under a large tent. Looking back, I believe something stirred within me, which I will get to later. Over the years, I listened to many of his sermons from The Billy Graham Crusade telecast, and I often felt like he was speaking directly to me, one on one. His message was so simple; he preached nothing but the gospel ~ the good news:

"God proved His love on the cross. When Christ hung and bled and died, it was God saying to the world, 'I love you.'"

Those words continue to resonate within my conscience and deep within my soul.

Prologue

The Simple Life, the Good Life
(A quick, flying review ~ more detail later!)

{It should be noted parts of the stories might even be accurate. I have an uncommon ability to shuffle things in and out of what "did" happen and what I "wanted" to happen. Life's journey has seen oh-so-many twists, turns, highs and lows, but as I begin to write each new chapter, I realize God's hand has been with me all the way.}

I never kept a diary. Oh, I made several half-hearted stabs at it, which probably lasted all of a week, at most, but I never really saw much of a need for one. Didn't give much thought to memory loss... HAH! What a mistake that has turned out to be. I have a good friend, Fred Kegel, who has kept a journal for as long as I can remember. Of course, he's a civil engineer; I guess it's embedded in his DNA.

I've been struggling to write my life story over the past several years, but where oh where does a person begin?

Hmmm?

Let's see, how are these for opening lines?

"All this happened, more or less..." ~ nope, won't work, Salinger used it.

"A story has no beginning or end..." ~ good beginning, but G. Greene beat me to it.

"It was a dark and stormy night..." ~ we all know that one, don't we?

"The first thing you'll probably want to know is where I was born..." ~ Salinger already used it, but what the heck, here goes...

I was born July 15, 1944, in Bremerton, Washington to Donald and Gail (Talich) Mills. How the two met is quite a story in and of itself, but I'll save that for later. (See the Family Life section) YES, I'm a "war baby" and not a "baby boomer". I believe being a war baby shaped my life immensely; we can save that for later as well.

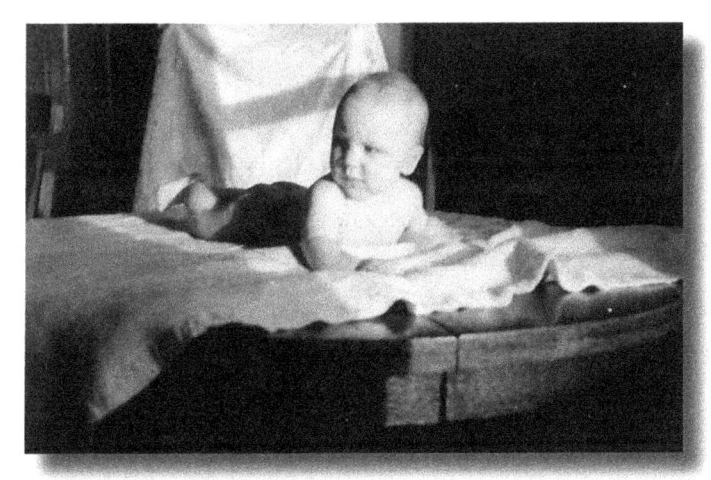

I was born at Harrison Memorial Hospital, when it was located on Chester Avenue; that was before its move to Marion Ave, then to Cherry on the "eastside", and now it's moving to Silverdale. Progress?

Mom and Dad made our first home on 13th St., behind the old TB and M grocery store, which was located on Kitsap Way and now is a Vape outlet. Dad was on the Bremerton city fire dept, and we were living outside city limits. The city, in its infinite wisdom and almighty display of muscle, mandated that all city employees must move within city limits. Mom and Dad then bought a house on Naval Ave, next to Evergreen Cemetery. What a playground that turned out to be!

The city's mandate, forcing employees to move within the city limits, was challenged in court, a common practice by today's standards, but not then. We eventually moved to National Avenue & B street in Navy Yard City, where I finished grade school at Navy Yard City Elementary, then attended Coontz Jr. High, and graduated from Bremerton's West High School. After an enlistment in the Marine Corps, and my marriage to Dalene, I graduated from the University of Puget Sound.

Life growing up in the '40s, '50s, and a portion of the '60s was so pure, so simple. We played marbles; I got a kaleidoscope for Christmas one year. Dad would always tell me a bedtime story. "The little boy that cried wolf" or "Jack in the beanstalk" … He would tell the story word for word; then every once in a while, he'd change the words tryin' to catch me. "No, Dad, Jack sold the cow for magic beans, not kernels of corn!" Before TV, we traveled the world through a "View-Master". I do remember a few radio broadcasts, but television added a new dimension.

I remember when television first made it into the average American home. My folks bought a huge console that consisted of a radio, a record turntable, and a whopping 10" television screen. There weren't many programs then, and I still remember Howard Kubli and I sitting in front of the TV staring at the "test-pattern". Remember the Indian in full headdress? {Editor's note: for those of you not old enough to remember, you can actually Google this!}

Serials on Saturday mornings were all about the cowboys ~ "The Lone Ranger", "Hopalong Cassidy", and "The Cisco Kid and Poncho". I loved Poncho. (I now have a framed photograph of the magnificent gate to his former casa.) When those shows came on, I immediately strapped on my twin cap-pistols, cowboy hat, and ruffled western shirt. I rode the range and fought the villains, side by side with my heroes.

I had heroes growing up. Hop-a-long Cassidy, Lone Ranger, Gene Autry, etc. Why did it take so long for me to see the real hero? God was preparing me my whole life; I just didn't know it. The haunting hymn ~ Amazing Grace ~ "I was blind, but now I see…" sums up my life.

Another great true-life western… "Death Valley Days" and, of course, the 20-mule team. I always tried counting to see if there really were 20 mules, but never finished. No stop action in those days. BTW, was I the only one thinking the "Lone Ranger" really was a ranger? Not until years later, when I saw him in an old-time western, did I realize he was just another actor. I was heartbroken.

A few years later, "Superman", "Sky King", and the "Mickey Mouse Club" entered the scene. The girls swooned over Spin and Marty. Do I need to mention the heartthrob for the boys? OK! Yes, it was Annette Funicello ~ WOW!

We also had great cartoons ~ "Popeye the Sailor Man", "The Adventures of Rocky & Bullwinkle and Friends", "Snidley Whiplash", and my favorite, "Mr. Peabody and Sherman".

We also had live local programs for kids:

"Sheriff Tex", "Brakeman Bill", and the iconic "King's Klubhouse" with Stan Boreson. The true stars of the show HAD TO BE the basset hounds "No-Mo" and "Miss Mo", along with Grandma Torvald, Pepita the Flea, and the singing phonograph, Victor Rolla. All that mattered in the 1950s was you'd make it home from school in time to see Stan play his accordion and sing the opening theme song: "Zero dockus, mucho crockus, hallaboolooza bub, that's the secret password that we use down at the club!"

Remember "Howdy Doody"?

"Iiiits Hoooow dee doooo dee time, its Hooo de dooo time..." was the opening song. And it had its cast of unique characters: Buffalo Bob, the mute Clarabell the Clown, and the beautiful Princess Summer Fall Winter Spring, puppets Kukla, Fran, and Ollie ~ the list is never-ending.

Good clean wholesome entertainment! Oh no, did I leave out "Wunda Wunda", "JP Patches", and "Captain Kangaroo"? Not really, I never liked those shows anyhoo - hehehe. (My editor thinks this is blasphemy!)

Night times were for homework and playing games. We played "pick-up-sticks" and "jacks". I vaguely remember a few of the old radio programs. Then TV was a family affair, nothing close to "Naked and Afraid". "Ed Sullivan", "Wonderful World of Disney", and who could forget Lawrence Welk with his bubble machine. Mom and Dad loved it, of course; it was painful for me.

Sundays were for church and afterward family dinner with Grandma and Grandpa, or an afternoon drive followed by a picnic at the city park or a lake in the country. The stories they would tell about growing up drew me in, but after the 100th time, hearing the same worn-out stories did get a little boring.

Immediate family and our church "family" dominated my formative years, and church at that time had a definite role in the community. No city league ball games of any kind were played on Sunday or Wednesday (Wed. was Bible study and prayer meeting night), and prayer before most games was pretty much routine.

The nightly news WAS news, and if a debate ensued or a differing point of view presented, it wasn't filled with contempt OR hate. There truly was respect for "my esteemed colleague on the other side of the aisle". Growing up, we had discipline and a deep respect for those in authority, but we also had a sense of morality and a strong work ethic.

Growing up in the Pacific NW, Thanksgiving was all about the family unit and a meal of roast turkey, dressing, mashed potatoes with giblet gravy, candied yams, and all the trimmings. Dessert always included a choice of apple and pumpkin pie.

A large gathering would include Mom, Dad, and the kids, grandparents, aunts and uncles, and cousins. It was a wonderful time to share memories of the previous year and reuniting with those we hadn't seen in a while. After dinner, the women would be in the kitchen doing the dishes; the men would sit around watching a football game and discussing politics. When they got bored, it seemed like they would instantly switch sides in the debate and never skip a beat. That's how I remember Thanksgiving.

Vacations

Yes, real family vacations, traveling in the family auto, not boarding a plane heading to Hawaii or some exotic location. Most families in the '40s and '50s visited state parks, our ocean beaches, and sometimes traveled to a national park, but it definitely was by auto and camping in tents.

When we went on vacation, it was in a 1940 Chev two-door coupe. Dad had the trunk so full he had to lash it down with rope and the back seat jammed to the point where I actually laid on the rear window ledge. And there was the pram on top of the car, which Dad artfully stuffed with a few more items. Quite often, on a stormy night, Dad needed to hold the tent upright to prevent getting blown over. Vacations were summertime affairs, which meant hot weather. The only air conditioning was an open window, and radiators in that day weren't anything to brag about, so there was a canvas water bag hung on the front bumper for when the radiator blew. Another thing about cars in the 40's & 50's - Rattles!

Every car we ever owned was full of rattles and they drove my parents nuts!

I remember my parents continually stuffing pieces of wadded up paper and match books from one side of the dashboard to the other. And the challenge to find the squeak was compounded by Road Noise!

Roads were nothing like the super-smooth highways of today. The roads even rattled.

Oh well, it kept my parents occupied…

My folks had steady jobs ~ Dad was a city fireman and Mom was a financial analyst at Puget Sound Naval Shipyard (PSNS) ~ albeit low paying, so we never left home with much money in case of an emergency. One time we were in Yellowstone National Park and my folks ran out of money. I mean, NOTHING! They had to wire home to Dad's parents for gas money to get back home.

Another time on the way home from Sun Lakes State Park in Eastern Washington, our car broke down in the small town of Soap Lake. Dad managed to limp to a small service station ~ Not just a gas station. In the '50s and well into the 60's we had service stations ~ honest to goodness service stations. An attendant would come to your car asking, "How can I help?" To which Dad would say, "Fill 'er up." After inserting the nozzle in the tank, the attendant lifted the hood to check the water and oil, and even wash ALL the windows. There was always the outside hope he'd forget about the gas hose and give us a bit extra, but that never happened.

Anyhow, we broke down in Soap Lake. I'm not sure what the problem was, but Mom and Dad didn't have much money and I heard Dad ask, "How much is this gonna cost me?"

The mechanic quoted a price and Dad said, "Say, how 'bout me trading you this cooler full of trout for the work?" The mechanic said, "Let me take a look." When Dad opened the icechest, the man's jaw must have hit the pavement.

"You've gotta be kidding; it's a deal! As a matter a fact, I'm gonna tell my wife I closed shop and went fishing. She's always after me to bring home some fish."

Boy Scouts!

Yes, let us not forget the Boy Scouts! My boy scout troop, complete with all the jamborees and the annual summertime 50-mile hikes exploring the Olympic mountains ~ unforgettable! Wonderful! (And more on this later, too! See the section on Scouting Life.)

Cruisin'

Bremerton was the cruisin' capital of the NW and all car radios were tuned in to Pat O'Day on KJR. Friday nights it was drive as slow as possible down Pacific Ave to the Navy gate, around the block, back up Pacific, out to the A&W Drive-In on Kitsap Way, then on to Kitsap Lake, circle Graham's Drive-In, then back to Pacific and repeat the process again and again and again. What was it all about? Well duh! Boys lookin' for girls and girls lookin' for... well, what do girls ALWAYS do? Of course, play hard to get.

Those were the days. My heart is truly heavy wondering what has happened to the America I grew up in. The things that shaped my life are eroding away with each new social media craze.

Kids today, and adults as well, walk around with a computer continually in hand. Instant gratification, non-stop "tweets", never-ending text messages, Facebook "friends", and news that really isn't news. (Yes, Fake!) Leave the phone at home, explore the forests, beaches, neighborhoods, learn who your neighbors are.

Our parents didn't need to tell us, "Go outside and play!" Not then! We were either riding our bikes, building forts in the vacant lot, playing cowboys and Indians, or fishing off a nearby pier. I barely made it home for lunch, but when I heard my dad bellow, "DAAAAAVID", I responded, "COOOOMING". I didn't dare say, "WHAT?" Had I, it would have meant the switch.

Nowadays kids, and adults, will sit in front of the tube and "play" THE LEGEND OF ZELDA: the Breath of the Wild, and be possibly consumed by the heart-pounding "Resident Evil 7". Did it really all start with PONG?

Today's television is filled with the "F" bomb, "casual" sex, and heavy doses of sexual innuendo that destroy the true beauty of romance.

Can anyone truly explain "soft porn"? What HAS happened to the America I grew up in?

Gail Mills, Jim Mills, Dave Mills, Don Mills

FAMILY LIFE

Parents

The "Greatest Generation" is a term used to describe those who grew up during the Great Depression and fought in WW2, or whose labor helped win it. The term "Greatest Generation" was coined by onetime NBC Nightly News anchor Tom Brokaw. Most of this generation fared unusually well in their adult years, because they came out of the hardships of the Great Depression (GD) with an ability to know how to survive, the strength to make do and solve problems, and they passed on their work and family ethics to their children.

The Great Depression was a severe worldwide economic depression that took place mostly during the 1930s. It was the longest, deepest, and most widespread depression of the 20th century. Nowadays, the Great Depression is commonly used as an example of how intensely the world's economy can decline. Construction, mining, and agriculture were all devastated. The recovery from the GD began in early 1933 and the US unemployment rate still stood at nearly 25%. Then came World War 2.

At the height of World War 2, approximately 10 million men were serving in the armed forces. The US was fighting battles in the South Pacific and across the Atlantic in Europe and parts of Africa. To fill the employment gap, women went to work in factories and shipyards taking on tough physical labor building ships and tanks to support the war effort. After the war, many products were being rationed. Each family would get ration stamps to purchase tires, automobiles, sugar, gasoline, meat, butter, and coal. Mother and Father were products of the Great Depression and part of that aptly coined "Greatest Generation". I've always had a strong work ethic and deep love of family, which I attribute to my grandparents, mother, and father.

Mother

Mother was born July 1st, 1921 to John and Bessie Talich in Giltner, Nebraska. It was the beginning of the Dust Bowl, a period of severe drought and dust storms that swept through Texas, Kansas, Nebraska, and portions of Colorado and New Mexico. The "Dust Bowl", as it became known, was largely blamed on a failure to apply dryland farming methods to prevent wind erosion.

When our pioneers began the great migration westward during the mid-1800s, they saw a sea of grass that stood six feet high and stretched all the way from Canada to Texas. THE PROMISED LAND! Homesteaders flocked to the prairie states, certain they had found the richest soil in the world and an ideal place to settle. The early pioneers began clearing the land and, for many decades, conducted deep plowing of the rich topsoil and planted wheat and corn. What they didn't realize was the displaced, deep-rooted native grasses had held moisture, which now ran off into creeks, streams, and rivers, basically carrying the land with it.

The stage was set.

With the advent of mechanized farm equipment, especially the small gasoline tractors, farmers converted more and more of the grassland. Then came a drought the like of which this country had never seen. (Was this global warming?) It came in three waves ~ 1934, '36, and '39 to '40, but some states experienced the conditions for many years previous. The agricultural devastation of this time in American history lengthened the Great Depression here, whose effects were felt worldwide.

It's a shame I don't know how Grandpa Talich ended up in Nebraska. All those from the immediate Talich family have passed away, and I didn't have the foresight to gather the family history. Grandpa Talich worked as a sharecropper cultivating, growing, and harvesting wheat and corn. Times were tough, income was meager at best, and he moonlighted for the railroad loading rail cars with grain.

Mother had two sisters, Charlotte and Norma, and two brothers, Eldon and Joe. They lived well below the "poverty level" by anyone's standard. Grandma Talich made dresses for the girls from flour sacks, and the boys wore pants and shirts patched with any piece of fabric available. Often, they went months without socks, and the soles of their shoes were lined with cardboard. The three girls slept in a single bed, as did the boys. Mom often told stories of life in Nebraska. There were no stories of fun times, playing with other children, or going to town, sitting at the malt shop enjoying a soda. It was a spartan life. Going to school was their only relief from drudgery.

One such story was how they typically found their way home from school.

All five would hold hands and be led home by one of the brothers through the blinding dust. Inside their home, the grit and sand blew in through cracks in the walls. Nowhere was there relief from the effects of the wind. I have watched John Steinbeck's "The Grapes of Wrath" several times. Mom could not watch; it brought back too many painful memories.

They did have electric lights, but often the heavy winds downed power lines, and they resorted to kerosene lanterns. They had no running water and no indoor plumbing. For a treat, once a week, their dad (Grandpa) brought home a candy bar, which got divided 5 ways to share. Yes, they were dirt poor.

"…They streamed over mountains, hungry and restless – restless as ants, scurrying to find work to do – to lift, to push, to pick, to cut – anything, any burden to bear, for food. The kids are hungry. We got no place to live…" (The Grapes of Wrath, John Steinbeck)

Grandpa Talich was one of those drawn west, "dusted out", seeking a better life. The family headed west and landed in Caldwell, Idaho where Grandpa found a job working in the woods logging. The kids entered school (Aunt Norma and mother finished high school in Caldwell, Id; Mother graduating top in her class. It's a shame that portion of her DNA wasn't passed on to her son.)

Times were really tough, and the boys dropped out of school in the 8th or 9th grade, getting jobs to help the family with expenses.

With the advent of World War II, employment on the west coast was booming. Grandpa and Grandma were settled and remained in Caldwell. So, the kids, seeking their own life, continued the westward migration.

Aunt Charlotte, the oldest, after graduating from high school, left Giltner for the "Big City" of Grand Island, Nebraska. She was the first one to leave the family. While working for the phone company, she attended a USO (United Service Organization) dance and met a fella, but nothing came of that encounter 'til years later. California beckoned, and Charlotte moved to Bellflower, CA, and found a much better paying position with the phone company. Once again, she was at a USO dance and... you guessed it. There was the same fella from Grand Island, Fred Reese. Didn't take long before they were married and made their home in Bell, CA. Uncle Fred worked for Burlington Northern RR, and Aunty retired from the phone company. They were married for 60+ years and never had any children. The two of them made several trips to the NW, visiting Mom and Dad, and we became good, close friends. I will never forget the good times we had together.

After graduating from high school, Norma left Caldwell, Idaho and worked in Bremerton, supporting the war effort, then met and married Ralph Hickox, who was working for Boeing Co. in Renton. Aunt Norma found a good job with the phone company in Moses Lake, Washington, where they took up their life-long residence. Uncle Ralph and Aunty Norma had three children ~ Sandy, Gail, and Bobby. Sandy passed away at a very young age, say 35ish; Gail resides in Kansas and Bobby in Oregon.

Mother, after graduating from Caldwell High, found her way to Bremerton and eventually met my father. She worked as a bookkeeper at Westpark housing, where Dad worked in the employee kitchen washing dishes.

Uncle Eldon and Uncle Joe worked on Eniwetok, an atoll in the South Pacific, where the United States first tested the hydrogen bomb. Both were wonderful uncles, and what a treat when either one or both of those nomads would re-enter my life every couple of years! They both loved fishing, especially for salmon, and together we took many trips to Sekiu or La Push. Uncles Joe and Eldon were nomadic individuals and found great jobs "here and there", but never really settled down. Oh, the stories that surrounded Uncle Joe and Uncle Eldon!

For instance, Uncle Joe loved the outdoors, especially being on the saltwater. My dad introduced him to salmon fishing which he took a likin' to. Uncle Joe didn't know much about the sport, but he had a remarkable ability to catch fish. He became so addicted one year he rented a boat from Curley's resort in Sekiu. We didn't have an outboard motor, so he rented one of their inboard motor fishing boats. Dad and I used to fish in them, and let me tell ya, they were horrible. Rowing would have been better, but the strong tides in the straits wouldn't allow for that. The motors were hard to start. You had to wrap a pull cord around the flywheel and pull like hell 7 or 8 times to get 'em started. The motor had neutral and forward, and the speed was way too fast for any slow trolling, and if you dare shifted to neutral, the engine would die. The motors were air-cooled, and oh ya, LOUD! That's all we had and guess what? We still caught fish.

Anyhow, Uncle was fishing in front of the caves, just west of Sekiu. He had caught a couple dandy chinook salmon, then hooked into a hard-fighting fish. As the story goes, he fought that fish for well over 45 minutes, dodging other boats, and trying to keep from snagging another line. After an hour passed, a fisherman pulled alongside and said, "Hey pal, you've probably got into a large halibut." And then the guy drifted off. Uncle fought the fish for a couple more minutes, more like seconds, and not knowing what a halibut was, cut his line. When he returned home and told the story, my dad hit the roof, and it wasn't a pretty sight. Enuff said.

When I owned my own boat, I was lucky enough to take Uncle Joe fishing, and duck hunting, many times. He and I were very close, and I will never forget the good times we had.

Uncle Joe was single for most of his life, then finally married a gal that flew a bi-plane in local airshows. I only met her one time, and so help me, I can't remember her name, but they had a lovely daughter, Kathlene "Holly" Talich Waude. Holly is married with two children, is the franchise owner of "Nothing Bundt Cakes", and lives in the Portland, Oregon area.

When Uncle Joe was in his mid-60's, he became quite ill and wanted to be close to his sister Norma, and silently passed away in a nursing home in Moses Lake.

Mom's brother Eldon, the youngest in the family, was a joy to be around. Neither Eldon nor Joe graduated from high school, but were skilled craftsmen. Uncle Eldon, like his brother, traveled the world and was never without a job. While he was, as he put it, "in-between jobs", he often would visit us in Bremerton. He wasn't as passionate about the outdoors as his brother, but Dad and I did take him salmon fishing a time or two. Uncle Eldon spent his final years in Bell, California near his sister Charlotte.

The Lord has blessed the entire Mills family with no finer set of Aunts and Uncles, and I loved each and every one.

Not long after watching "The Grapes of Wrath" for the umpteenth time, I felt the need to connect with my mother's hometown of Giltner, Nebraska. Dalene and I discussed our itinerary and how to go about it. Should we simply fly to Omaha? Rent a car and drive to Giltner? But not knowing if there would be accommodations along the way and besides, we owned a fully equipped travel trailer, we opted for: ROAD TRIP!
As it turns out, we could not have made a better choice, but see the section "Other Outdoor Life ~ Travel Trailer Life" for the goods on this!

Charlotte (Reese), Eldon Talich, Gail (Mills), Norma (Hickox) and Joe Talich

Left: Grandma Bessie Wright Talich,
Right: Grandpa John Talich and daughter (my mother) Gail Talich

Grandparents

Knowledge of mother's parents is very sketchy at best. I never met Grandma Talich (Bessie Cornelia Wright). Mother's father, John Arthur Talich, of Bohemian descent, was born, married, and raised his family in Giltner, Nebraska where he worked as a sharecropper. The dust bowl era drove the family westward and he settled in Caldwell, Idaho and spent time in the woods logging and was crippled from the waist down by a freak accident where logs rolled off a logging truck and crushed his legs. Grandpa Talich was a big strong man with a warm heart.

I'm much more familiar with the Mills/Fairbanks family history due to their proximity during my growing-up years.

Grandpa Mills had been a cook in a lumber camp in Minnesota prior to moving out west. He also cooked in a logging camp in Alaska and was considered "The Bull of the Woods". He left Alaska for the Puyallup valley, where he met Grandma, and eventually opened his own restaurant in downtown Puyallup called the "Good Eats". Clever name, huh?

Bremerton was a boomtown. The shipyard was at full employment, and there were plenty of service industry jobs available. In the 1930s, Grandpa was considered a chef. Not like chefs of the modern-day, but nobody could make gravy as good as Grandpa. He said, "The secret to bein' a good cook was knowin' how to make good sauces." and that is true to this very day.

He was a fixture in Bremerton during the '30s and '40s. He cooked at the Crow's Nest, located on Pacific Ave, just around the corner from the shipyard's main gate. Back in the '30s, it was THE place to eat. Later, he was also head chef at The Palace, also located on Pacific Ave, and was a popular restaurant long into the '70s.

Grandpa was also noted, around Bremerton, for his feats of strength. At one point in his life, it was reported he "dead-lifted" a world record for a light heavyweight. Of course, that report was totally unofficial. Grandpa's forearms were Popeye-like, and he could bend railroad spikes in his bare hands. Every 4th of July, he would lash a rope to a fire engine and pull the truck down Pacific Ave with that roped clutched in his teeth.

Grandpa and I had a special log on just about every lake in Kitsap and Mason counties. We didn't own a boat, so we would sit on our special log for hours and fish for trout and perch. Sometimes we had to park alongside the county road and find our way into our secret spot. So as not to get lost, Grandpa would always break a twig on a bush, marking our path. It reminded me of the fairy tale about Hansel and Gretel dropping bread crumbs. And, of course, we always got lost, and even after multiple trips to the same hidden lake, there were so many broken branches, we never did take a straight line. On the way home, Grandpa would let me drive. He always had a Buick, and I would "hafta" sit on a catalog to see out the window. Fortunately, my toes barely touched the brake and gas pedal. Grandpa would often say, "Don't tell your dad I let you drive."

He loved baking, and every Saturday morning, we stopped by Grandma and Grandpa's house for a few cinnamon rolls and Grandma's famous sugar cookies. When we entered the house, he had several pans of dough staged by the heat register. When the dough had risen juuuust right, into the oven they went. I still can smell those oh-so-tasty rolls.

Grandpa Mills retired from cooking after working at "Bixby's", a classy little restaurant in Chico, Washington, and finally at "King's Garden", a private Christian high school in Seattle.

Grandma was born Ivy Myrtle Fairbanks, March 1891, in Hokah, Minn. She had a sister Lois, born March 1895, and twins Rufus and Ruth, born in 1893. They left Hokah, Minnesota circa 1908 and settled in Puyallup, Washington. Grandma would tell about crossing the bitter cold Great Plains and gathering buffalo chips for heat. Rufus died in 1982; Ruth Fairbanks Parrish died in 1977. Lois Fairbanks Siebert died in 1972,

Grandma spent many hours of her day in prayer. I deeply regret losing her Bible, but I still remember a long list of those people she prayed for daily... Daily. Grandma was a true prayer warrior. She went to be with Jesus in 1984.

Looking back, my grandparents had a profound influence on my behavior and they always lived near-by which made for a strong relationship. I spent quality time with Grandpa on our favorite "logs" and by his example, he taught me respect for others. Grandma and Grandpa provided me with unconditional love. At the time, I was too young to realize what was happening, but they instilled in me lifelong values that can never be erased. Nothing can replace the memories of Grandma and Grandpa, but one of God's greatest gifts to me is MY grandchildren. I pray I will be able measure up to the task of being a positive influence in their lives.

Grandpa Talich bottom row far right
Derek and Grandpa Talich are spitting images of each other ... I think!

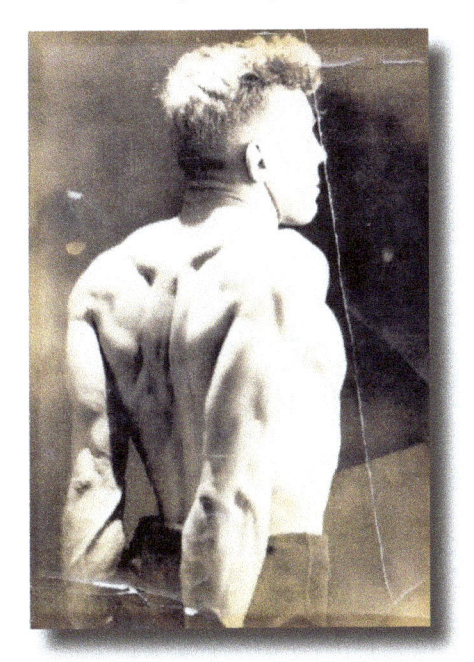

Strongman George Mills

MR. AND MRS. C. G. MILLS
Celebrants

C. George Millses Wed 50 Years

Sunday begins a 50th wedding anniversary celebration for Mr. and Mrs. Conrad G. (George) Mills that won't end until Thursday.

That is the day when the couple will be guests of the W. F. Jankes at Western Washington Fair, Puyallup. The Jankes, candy manufacturers, have had a taffy booth on the fairgrounds for 50 years and selected Mr. and Mrs. Mills as a golden anniversary couple to share the celebration.

As it turns out the whole thing is perfectly timed.

Sunday, on the date of their 50th anniversary, they'll be honored with an open house given by their children at the home of a son, Don Mills, 1225 National Ave. Friends of the couple are invited to drop by between 2 and 4 p.m. to extend best wishes.

And Thursday — the day the elder Mr. and Mrs. Mills and their son and daughter-in-law will see the fair, attend the grandstand show and have dinner as guests of the Jankes— also is the elder Mr. Mills' birthday.

Besides, Mr. and Mrs. Mills "saw Western Washington Fair grow up."

They met and were married in Tacoma and made their first home in Puyallup where all three of their children were born.

They moved to Bremerton in 1922, and Mr. Mills, a chef, was employed for 20 years by the late George and Johnny Mattock at the original Crow's Nest, during World War II worked at Tiny's and finally worked as chef at the cookhouse when the Westpark housing development was built. He retired in 1953.

"We really had a hand in building the place we live now," said Mr. Mills speaking of their home at 22-E McNeal Ave.

Of the couple's three children, sons Don and Laurence live in Bremerton and daughter Mrs. Earlene Trainer is from Seattle. The Don Mills have two sons, David, 18, and Jimmy, 9; they all will be hosts at Sunday's open house.

Mr. Mills was born in Chicago and moved to Michigan with his family when he was 12. He left home to serve a three-year apprenticeship as a chef at the Paxton Hotel in Omaha, then went to Saskatchewan and from there came to Tacoma to take a job at Fanny Paddock hospital; now Tacoma General.

Mrs. Mills was born Myrtle Fairbanks in Hokah, Minn., but moved to Puyallup with her family when she was 15 and took up work as a housekeeper. Through this route she arrived at the Fanny Paddock hospital as a laundry employe and it was there they met.

Both are now members of the senior citizens group and also belong to the Christian Missionary Alliance Church. Mr. Mills is a fisherman and gardener in his spare time and Mrs. Mills is a crossword puzzle fan but says she doe put them down once in a while to embroider.

Of 50 years of marriage, they says it has had its ups and downs but there's nothing can beat it.

MR. AND MRS. C. G. MILLS
On Wedding Day

Father

Father was born September 14, 1914 in Puyallup, Washington to Conrad George and Myrtle (Fairbanks) Mills. During the summer months, Dad would spend a good deal of his youth in the Puyallup and Sumner valleys. In those days, there still were swimming holes, horses roaming "wild", and fishing creeks. He often told stories how a local farmer allowed the "gang" to rope and ride his horses, camp out by the swimmin' hole, and fish the creek.

During the Great Depression era, Gypsies traveled throughout rural America and many camped in the Puyallup valley. Gypsies dressed differently, spoke a different language, and looked different from the locals. Gypsy men were often good horse handlers, and the women made jewelry and baskets and would tell fortunes at county fairs. Quite often, Gypsies were unfairly accused of stealing from the locals, but Dad and his gang of "ruffians" had no fear and learned how to rope and ride horses from the Gypsy men. He told about times they had sitting around the Gypsy campfire listening to stories ~ didn't matter that they couldn't understand the language, the boys just loved bein' there.

Dad graduated from Bremerton High School in 1933 and was a stand-out athlete in basketball and track. To this day, I can't find anyone who remembers this: after a made basket during a basketball game, the teams would "jump ball" at center court. Dad told me he never lost a jump ball.

In track, Dad did the high jump, with a personal best of 6'2", using the scissors method ~ the western roll or Fosbury Flop had not been invented. He also did the broad jump, typically jumping 19', and had patterned his style after the legendary Jesse Owens.

When Dad was alive, he would never miss reading the high school track times and would simply shake his head saying, "If I was still in high school, I would be beating all these times." And this without the current track technologies! In his day, high school sprints were run on a cinder track and starting blocks were not used. Sprinters would take a spoon to the starting line and dig a slight depression for their cleats.

But speed was Dad's best attribute. The 100- & 220-yard dash and the 4x100 yard relay are where he excelled. Often the first man in a relay is the weakest member and the last man, the anchor leg is the fastest. Dad, though, led off the relays because he would have such a long lead after his leg, the other teams were shell-shocked and the race was pretty much over. As with most great athletes, he wouldn't brag about his speed and always said, "Chuck Lombard was the best man on our team." History is a bit sketchy, but the 1932 Bremerton track team won the 4x100 relay, with Dad placing second in the broad jump and a personal best jump over 20'.

After high school, jobs were few and far between, so Dad and a buddy hopped a freight car out of Puyallup. They rode the rails across the country living in hobo "jungle camps" and bummin' off the land. After that, he joined the army and spent his entire tour of duty at Schofield Barracks on the island of Oahu. He loved the islands and competed on the All-Army track team, where he finally ran on a tartan track and used starting blocks. He was so proud that he broke 10-flat in the 100-yard dash, running a 9.9 hundred.

After his tour in the Army, he returned to Bremerton and helped build the military housing, commonly referred to as Westpark and East Bremerton Housing. That's where he and Mom met. She was a bookkeeper for the housing authority and he was washing dishes in the employee cafeteria. It just so happened Grandpa Talich was visiting his daughter and working in the kitchen as well. When Dad found out Gail was John's daughter, he asked if he could ask her out on a date. They dated for about a year and were married September 14, 1941, making their first home in an apartment at the end of Warren Ave.

Yes, there was "an end" to Warren. Just a steep cliff down to Dyes Inlet, where now sits the Warren Avenue Bridge.

After marriage and Westpark, Dad tended bar at the legendary ~ yes, legendary and historic ~ Maple Leaf Tavern and a top payin' job it was.

That's right.

Top pay.

WW2 had just broken out and a friend, who was on the fire department, came to Dad and said, "Hey Mills, why don't you join the fire department?"

Dad said, "Why should I do that? I make twice as much as you tendin' bar."

His friend told him about the medical, dental, and retirement benefits and said, "Firemen are exempt from the draft." And that's all she wrote!

Dad's ties to the Puyallup Valley never left his spirit. When I was a young lad Mom, Dad, and I would spend many Sunday afternoons visiting the many aunts, uncles, and numerous cousins. We made several trips to the old swimming hole, and his favorite fishing spot on Clark Creek. We never wetted a line. He would simply stand silent, looking over the surrounding valley, and once in a while talking about the horses and his old gang.

What has happened to the America I grew up in?

Dad's younger brother Lawrence was a true war hero. While fighting in WW2, he stepped on a land mine and lost his right leg from the knee down, but that didn't slow him down one bit. He never owned a car, that I can remember, and would walk everywhere. Even with his prosthetic, I had to run to keep up with him. My dad was a speed burner on the track and often told me Uncle Lawrence could whip him in the 100-yard dash. Uncle often would take me to special events sponsored by the VFW, where he was quite active. Uncle Lawrence was a believer in Jesus Christ, but the effects of the war took a toll on his emotional life. He never shared much with his family about his personal feelings and suffered from alcoholism. He was married, AT LEAST seven times, twice to the same gal, but never had any children that we know about. Then for some unknown reason, he drifted off, unannounced, and died in a motel room in El Paso, Texas. Before he left, he told my brother, "That's where God wants me to be." Mom and Dad found out about his death because he left them a note, which I never became privy to. I truly loved Uncle Lawrence.

Dad had a younger sister, Earlene. She was a beautiful gal. I don't know much about her early life growing up. The first time we met was at Grandpa and Grandma's house on Elizabeth Ave, with her husband, Johnny Trainer. Aunt Earlene had taken Hula lessons while in Hawaii, and I remember she danced for us, wearing an authentic grass skirt. It was quite the show. Uncle Johnny was in the Navy and the two of them had just returned from Pearl Harbor after a long enlistment. Uncle Johnny was a hospital corpsman serving on the USS Solace, which was bombed by the Japanese and severely damaged during the December 7th, 1941 raid on Pearl Harbor. Remember the President's address to the nation and those famous words, "A day that will live in infamy."? Fortunately, Uncle Johnny was off duty that Sunday morning, but his ship was quickly repaired and turned into a hospital ward.

Aunty was a "live wire", always on the go, and Dad and Uncle Lawrence had given her the nickname "Boonus". She seemed to like it, but don't ask me where that came from. I have no idea of its origin, but it was funny at the time. Uncle Johnny was as cool and calm as a glass of ice water. Go figure. Uncle's last tour of duty, before retirement, was at Bremerton's Naval Hospital, which at that time, was located inside Puget Sound Naval Shipyard. Mother was a budget analyst for the Supply Department and Uncle would often stop by her office and have lunch. She said, "When Johnny came into the area, all the women stopped working just to watch him walk past."

One Christmas, they gave our boys ten hand-made pillows decorated with cute, little stitched animal figures wrapped in a large cardboard box. Doug and Derek, probably 3 and 5 years old, tore into the gift-wrapped box, threw out the pillows, spent the entire day playing in the box, and ignored the pillows. Aunty was so offended, and that turned out to be the last Christmas gift she gave the boys. Not sure why, but the two of them never had any children. Would have been nice to have cousins from them AND Uncle Lawrence. Oh well. Still, I have many fond memories of Uncle Johnny and Aunty Earlene. I will always love them.

Uncle Lawrence in France

Jones' First Track Meet

A kind note from a reader asks what has become of the relay team of a couple of years back at Bremerton high school. The team he meant was composed of Don Mills, Howard Carlson, Chuck Lombard and Chuck Jones.

Mills, one of the best trackmen Bremerton ever boasted, is now in the army. Carlson, who dropped out of the local high school to finish his prep education in Oregon, became something of a sensation in Oregon track meets and is now enrolled in Oregon State college, according to my best info.

Lombard and Jones are still in Bremerton. The latter, of course, is still going to school. He'll graduate in June and next fall will see him enter the University of Washington. Those four were really fine performers on the cinder paths, too. Speaking of Jones as a tracksters reminds of the time the inter-class track meet was being run off at Washington field and Jones won the 220 in his baseball suit.

Darrell Floyd, a good 220 man himself, was running in the meet for the seniors. Jones, who was at the field turning out for baseball, decided to step into the race for the sophomores. With baseball shoes and the bulky plus-sixes of the diamond as attire, the fleet-footed sophomore nosed Floyd out after a mighty stretch battle. That was Jones' first track meet.

Left: Dad's high school graduation 1933, Right: Army Scofield Barricks, HI

Four Bremerton High Grads:

Douglas 1979, Dad 1933, Derek 1981, and me 1963

Brother Jim
(or the sibling effect)

Jim, my baby brother, no matter what, will always be my baby brother.

He was born June 24, 1954. I was born July 15, 19-FORTY-FOUR.

I had been an "only child" for ten years.

It was MY bedroom. It was MY backyard. It was MY back seat in the family auto.

I didn't have to share ANYTHING.

Oh yeah, I've read about: The only child depression syndrome

The only child loneliness syndrome

You name it, there is an only child syndrome about sumpthin'. Give me a break. I think it's all a bunch of Hooey. I wasn't a bratty or spoiled child - quite the opposite. Dad believed in the "spare the rod, spoil the child" syndrome. Now there's a syndrome I DO believe in!

Did my parents prepare me for the new arrival?

Heck, I really don't even remember Mom bein' pregnant. One day she came home from the hospital carrying my baby brother. But it didn't take long and there was a crib in MY room. And the nighttime feeding, in MY room.

The toy box became HIS toy box.

And bunk beds, are you kidding?

I couldn't take it any longer and moved to the basement where Dad once had a room full of tropical fish. I still remember the smell of brine shrimp.

Then came family vacations.

No longer was the back seat of the family auto MINE. I had to share it with my baby brother.

Jim had Mom wrapped around his finger. We'd be on a long trip or on our way to church and he'd pull the same ol' thing. I'd be staring out the window, minding my own business, and with a whiney voice, Jim'd say, "Mom, David made a face at me." Naturally, Mom's response? "David, stop that!" It didn't matter who we were with, and we didn't even have to be in a car. His favorite was cookie Grandma: "Grandma, David stuck his tongue at me." Without knowing anything, she'd simply bark, "DAVID!" I contend I was always innocent of ANY provocation. Ok, maaaybe once in a while…

Over time we did quite a bit together. I became his big brother and today he still calls me, "Big Brother". After I graduated from high school and was exploring life on my own, Mom and Dad moved to Erland's Point and Jim spent his elementary and high school years in the Central Kitsap school district, graduating from CK in 1972.

Jim was an excellent trombone player, marching in the high school band, and was the lead trombonist in the dance band, where he received the nickname "Bones". After high school, he marched in the local drum and bugle corps, meeting the love of his life, Cindy Erlandsen. While the two dated, Jim worked in Bremerton at various restaurants and became an accomplished fry cook at the VIP restaurant on Kitsap Way.

Jim was not much for paying traffic fines; in fact, he had a mountain of parking tickets and decided it was best to leave town. I think there was some encouragement from Dad, so Jim joined the Army.

Great move.

(Not sure what happened to all the tickets, but Mom and Dad had their hand in it somehow.)

Jim's Army career took him to two tours in South Korea, various Army bases around the United States, and a tour in the Berlin Brigade with A company, 3rd battalion, 6th infantry regiment. The Berlin Brigade was a US Army brigade-sized garrison based in West Berlin during the Cold War. After WW2, under the conditions of the Yalta and Potsdam agreements, the Allied Forces occupied West Berlin.

Jim and Cindy were married April 25, 1981 and lived in Berlin with their first child, Steve. Steve was born on base in Germany. Steve and I became quite close when Jim was on his tours in South Korea. More on that later.

Dalene and I were about to celebrate our 17th wedding anniversary. Douglas was in the 6th grade and Derek in the 4th at Haddon Elementary. Mom and Dad had never been to Europe and decided to take our boys and go to Germany. They could NOT have given us a better anniversary gift. I believe we were away from home as long as Doug and Derek were!

After a 20-year stellar career, Jim retired, joined the Pierce County Police Department, worked another seven years, and is now fully retired.

Jim and Cindy are currently living in Bremerton, and are members of the Bremerton Yacht Club. They have three children and seven grandchildren. Their son Steve served in the United States Navy and gained valuable experience as a nuclear engineer. He is now a supervisor at a nuclear plant in New York, is married to Jennifer, and has four children: Luke, Warren, Elana, and Dianna. Jim & Cindy's daughter Christy lives in Colorado Springs, married to Joseph Gray, and they have two children, Isaiah and Leila. Jim & Cindy's youngest daughter Brianna lives in Bonney Lake, married to Jason Favors, and they have a son, Douglas.

When Jim was stationed in Korea, he asked me to watch over Steve ~ be a father to him. And boy-oh-boy did I enjoy my time with him! We spent many days in the duck blind and countless hours salmon fishing. In Washington state, youth are required to attend a hunter safety program. I sat in the classroom with Steve and was there when he passed all the tests. That Fall, I took him duck hunting and he was a natural shotgunner. His first day in the blind he knocked down a double on widgeon drakes. There was one incident in the blind that became a "father and son" moment. Something special between the two of us that shall remain our secret. I had his first duck mounted, and it's at Jim and Cindy's home still. When I go to their home and see that duck, it brings back fond memories.

I also took Steve salmon fishing. I will never forget the first time he hooked a blackmouth. We were at Point No Point and the fish was giving him all he could handle. All of a sudden, the fish took off and Steve's reel was peelin' off line. I knew the fish was about 8 lbs., and no 8-pounder could run that fast and hard. I looked up, and sure enough, a seal had grabbed his fish. The seal eventually broke the line and we lost the fish. Steve broke down in tears. There were plenty of other days and many more fish.

I also feel a closeness to Christy and Brianna. Dalene and I had two sons, and if we were to have daughters, I would want them to be exactly like these two. Like our boys, Christy and Brianna are as different as night and day. Bri was a bookworm. Christy? I'm not sure what she had goin' on. Ah, come on, just kidding. I love 'em both!

Those who know me know this ~ there's always one more thing:

For My Brother

Jim, those were GEESE, not seagulls

Jim, those were DOVES, not bagpipes

If I wear my bedroom slippers on the wrong feet, that hurts... ski boots?

*My brother had an outstanding career in the army:
20+ yrs. including two tours in Korea and one in Germany*

Brother's family: Steve, Santa, Christy, Cindy, Jim, Briana

Steve's family: Steve & Jennifer, front row l to r: Luke, Warren, Elana, Dianna

Left: Christy's family: Joseph & Isaiah, Christy & Leila, Right: Briana & Jason with Douglas

When my brother was in Korea, I had the pleasure to take Steve hunting and fishing. First day duck hunting, oh my! "Steve! Mark! On your left—a mallard drake, wings cupped, take him!" First shot ever he folded a fat mallard drake. Left picture: with a nice 8# Blackmouth from mid-channel bank.

MARRIED LIFE

Our Wedding
(but it's really all about the honeymoon)

The most beautiful, glorious thing that ever happened to me was in September 1964 when I sat behind a gal in Geology class at Olympic College. All I saw was the back of her head, and a raincoat draped over the back of her chair, but I was drawn to the empty seat behind her like something I had never experienced.

When it came to talking to … a girl… I was afraid. I wasn't a shy person, just afraid of GIRLS. I felt awkward, and I knew rejection was simply one "hello" away.

After that first day, the seating arrangements were pretty much established, and on day two, I found myself sitting behind the same girl, with the same green raincoat hanging on the back of her chair. I had yet to say "Hi"; heck, I hadn't even seen her face, but I knew something was different.

On day three, when I entered the classroom, she was sitting sideways in her seat, talking to someone across the aisle. Oh my, she's pretty. I sat down; she turned my direction and smiled. Not one rational thought came to mind and I said the stupidest thing ever, "Hi, do you think this rain will ever stop?" What a fool! But that was all it took. Neither of us knew at the time, but our fate was forever sealed.

On Valentine's Day 1965, I gave her a pearl ring and asked her to be my "steady".

It was June 1965, and I hired on for another summer of logging with Simpson Timber Company. I didn't own a car, and on weekends Dalene would drive to Grisdale and pick me up after work. We would spend the weekend either at my parent's house on Erland's Point or with her parents in Yelm. When we spent the weekends at my folk's place, we did a lot of lake and salmon fishing. My brother often tagged along, and adopted Dalene for a big sister.

I worked the rest of that summer logging. Then for lack of anything better, I returned to Olympic College for the Fall quarter. I found a job at Friedlander and Sons jewelry store, working in the stock room. I remembered Dalene's ring finger size and, on my own mind you, picked out a wedding ring.

One weekend, on Dalene's birthday, September 18th, we decided to visit her parents in Yelm, where I was going to "officially" propose, but somewhere along the highway, as we were passing through Fort Lewis, I pulled over. I couldn't wait any longer. I pulled the ring from my pocket, and without getting down to one knee, I proposed in the front seat of her Rambler Classic. She said, "David, I love you. Yes." And we sealed it with a kiss. Ok, two or three or four would be more accurate.

When we arrived at her folk's place, I stood before her father, Dale, told him I had just proposed marriage to his daughter, and asked for his blessing. Not exactly sure what made me do that, must have seen it on TV or sumpthin' like that, but I felt it was the right thing to do.

Dale was a very soft-spoken man; he shook my hand and said, "You have my blessing." I believe, deep down inside, he was thrilled.

The very next Monday, I got a letter from my Uncle Sam with a new draft status... 1A.

At that point I "officially" dropped out of school and spent the next few months fishing, hunting, and working at Friedlander's jewelry store. Hey! Why not!

I left for Marine Corps boot camp on February 14, 1966, and after eight weeks of boot camp and another 4 weeks of advanced infantry training, I headed home on a 30-day pass.

May 28th, 1966
Pastor John Sara First Covenant Church

Dalene with her father Dale. When I saw the two of them in the doorway to the church my knees literally buckled. Yes, we were a bit late, but "Jack" was the culprit.

The most unforgettable moment in my life was May 28th, 1966. I was standing at the altar of First Covenant Church with Jim Bennett, my best man, at my side and Howard Kubli and

Tom McMullen my groomsmen. Fred Kegel, still in school at Pullman, rushed home, made it to the wedding just in time. We were quite late for the ceremony, and I heard later some thought I got "cold feet" and wasn't gonna show, but that was not the case. To say I was nervous would be a gross understatement, so Jim and I spent more time than we should have at his house with a bottle of Crown Royal on the kitchen counter. Need I say more?

We finally arrived, met with my groomsmen in the pastor's chambers, and then made our way to the front of the church. The church, the one I grew up in, was packed. Alfred Kubli, Howard's father, was all over the place taking pictures. There was Mom and Dad sitting in the front row. I spotted Mrs. Bandy, my grandparents, aunts, uncles, and many of my former classmates. I saw Dalene's mother, Betty, and Dalene's grandparents, Harold and Evelyn Jackson, and Olga Aimer.

As we took our places, my brother Jim and Dalene's cousin Robert lit candles; her brother, Mark, came down the aisle with rings on a pillow. Oh ya, I watched everything. Then came the bridesmaids, Dalene's two sisters, Kathy and Norma, and her cousin Teresa. As the organ music changed tempo Dalene's cousin, 4-year-old Kelley, tossed rose petals on the runner along her way. And then it happened, the organist started playing, that's right, "Here Comes the Bride". I looked down the aisle to see Dalene, clutched in her father's arm. The front doors of the church were open wide with the sun at her back. The golden rays of the setting sun glistened through her veil and lit up a warm, loving smile on her face. My knees turned to jelly, and my heart sank down to my toes, but I was looking at the most beautiful woman in the world, and we were about to become one!

Dale placed Dalene's hand in mine and we turned toward Pastor Sara. I know Pastor Sara said something, but I have no idea what. At this point, I was in a fog. We recited our "vows", said "I do", kissed, and Pastor Sara then introduced Mr. and Mrs. David and Dalene Mills to our guests.

How we settled on our vows is an interesting story. Pastor Sara counseled us a few times before the wedding, where we discussed roles as a married couple. Pastor Sara was very much "old school" and stressed that the man is the ultimate authority in the household and the wife must obey her husband. We listened respectfully, but when alone, we agreed that marriage was an equal partnership. We talked about our vows with Pastor Sara, and the word "obey" in the traditional "Love, Honor and Obey" didn't sit too well with either of us. To be totally honest, I never gave much thought about what we should say, but thankfully Dalene did! However, to this day, neither of us can remember what we actually said, but we do know the words love and honor were in there.

After the wedding, we spent the weekend at the Tyee Motor Inn in Olympia. We had breakfast, lunch, and dinner at the Inn and had a great room with our own private swimming pool/sauna. Although Fred Kegel sabotaged our honeymoon suitcase with a bouquet of Iris flowers, which by the way, turned one of Dalene's dresses PURPLE.

I was making a whopping $89.50 per month and the Tyee Inn took all our money. We still wanted to go on a honeymoon, but were broke. Hawaii was not doable, and I couldn't leave the continental US anyhow. Olympic Hot Springs was out of the question; room rates were $50/night.

Now what? Ahhhh, Mom and Dad to the rescue.

"Why don't you kids take our camping trailer and head down the Oregon coast?"

Now you might think spending our honeymoon in a 16ft. teardrop camper, pulled by a 1965 4-door Buick LeSabre "lead-sled" doesn't sound very romantic. A "Terry" travel trailer for a honeymoon suite? Even now, I hafta laugh. But we had a great time. Didn't matter where we "slept". We were in love. Mom and Dad chipped in enough money to finance the trip and gave us their Standard Oil credit card. We were on top of the world.

We camped all along the Oregon coast from Astoria to the Sea Lion Caves. Funny how a thirty-day leave evaporates into thin air, but we had just enough time for one more adventure.

What else? You guessed it.

"Dalene, I think we have just enough time and money for a weekend at Westport. We can dig razor clams, that's free, and then go salmon fishing on a charter boat." In 1966 a charter boat only cost $8 per person, such a deal.

I still can't believe she agreed, and to this very day, neither can Dalene, but what a fabulous ending (for me) to our honeymoon.

After our wedding and honeymoon along the Oregon and Washington coast, I returned to Oceanside, California to continue advanced training, and then was transferred to the Marine Air Wing in El Toro, Calif. Dalene and I made our first home in Santa Ana, California. Dalene had a job at Budget Finance in Tacoma, gave her two-week notice, and then drove to Santa Ana.

Dalene had just enough money to cover expenses for the trip south, but the clutch burnt out in San Francisco. She got that fixed, but had to spend an extra night at a motel. After leaving 'Frisco, Dalene was in a bit of a rush and got a speeding ticket in San Jose, another $75 bill. When we met up in Santa Ana, we had a mere $25 to our name.

There were no quarters on base for a married PFC making $87.50/month, so we looked for an apartment off base. We searched and searched for an apartment, but the landlords required a $100 deposit. After a few rejections, we got lucky and found a nice couple that rented us a room. I'll never forget Bill and Vivian Shay. I'm not sure what the monthly rent was, but they allowed us to stay by lowering the cleaning deposit to... guess what? Yup, $25. I'll bet they paid the balance out of their pocket.

But now what? We were penniless.

Our complex was home to a lot of young people, and there was a BBQ poolside every day. Everyone knew our situation, so they invited us to eat without adding anything to the table.

A person can go without food for one day, but there is one necessity you cannot do without. Toilet Paper. Sounds gross, right? But that's the truth. There was only one option. Now you can borrow a cup of sugar from your neighbor, but NOT toilet paper! So, I walked down the block to the local gas station and stole - that's right STOLE - a roll of toilet paper.

What a humble beginning.

Trust me when I say, "Dalene CANNOT lie." She can't even tell a politically correct lie. The next day she went job hunting and somehow found Cadillac Plastics, a small industrial supply company that was in need of office help. As she was filling out an application, a gal in the office asked if her husband was in the military. Of course, Dalene said, "My husband is in the Marine Corp stationed at El Toro." The gal told her, "Do not tell the boss. He will not hire you."

When the boss interviewed her and asked about the military, she LIED. It was the hardest thing she ever did. After a few days, her conscience got the best of her, and she confessed. The owner said, "I sorta figured that all along, but we needed a gal of your ability and took a chance." To this very day, Dalene feels a touch of guilt for LYING.

After we settled in, we still had trouble making ends meet, so Dalene kept score during league play at a bowling alley, and I worked in the kitchen washing dishes.

That's the America WE grew up in.

Doorway of our home on Erland's Point

Our Life Renewed

My Near-Death Experience in Fall 1969

Dalene and I were living in Tacoma, WA.

She was working at Olympic Savings and Loan Association in Bremerton; I was about to graduate from the University of Puget Sound, and I was not in fellowship with the Lord. All I thought of was my own self-interest. Not a proud period in my life.

In a couple days, Dalene and I were to go with my dad to eastern Washington for the opening of pheasant season, but the Lord had other plans in store.

After a night of drinking with two classmates, we decided to stop off at another college watering hole. We were driving south on I-5, missed the 38th street off-ramp, hit the Jersey barrier, careening across the southbound lane, and ending up on a guard rail in the northbound lane. The guardrail split the right hand door like a hot knife through butter and totally destroyed the passenger seat where I was sitting.

When the medics arrived, I was sitting in the middle of the freeway. I remember some chatter going on around me, was somewhat aware of my circumstances, could tell I was sitting in a puddle of blood, but there was no pain. None whatsoever! My college buddies were still in the car. The tow truck driver had to use the "jaws of life" to get them out and they both escaped with just scratch here and there. Nothing major!

How did I get out? No one knows. No windows were shattered. At the time, it was a mystery. Now I know - an angel. Yes, God was with me yet again.

I drifted in and out of consciousness. I remember being placed on a gurney and driven off to the hospital. I clearly remember Dalene standing by my side and I said, as only David Mills could possibly come up with, "Dalene, we're not going pheasant hunting this weekend."

There are many sounds and memories which fade away with time and I wish they would, but for some reason the Lord won't let me forget being under the bright lights in the emergency room and the doctor using a knife to remove my blood soaked jeans. Think about it!

I spent 8 weeks at St. "Joe's" Hospital, and the first two were in a coma. Now and then my eyes would open to see the same nurse holding my hand and praying to God for my recovery. After my release, I tried to find her, but no one in the hospital knew who she was. As hard as I searched and asked staff, it was as if she never existed, but I KNOW she did. Hmmm?

Not until I was in conversation with my publisher, Ingemar Anderson, had I considered this a Near Death Experience. I didn't even know Near Death Experience was a thing. Okay, like everybody, I heard about people who died and saw the white light and that sort of thing, but I didn't think this "counted." My publisher (who's done a good bit of research into this) kindly said, "Think about it, I believe it truly was an NDE for you." Oh my! Ooookaaayyyy...... My pushy editor said, "Go research NDE and then we'll talk…" So, I did, a little bit.

NDE is not a new phenomenon. It can take many forms and yes, it's a very subjective personal experience that can occur during life threatening events. Some people that experience NDE will have destructive side effects; blessedly, I had a very positive, life-changing experience.

I was near death sitting in the middle of the freeway and it's safe to say I was pulled from that wreckage by an angel.

I was near death while being in a coma for two weeks and every time I woke up, I know I was clutching the hand of an angel.

Was I a perfect angel following my NDE? By no means, but my life was changed in ways only Dalene and I can understand.

Renewal

A few months after my release, Dalene came to me and, with tears in her eyes, said, "David, I want a divorce."

To say the very least, I was speechless, but I asked, "Why?"

"Because all you ever think of is yourself. You have no time for me, and you're not the same man I fell in love with."

I was shocked. Of course. What else from someone so absorbed with his own self?

I realized we had a good foundation. I believed God brought us together, but I was not living a life pleasing to God.

I asked her if she would like to meet with Hank and Charlene Bergquist, friends from church. She agreed. I called Hank to set up a meeting. When we arrive at their house, we sat in the kitchen and told the two of them what was going on. I figured we'd talk about how married couples need to act. How they need to share. How they need to be concerned about one another's feelings.

But guess what? Not one word about marriage. Not one. It was all about Jesus Christ.

That night, Jesus Christ saved our marriage. Hank and Charlene were the vessels. They wanted no credit. To Christ be the glory.

That's the America I grew up in.

Hank & Charlene Bergquist

God's Provision ~ 1st Hand

Dalene and I were living in Purdy. Doug and Derek were maybe 8 and 6 years old? We were down to our last penny. As we sat down for dinner, we held hands and I prayed the Lord would provide. No sooner had the words left my lips, there came a knock on our front door. I saw that it was Fred Kegel and let him in. Fred had his own business surveying land and had me do some work for him a while back. We sat and talked for a while, and then he said, "I just got paid for the job you and I worked on last month. Here ya go." He handed me an envelope and then shoved off. After he left, I opened the envelope and found a check for EXACTLY how much we needed. Oh, how the Lord does provide if we only have faith in HIM.

A "Death" in Our Church Life

I grew up in the Covenant church. Taught Sunday school class, was Sunday School Superintendent, served on the Deacon Board, and was elected as Chairman of the Church. Oh, such a lofty position. Well, that's what you might think.

Annual church meetings were awful. There was always someone demanding we stick to Roberts Rules of Order. I often thought, "This is a church meeting, with Christ as our leader; what's with all the rules? There should only be one Authority." But I let it go ~ after all, others were much older and supposedly much wiser.

Our pastor, Curtis Jennings, indicated his interest in retiring. We set up a committee to seek candidates, invite them to church, and address the congregation. After several speaking engagements, a young man and his wife were invited to become our pastors. What ensued lingers to this very day. As in any "election", there will always be disagreement, but you would think members of a church would accept the will of the people and be gracious. Nope. Just like in the "real world", some just can't let it go. They make waves until, eventually, so much grief has been shed, the rest of the congregation relents.

Well, I was chairman of the church and decided the fight was not worth it. When our new pastor gave up the battle, our family did as well. It took years before we found our way back "home".

And let me just say here that much later we came back to a Much different situation! The present pastor preaches grace and truth, straight from the Bible, no legalism at all. I've asked some of the younger families, "Do your kids know how lucky they are being raised in a church like this?"

Phil Linden

I'm not exactly sure how this all came about, but let me try and explain.

The first 7 years of my life were spent going to Naval Avenue Elementary School. We lived on Naval Ave at the corner of 13th street, next to Evergreen Cemetery. Across the street and two houses down on 13th lived Phil Linden. We did a few things together, but to be honest, I'm not sure what. Today we talk about the neighborhood like we were joined at the hip. All the kids, that nasty bulldog roamin' the nursery across the street from his house, and especially our second-grade teacher, Mrs. Lubeke. Phil remembers her well. I just have a mental picture of her in a long black dress, hair rolled up in pigtails wrapped around her head, standing in front of the class with that penmanship thing on the wall above her head. You know, Aa, Bb, Cc, all in cursive. Can you believe Phil says Mrs. Lubeke was the best teacher he ever had? A SECOND-GRADE TEACHER WAS HIS BEST? COME ON!

Then we moved to Navy Yard City, where I attended Navy Yard City Elementary School and West High, never to see Phil again 'til 1962. I knew Phil moved to the east side and attended East High, and I knew he went to Sylvan Way Baptist Church, but for the life of me, I can't explain how I knew. Maybe it was because we competed against one another in a city-sponsored church basketball league, but there we were, as if we had never parted company, posing for pictures at the Bremerton ferry ramp waiting for the Seattle Ferry. The two of us were part of a group of Kitsap teens headed to Washington, DC to attend a Youth for Christ conference. We spent some time together on the train, even roomed together in DC, and here I go again, I don't remember many of the details, but something was holding us together.

After the DC trip that was it until - get this - 1985 or was it 1986? Does it really matter? Nah! Fate enters my life once again. Fate? HAH!

Dalene and I took Douglas and Derek to a Young Life kickoff event at the Bayview Holiday Inn and guess who I spotted, all by himself, leaning against a wall in the far corner of the banquet room. That's right. Phil Linden. Remember now, I had not seen Phil since 1962, but I was drawn to him by some force I cannot explain. No introductions were needed. We just started talking as if we had never lost contact with one another. Oh, we had a lot of catching up to do, don't get me wrong. We filled each other in on marriage, kids, careers, and all the mundane stuff, but before we parted company that night, we made a date to get together and REALLY re-connect.

The next Friday, Phil and his wife, Bonnie, and Dalene and I met at the Boat Shed restaurant, and we've been as close as the skin on an onion ever since.

Phil and I are friends and will never part company again. Did I say I was drawn to him by some "cosmic force"? I did, but you and I both know what force brought us together. Of course, it was the Holy Spirit. Phil and I have become spiritual springboards for one another. I live in the "real" world, and Phil lives as much by the Spirit as anyone I know. The two of us are able to share and confess some of our sordid past. We've laughed, we've cried, but we know who is ultimately in control of our lives. Jesus Christ.

Now, THAT'S the America I am growing up in.

I had trouble locating a current picture of Phil. Here's one from his teens.

And Now as Parents of Adult Children

Derek and Jennifer Meet

Dalene and I met in September, 1964 and were married 19 months later, May 28th, 1966. Douglas and Susie met in November 2010, were married on October 19th, 2013, approximately 36 months later. Neither of which you would consider whirlwind courtships. Derek and Jennifer met in the summer of 1994 and were married August 25th, 2001. Now, THAT'S a courtship for the ages. Of course, there were plenty of circumstances, and it's going to be a joy to tell the story.

It was the summer of 1994. Jennifer was attending UCLA and would spend summers with her father in Silverdale. Her step-sister Carrie was dating one of Derek's best friends, Steve Balodus. Steve and Carrie thought it would be a good idea to introduce the two of them and take them on a double date. Jennifer's father had a small runabout boat, and the four of them cruised the local waters, but as the old story goes, this time the boat ran out of gas, not the car. Fortunately, they were able to tie up to the Boat Shed restaurant pier. Steve and Carrie took off to get gas and left Derek and Jennifer alone, hoping things would "work out". At summer's end, Jennifer returned to UCLA, and Derek went back to WSU. Something must have "clicked", being left alone in the boat, because it wasn't long before Mom and Dad heard, through the grapevine, about a "road trip" to LA.

Meeting Jennifer's Parents / The Courtship Continues

Jennifer's father, Joe, lives in Silverdale. Being so close geographically, we met with him, her sister Judy, and others of the family, several times and we had become good friends. During the school year, Jennifer moved back to California and enrolled at San Francisco University Law School. Derek was working at Indian Valley golf course in Novato and was coaching the Novato High School boys golf team. That's when Mom and Dad received an invitation to meet Jennifer's mother, Joan, and step-father, Jack. We attended church where her mother was pastor and had dinner at their home in Sausalito. Oh my! Joan and I still talk about that beautiful evening.

After law school, Jennifer went to work for the law firm of Stanislaw & Ashbaugh in Seattle. Derek moved to Blaine, Washington where he became greens sup. at Semiahmoo golf resort. New Year's Eve 1999, at Whistler Blackcomb ski resort, Derek proposed, and they "finally" set a date for their wedding.

Rehearsal Dinner / The Wedding

At long last, August 24th, 2001 ~ the night of the rehearsal dinner ~ had arrived; the dinner was held at the Port Ludlow Marina. As the parents of the groom, this was our responsibility and our pleasure, truth be told.

This week in August had been picked partly because the weather is almost always good. Except this year, the 3-4 days leading up to the wedding had been rainy, and not just rainy, but a downpour. So, we had to hustle to find tents to rent, just in case. Any other week of the year, that wouldn't have been difficult, but this was also the week of the Kitsap County Fair & Rodeo, so most rental outfits were out of tents. We had to go elsewhere to find them.

Since we live in the Pacific Northwest, and Derek and I are avid salmon fishermen, it only seemed logical to have a seafood dinner. Dalene and I catered the dinner ourselves. For the main course, we had barbecued salmon, tons of oysters – any way you like 'em, and for non-seafood people - marinated chicken breasts. There were all kinds of salads and plenty of other food to go along with the main dishes. Our good friends Ted Hauschel, and his wife, Jan, volunteered to help with the BBQ, and they were a great help, as were Dalene's brother Mark and his family.

It turned out to be a wonderful evening with a beautiful sunset. Everyone enjoyed the evening, and I'm not sure if anyone rehearsed because the celebration lasted well into the night. All of the family stayed at the Heron Beach Inn on Ludlow Bay that night and the next night.

The morning of August 25th, the wedding day, naturally was full of everyone getting ready for the wedding. Family photos were being taken that afternoon. This wedding was extra special to us because my mom and dad, Dalene's mother, and my two aunts, Charlotte and Norma, were all able to attend. We had plenty of time to visit with them and other friends who were in from out of town.

The wedding was an eloquent affair. It was a sunny day, and surrounded by beautiful blue water, with the magnificent mountains in the background, the immediate setting for the wedding was next to a totem pole on a point of land in front of the Inn, next to the marina. Jennifer's mother, the Rev. Joan Carter, officiated the ceremony.

There was yet another spectacular buffet dinner. A large, white tent was set up with a dance floor and band for the reception, so there was plenty of music and dancing. Douglas absolutely lifted the tent off the ground with his "toast/roast" to the bride and groom. The entire day, and evening, was a great event. I must say, it was quite the courtship.

Doug and Susie: The Engagement Party

I've been told a million times how Susie ended up in Alta, Utah, and I forget most of it, but what I do remember is how Doug and Susie met. Doug was "hosting" a potluck Thanksgiving party at the Ben Hame Lodge, where he works as a personal chef. He is also part of a large network of young people that work on the mountain at Alta and Snowbird. Some are on the ski patrol, some work in restaurants, but most live on the mountain. One of Doug's friends brought Susie to the party. She was on the ski patrol at Brighton. After being introduced, it took a mere two weeks, and Dad got a phone call.

"Well, old man, you've never gotten a call like this from me, but I've got a girlfriend, and it's pretty serious." I immediately had Dalene listen in and we got all the details. Dalene had always said, "When the right gal comes along, it won't take long, and he will know it." And she was right, as usual.

I had been to Charleston many years prior to the engagement party, but never had a chance to discover its rich history. Susie was born on "Rainbow Row", a series of 13 brightly colored pastel-painted houses along the waterfront - a top tourist attraction, just south of the French Quarter.

The engagement party was held at the home of her mother SuSu and step-father Charles "Pug" Ravenel on Legare Street. The architectural style of their home was the "Charleston Single House". It was multi-story with many rooms. Some homes are 10 feet wide, some 25 feet wide, but they always sit with the narrow part of the house facing the street. The house is open to its own side yard with facing porches and large windows. The house is impressive and was once occupied by General William T. Sherman. General Sherman was so impressed with its beauty, he saved it while Charleston burned.

The engagement celebration was quite the affair with many toasts to Doug and Susie, but quite frankly, I felt a bit out of place until Susie's step-father pulled me aside and introduced himself. What a wonderful man. He showed me every nook and cranny of the house inside and out. He made me feel like family. "Pug" was an amazing man. He had a lavish family history in Charleston and told stories of his days as a quarterback at Harvard. Because of his short stature, he invented the jump pass. We drove to a grove of trees outside of town, which he was cultivating, and he shared about his run for Governor for the state of South Carolina. We had known each other less than 24 hrs, but neither of us was afraid to share stories about our past. I have never experienced a bond with another man as I did with "Pug". Dalene and I spent the night at "Legare". We both lay in bed for hours, listening to the creaking of footsteps along the hardwood floors, and talking about how amazing it was to spend a night in such a "southern mansion" with its rich history.

In the morning, we woke to the aroma of baked biscuits floating up the stairs and something else. It was a familiar smell, but we couldn't quite identify it. We dressed and headed for the kitchen to explore... shrimp and Grits?!? What could be more traditional than Grits? Ok, to a Northern boy, it was simply cream of wheat, but the shrimp was quite a treat.

Thanksgiving 2012 at the Damon Hunt Club

After breakfast, we headed for the Thanksgiving picnic near Darlington. From Charleston north to Tanny Town, past Moncks Corner to Greeleyville, Shiloh, Lynchburg, Timmonsville, and then Darlington. Susie led us off the main highway, along a bumpy, dirt road to the club deep within the forest. When we arrived, I was shocked to see hundreds of cars parked around the grounds.

Every year since WWII, the Damon Hunt Club in Darlington, South Carolina has hosted the largest "private" Thanksgiving in all of SC.

The Coxe family has owned thousands of acres of swampy hunting grounds along the Pee Dee River for more than a century. Tom Coxe set up the club in the 1930s as a place for his friends to bring their hounds on Saturdays and holidays. Legend has it the men's wives were none too happy about them choosing to celebrate Thanksgiving that way, so the two sides came up with a compromise. The ladies would bring a dish to the club, and the men could still hunt.

From there on out, Thanksgiving would be brought to the club. And so, a tradition was born and every year since the Damon Hunt Club has hosted Thanksgiving for its members, family, and guests, drawing up to 400 people annually. It became custom that once you're invited, you become a permanent guest.

It's a sprawling affair. Families spread blankets and lawn chairs around the grounds. The centerpiece is line after line of banquet tables loaded with food. People bring their favorite dish, and it's a spread unlike any other. There was pasta salad, fruit salad, potato salad, cranberry salad, shrimp salad, turkey salad, grape salad, and sweet potato salad. Roasted oysters, peel and eat shrimp, clam chowder, butter beans, carrot souffle, Spinach Madeleine, collard greens (yuck), scalloped apples, and that's just a partial list!

So now imagine the dessert list: apple pie, pecan pie, chocolate pie, chess pie (made with buttermilk and chestnut flour), and peach leather.

Then domestic and wild hog, venison sausage, venison stew, and sugared sweet potatoes, which did not last long. One lady said, "If the 3 little pigs had made their house out of sugared sweet potatoes, it would never have blown down ~ it's like glue!"

Chicken pot pie, crab pie, dirty rice, mushroom rice, wild rice, corn pudding, and tomato pie.

Hunt Club member Alan Hubbard arrives the day before to fire off his cooker, which holds 25# of sausage, 8 Boston butts, and 4 hams. Of course, there's plenty of turkeys (domestic and wild) and different kinds of dressings.

I will never forget this highlight of this magnificent affair: After my second time through the buffet line, I realized I hadn't seen any mashed potatoes and gravy. I said to the lady standing next to me, "Somehow, I've missed the mashed potatoes." In the sweetest, deepest, most memorable southern drawl, she said to me, "Honey, in the South, we don't have mashed potatoes; we have grits." I fell in love with that lady right then and there.

I can hardly wait for my next Thanksgiving at the Damon Hunt Club. Might be a trite saying, but if you went away hungry, 'twas your fault.

The Most Memorable Thanksgiving Ever

Doug and Susie's Wedding

Doug and Susie's wedding, October 19, 2013, was held at the home of her father, Bright Williamson, in Darlington, South Carolina, about 2 hours north of Charleston. He owns and lives in a beautiful southern style, large, white, two-story wood-framed house with a wrap-around porch on a former tobacco plantation, complete with all the related barns and out-buildings. The property was alive with quail, doves, turkey, and whitetail deer. It was a beautiful setting for Susie and Doug's wedding.

Dalene and I were staying in Charleston along with Derek, Jennifer, my brother Jim, his wife Cindy, and many other family members. To transport all of us, and many of Susie's family and friends, to Darlington would have been a transportation nightmare. Bright reserved three railroad passenger cars for the round trip.

The weather was perfect for an outdoor wedding… complete with a fabulous buffet and TONS of oysters. I feel totally inept at describing this event (a rare thing for me, obviously) ~ the wedding, the setting, the great food and feasting, the delightful dancing! I should, I'm sure, put some "girly stuff" in here, on the beauty of the dresses, gowns, attendants, and bride, but again I'm feeling inept ~ perhaps because that is really their story to tell, not mine? There are, of course, a couple bits I can readily share ~ Derek returned the favor in fine style, totally roasting Doug with his "toast". (I hope my toast to Susie and Doug is lost in everyone's memory 'cause it was not good.)
The train ride from Charleston to Darlington had been uneventful. But on the way home… it turned into party central. It was a train ride I will never forget. Did I mention the "car wash"? Enough said.

My Two Sons

(ok, my three sons)

Derek, Douglas, and Mike

Writing my life story has been quite a challenge. I thought it would be easy: tell when and where I was born, and a few stories about hunting and fishing. How tough could that be? Now, three years after I first put pen to paper, I haven't quite finished. I have enjoyed writing about the past and placing myself back in time. One story would lead to another and another; then I would pause, remember something not even related, and go off on a tangent. There were moments when I felt like I was actually in a duck blind with my father back in the '50s; I cherish those memories. There were times when I laughed. Times when I shed a few tears ~ some were joyful, some were sad.

All the while, in the back of my mind, I knew I would need to write a personal letter to each of you, but a separate letter to Douglas, and a separate letter to Derek? Impossible. Because I love each of you equally, with all my heart, how could I say something to one and not the other? Even though you are unique individuals, that didn't work for me because I feel a oneness with both of you.

When each of you came into this world, opened your eyes for the first time and I proudly stared into your face, I fell in love. Didn't matter that my life was about to change, I was in love.

In this book, I've shared many stories, some involving you, but now I want to speak directly to both of you, and it ain't EZ. So many joys, and yes, there were a few heartaches along the way.

Back in the '70s, expecting parents didn't have the high-tech ultrasound doctors use today. Heck, no one knew the sex of the child until the actual delivery. And "gender identification" parties? Who thought that one up?

Yes, and just like in the old-time movies, I nervously paced in the waiting room (fathers weren't allowed in the delivery room in them days), waiting for the nurse. Back and forth I shuffled. Sit on the sofa, lay on the sofa. Up and down, oh-so-nervous, until the nurse entered the room and said, "Mr. Mills, you have a healthy boy, and the mother is doin' just fine." Moments later, another nurse came in the room holding the most beautiful sight I've ever seen. They say newborn babes cannot see, but I'll tell ya, both you guys looked straight into my eyes and my heart melted. Yes, I handed out cigars to friends and family; that's what fathers did in them days.

Right now, I'm thinking I would like to share a few stories about your childhood, but I think it best to keep most of them locked in my vault. With that being said, I need to share a couple amusing tidbits. Here goes:

We had so much fun as a family. Camping trips (in a tent) to Sun Lakes State Park, where "it never rains." Right? After a time, we were able to buy a camper and spent time at the ocean, Yellowstone, Sun Valley, and Moses Lake.

Remember the time when, as a family, we took Douglas to WSU, his freshman year? We camped at Moses Lake and played golf in Warden. On the way back to the camper, as we passed a cornfield, I decided to snitch four ears of corn for dinner. OK, steal four ears. Anyhow, I stopped alongside the road, jumped out of the truck, jumped over a drainage ditch, and ripped off four ears. Oh Boy. Fresh corn with our meal. Back at the camper, I cooked burgers on the BarB and Mom boiled the corn. I think I was the first to bite into the corn. Oh My! Field Corn! It was like biting into a cardboard box. I still laugh at that.

In high school, you boys fought continuously, but one week after dropping Doug off in Pullman, Derek HAD to go visit.

I also remember we gave you a car to travel to and from home. A Chev Celebrity. The "Bad Boy". Come on now, be honest with the old man. Never mind the story that a local mechanic couldn't fix the engine. Fix? I probably will never know the real story, but legend has it the Bad Boy ended up buried in some remote wheat field between Pullman and the Snake River.

"Not Everything, Ol' Man"

As you well know, my dad was a Bremerton City fireman, and by default, he knew most of the policeman on the force, and many a time and oft he would let me know, "David, no matter what you do, I'm gonna hear about it. Word will get back to me." That's how I grew up, with the fear of livin' in a small town where everybody knows everybody. I tried using those words to you guys. "Ok boys, you can't get away with anything because I will find out. I know a lot of people, so be careful."

Other than a short stint in the Marine Corps, I have lived my entire life in this area so, of course, I know a lot of people. Things you boys did would always work their way back to me, and I would hold that over your head. "Boys, you can't do anything that I won't find out about." How many times did I confront you with that one?

Well, one weekend, your mom and I took off for a couple days. No need for a babysitter; you were in high school. Ok, that wasn't funny. When we returned, everything "seemed" normal; life was back to our normal routine.

A few years later, when the two of you came home from Pullman for a weekend visit, all of us were in the family room on Chrey Lane. I HAD to say the old worn-out line, the "I know everything.", when both of you said, "Not everything, ole man."

You both kept looking over at the wall and then back at me. To the wall and back at me. As the conversation continued, I wouldn't let up, and you guys would continue with "You don't know everything." and kept staring at the wall near the bottom of the staircase.

After a few minutes of staring at the wall, I got up from the couch for a closer look. As I rubbed my hand over the textured wall, it became apparent. Oh my! What a magnificent sheetrock patch for what was about a 24" diameter hole in the wall! I was shocked. How did I not see that patch for so many years? Or better yet, how did I not "hear" what happened? It was then you let the story out. I won't go into all the details, but the two of you made about a dozen phone calls, found a guy who would come on an emergency basis and repair the wall. You had one over on the old man. I still don't know the whole story and not sure I want to. I'm sure there's more, but brothers always stick together.

Family Memories

When you were in high school, I was pretty fit. I ran 7 miles a day and competed in a few local distance races. My ego got the best of me, and I challenged the two of you to a triathlon: swim a short distance around Tahuya Lake, bike to NAD park, and run home. The Greggs and Kublis were there, and after the race we had a fun party. Anyhow, let's just say we finished the race without incident, and Doug "smoked" both Derek and me. Say, whatever happened to the trophy we gave you, Doug?

Don't ever forget the great times we had together as a family. The time at Pier 4 campground in Moses Lake with Grandma and Grandpa? We couldn't stop Derek from fishing, and he came back to the trailer with a "dinner plate" size bluegill? That was the same trip where we spent the night in a gravel pit in Sun Lakes, on our way to Yellowstone, because all the campsites were full.

Camping trips to Sun Lakes State Park with the Kublis and Greggs? Fishing, waterskiing, and jumping off the rock cliffs in that small cove on Blue Lake?

Remember our road trip to "P" creek? Unbelievable! We stopped at a local fly shop along the Snake River and the gal swore, "Here's the pattern you need." Remember what it was? I do. Probably the best day ever on a small stream, and you guys gave me the nickname "King of the Misses". Even with all the misses, we probably caught a hundred fish that day. And that sneaky little pond just off the main stream? I didn't miss 'em there, did I? What a great trip! Digging up potatoes from a farmer's field for dinner and watching the Northern Light display one night somewhere in Wyoming. Oh, and that road grade operator that deliberately ran us off the road?

Ah, that day on the Lost River in Idaho near Mackay? How that rancher tried playin' "Billy Goat Gruff" with us while his young daughter sat on the quad? He tried to kick us off the river, saying it was private property. Then he played his last card in the deck; he stuck out his chest and said, "I'm gonna call the Sheriff if you guys don't leave NOW!" Didn't work, did it? That night we camped out along the river just below Mackay reservoir, and Pepe Le Pew kept trying to crawl in Doug's sleeping bag.

So many fond memories together, but at some point, I need to stop. Don't forget the stressful times growing up; use them wisely with your children, and savor the fond memories we had and pass them on.

One more. OK?

A favorite memory of mine is when the three of us sat on the bank of the Big Lost River near Mackey, Idaho. We sat in the grass looking out at the Saddle Mountain Range. Trout were rising up and down the stream, but we had caught so many fish we really didn't care, and we didn't have a care in the world. We laughed about all the fish I missed and how you "out-fished" the old man. I told you about the time Dad and I fished this same stretch of water and the good times we had. Both of you shared thoughts about your future plans, and there was some guy talk. I believe I sang the chorus to "Mary McCarty" a time or two, "whiskey and gin, whiskey and gin, Mary McCarty loved whiskey and gin." I'll leave the rest to your imagination. At that moment, it wasn't just a father sitting on the edge of a stream with his two sons; we were buds. "Buds for life… I think."

That should do it.

A Trip I Will Never Forget with Derek

A Trip I Will Never Forget with Douglas

Boys, I have a love for you that time nor circumstances can erase.

After you left home, I never told you how to live your life. Oh, there were times when I was disappointed. There were times I wanted to step in and give you my unsolicited advice. I would go to your mother for comfort and she would calm my spirit. Let's face it, your mother is a saint and everyone knows it. There were times when I asked God for the strength to keep my opinions to myself and allow you to become your own individual.
I truly believe God kept His hand on my lips.

I recognize the two of you have different personalities even though raised by the same parents, with the same standards, and under the same roof. Of course, I would not be honest with myself or you if I didn't say there were times when I thought, "What did I do wrong?" "What could I have done differently?" I imagine a few parents have had similar thoughts, but that didn't make me feel any better. As Proverbs 22:6 says, "Start your children off on the way they should go, and when they are old, they will not turn from it." You have a solid foundation and have made me a VERY proud papa.

When Jesus ascended back into heaven, He didn't leave you to fend for yourself. He left the Holy Spirit to live within you, to guide and comfort you throughout your lives.

John 14:27 Peace I leave with you; My peace I give you. Do not let your hearts be troubled and do not be afraid.

Let me leave you with the following:

Douglas:

I saw the joy in your eye when you got married, and I've watched the overwhelming love you have for Conrad. I am so blessed how you have grown into manhood. You are a fabulous skier and awesome chef and well respected amongst your peers. I want to leave you with a couple bible verses:

Romans 8:31 I will paraphrase ~ If God is for you who can be against you. You can have a strong witness for the gospel of Jesus Christ; use it. You have some great friends, and some need your witness.

Matthew 7:11 As a father, this is a great verse, and interesting that 7:11 was what you weighed at birth.

If you then... know how to give good gifts to your children, how much more will your Father in heaven give good gifts to those who ask Him!

And a follow-up verse, Psalm 84:11 For the LORD God is a sun and a shield; the LORD will give grace and glory; no good thing will be withheld from them that walk uprightly.

Derek:

You display so much love for Sophia and Davis; what a beautiful thing to witness, and you also are an amazing father. Derek, you are a talented athlete; be humble and give all the credit to Christ who richly deserves it, and be a good witness to those around you.

Listen, GOD blessed you with a great deal of talent, and your "skills" can also be a strong witness for Jesus Christ; use it. I have a couple verses just for you also:

Galatians 1:3-5 To God be the glory forever and ever! Amen.

and 1 Corinthians 10:31 ...whatever you do, do it all for the glory of God.

Matthew 6:11 A verse for you and also interesting 6:11 was what you weighed at birth.

"Give us this day our daily bread and forgive us our debts, as we forgive our debtors and lead us not into temptation, but deliver us from evil, for Thine is the kingdom and the power and the glory forever. Amen."

(For You Both) Listen:

Boys, the enemy wants you to believe living the Christian life is difficult. You will lose friends and not have any fun. That's such a lie. A BIG lie. The truth is quite the opposite. Stand by your Christian values, your relationship with Christ will grow, family and friends will admire you all the more, and you will GAIN friends.

Remember, never be afraid to admit when you have erred, you will be blessed for so doing. Keep Jesus Christ at the center of your household, love your wife, and raise your children in the ways of the Lord.

The greatest gift you can give your children is to introduce them to the love of our heavenly Father, teaching them never to be afraid to proclaim the truth...

I'm challenging you to maintain and defend, at all cost, and never shrink from the doctrine of complete atonement for our sins through the blood of our Lord and Savior Jesus Christ.

Life is not about situational ethics, a term that came about as society drifted from God. Deep down, you know right from wrong.

I urge you to walk with the Lord. God has a plan for your life. Allow Him to direct your paths.

Both of you know Phil, one of my dearest and closest friends. He directed me to a message from his alma mater, Bethel Bible College. I have taken the liberty to paraphrase, but this comes from my heart:

My desire is that God will use my words to inspire you with courage in the cause of truth. My prayer is that you will overcome all fear of speaking the truth of scripture and that you will have the courage and strength to stand for the Truth.

2 Timothy 4:3-4 For the time will come when they will not endure sound doctrine; but wanting to have their ears tickled, they will accumulate for themselves teachers in accordance to their own desires, and will turn away their ears from the truth and will turn aside to myths.

Shy away from the assumption that we have the right to determine what is good and bad, what is right and wrong, what is true and false, without submitting our judgment to the ultimate authority, Christ. Today, it is unpopular to take a strong stand on anything except tolerance.

Don't be afraid to speak openly about what Christ has taught you, even if it costs the loss of your church or loss of friends. Be courageous to speak the truth of scripture, openly, for all to hear.

Let me add Isaiah 41:10 Fear not, for I am with you, be not dismayed, for I am your God. I will strengthen you, YES, I will help you with My righteous right hand.

The single hardest part of being a dad was trying to balance discipline and being pals. My memory has a host of things rattling around, but I will keep them to myself. I love you guys more than life itself. As I enter the latter stages of my life, I want you both to know you are an inspiration. When I'm alone, I feel old. When I'm with you, I feel alive and twenty years younger.

Mikey (Mike Neimann):

I haven't forgotten you. How could I? God blessed Dalene and me with the opportunity to receive you into our home when you were struggling. (Douglas was enrolled at Washington State ~ GO COUGS! ~ so Mikey took over Doug's bedroom.) It seemed like you preferred sleeping on our couch in front of the fireplace more than in the bedroom, and many a morning I tried to get you up and moving. I would shake you, turn the TV volume up so loud it would wake Dalene on the 3d floor, but you would not move. It's another moment in time etched into my memory bank.

If truth were to be told, and I guess I'm about to tell the truth, I never thought you would get out of bed or even off the couch. From couch potato to a successful businessman, devoted husband, and loving father. Shall I tell the story? I think not. You have an amazing story to tell; someday you will write a book about your exploits, and it will be a best seller.

Mikey, I want to leave you with these words and a bible verse. It was only by the grace of God, my savior, we were able to help. I pray you will become the spiritual leader of your family. Remember, there is no greater love than the love God showed when He shed his blood on the cross for YOU. One of my favorite passages: Ephesians 2: 8-10 For it is by grace you have been saved, through faith and this is not from yourselves, it is the gift of God, not by works (so that no one can boast). For we are God's handiwork, created in Christ Jesus to do good works, which GOD prepared in advance for us to do.

Mikey, I love you. We BOTH love you.

To all of 3 of you:

I know, I know, it's always "one more thing", but allow me to offer the following bit of guidance. When you married and started raising a family of your own, I purposely kept silent on how to raise your children; hopefully, I set a good example for you to follow as you were growing up. That is your number one responsibility as a parent, set a good example. Yes, your children will ALWAYS be your children, but there will come a time when you need to loosen the reins and set them free. There will come a time when they need to make their own decisions and live with the consequences. Sometimes they will fail; that's simply part of growing up, part of the learning process. Yes, there will be moments for you to step in, offer parental advice, but only do so prayerfully. Allow them to become adults.

My father had much difficulty cutting the "apron strings". For example, and this might seem a bit silly to some, but I know you will understand. Dad and I were hunting ducks in the potholes near Moses Lake. I was in my mid-50's, so I had been hunting birds the better part of 40 years. I knew how to set a spread of decoys; Dad was an expert and taught me well. But this morning my setup wasn't good enough for him. He got mad at me for not doing it right. Doesn't matter that it WAS right; he just could not accept that I was an adult and not a teenage boy. I honored my father and changed the arrangement a bit, but boy-oh-boy did that incident put a strain on our relationship. Don't get me wrong, I never considered myself his equal, but I was now long past puberty and able to accomplish things on my own without the constant critique and disapproval.

Boys, adulthood for your children will be here before you know it. I have already witnessed Sophia becoming more mature, more independent, and Davis ain't far behind. At the time of this writing, Conrad is only three years old, but let me tell ya, he's gonna be his own man, that's for sure. Prepare yourselves for time to fly – and I mean REALLY fly – so pay attention! Dial in on what's happening NOW with your family and take advantage of all the moments you can to enjoy this oh so special and oh so brief time in your lives! I know it doesn't seem "brief" while you're in the midst of it, but believe me – 'cause I've been there, done that – it will pass on before you know what happened if you don't pay attention.

3 John 1:4 I have no greater joy than to hear that my children walk in truth.

Store that in your heart and never let it go; submit to HIS leading.

And For All 3 Couples

Douglas & Susie, Derek & Jennifer, Mike & Tauna

I'm not all that excited about televangelists, but there is one preacher on television I've listened to many times over the past 30+ years and that's Charles Stanley, Pastor Emeritus of the First Baptist Church in Atlanta, Georgia.

I happened to catch his broadcast on television a while back and the message was so timely and powerful, I would like to share a couple key points you as parents need to adopt. (Okay,

I know that's a powerful, pushy thing to say, but I'm gonna leave it there so you'll know how much this means to me.)

We are living in a time when this country's customs and codes of behavior are under attack. You as parents have a Divine obligation to teach your children the truth of God's word. Teach them by instruction and example. Now be VERY careful, because your "example" will win out over verbal (do as I say, not as I do) EVERY time and it is your responsibility to introduce your children to the Lord.

Christ has kept our family together by grace, the faith and prayers of my parents and grandparents, and He has given me the assurance that my role as grandfather to Sophia, Davis, and Conrad, and to Harrison as well, will be grounded in Christian truth.

You have been saved by the grace of God.

You have a testimony and you have a story to tell.

Be strong in Christ.

Listen, my people, to my instruction;
Incline your ears to the words of my mouth.
I will open my mouth in a parable;
I will tell riddles of old,
Which we have heard and known,
And our fathers have told us.
We will not conceal them from their children,
But we will tell the generation to come the praises of the Lord,
And His power and His wondrous works that He has done.

For He established a testimony in Jacob,
And appointed a law in Israel,
Which He commanded our fathers
That they were to teach them to their children,
So that the generation to come would know, the children yet to be born,
That they would arise and tell them to their children,
So that they would put their confidence in God
And not forget the works of God,
But comply with His commandments,

> And not be like their fathers,
> A stubborn and rebellious generation,
> A generation that did not prepare its heart
> And whose spirit was not faithful to God.
>
> ~ Psalm 78:1-8

Ok, that's enuff, I said my piece...

Sophia, Davis, and Conrad:

Oh, how I wish I could lay claim to the following passage, because this truly comes from my heart, but who can say it better than Jesus Christ himself:

John 16:12-13 (Living Bible) Oh, there is so much more I want to tell you, but you can't understand now. When the Holy Spirit, who is truth, comes, He shall guide you into all truth, for He will not be presenting His own ideas, but will be passing on to you what He has heard." And what He has heard comes from our savior Jesus Christ.

Sophia:

You are my first grandchild and oh so beautiful! You will always be my first. I was at Swedish Hospital in Seattle when you were born. As I paced the waiting room with a few others, waiting for your arrival, I was so proud when the nurse came into the room, walked by everyone, and gently placed you in my arms. Oh, I was overwhelmed with joy, wept tears of joy. I experienced the same feeling when I held your father in my arms; another love affair was formed. That day will be etched in my memory bank forever.

I know you remember the first time I got to babysit you, and I will never forget the day your mom and dad needed me to babysit. Let's face it, all other options had to be unavailable; why else would they resort to a 65-year-old GRANDPA to spend the entire day with a 3-year-old? It had been so many years ago that I babysat anyone; I had no clue what I was doing. Diapers? Not sure about that...

First of all, you hated taking a nap, so laying you down in your crib didn't happen, and I really didn't know how to play with dolls and dress them up.

I totally forgot what your mom left for lunch and I asked what you like best. You said, "Booty." "What the heck is Booty?" You went to the cabinet and pulled out a bag of… BOOTY! For those of you that don't know, Booty is aged cheddar cheese puffs (best as I can remember) much like corn puffs and yes, you get cheddar cheese residue all over your fingers. That was the best part. When your mother got home, she asked, "Sophia, how was your day with Popi?" You said sumpthin' I can't remember. After Jennifer looked in the frig, she asked, "What did you have for lunch?" You replied, "We ate Booty all day. It was good." Do I need to say anymore?

Sophia, God has blessed you with an amazing gift. When I was in the hospital with a broken back, you and your mother often visited me. One day, as I recall, you sat in the far corner, next to the window, drawing a picture, and said very little to Popi. I still have this mental picture of you, leaning against the window, drawing. I was a bit disappointed ~ not in the best of shape, drugged up to relieve pain ~ but after you and Jennifer left, the nurse came up to me and said, "David, would you like to see the picture your granddaughter drew?" OH MY! It was us ~ you were holding my hand with a giant heart above us and the caption, "I love you popi". Wow! Tears flowed from my eyes like you can't believe and I still shed tears when I look at it. Sophia, Popi loves YOU. The Lord had blessed you with a great gift. Do not hide it under a bush.

I have constructed houses from the ground up, but the single most challenging thing I ever built was your hope chest. I traveled all over the NW looking for the most beautiful and perfect wood for such a project. I spent hours making sure everything was square. Unlike building a house, where you can kick a 2x4 over a bit to square up a wall, that doesn't work with hope chests. I did "waste" a few boards and got help from your grandmother, and I even called on Phil Linden to help with the hinges, but I am so proud of the end project. I hope it will stay with you all your life and you can show it off to your children.

In the short 12 years of your life, I have seen quite a change. Remember the first time I skied with you? We had just finished lunch at Campbell Basin. We stepped outside, got our skis on, and you said, "Ok, Popi, follow me and make every turn I make." Sophia, I bubbled over with joy to think you cared that much about your grandpa. Brings a smile to my heart right now.

Sophia, you have so much talent. I love how you will try anything. Soccer, track, piano, violin, voice lessons, skiing, and knitting. What did I miss? You are the most multi-talented person I know. Keep it up. You never need to promote yourself; your talents will speak for themselves.

Let me finish with this: at times you seem to be, shall I say, "stand-offish"? But I know, still waters run deep. I have witnessed first-hand your reserved manner, but I know you have an over-flowing love for friends and family.

I love you.

> Verses for you ~ Proverbs 3:5-6
> Trust in the Lord with all your heart
> And do not lean on your own understanding.
> 6 In all your ways acknowledge Him,
> And He will make your paths straight.
>
> And 1 Peter 5:7 Cast all your anxiety on Him for He cares for you.

Davis:

You're another first, my first grandson.

You're my bud. I missed the day you were born. I had just returned from a hunting trip in Canada and had been exposed to the Swine Flu and needed to be under quarantine. What a thrill to hold for the first time in my arms and I sang the song "Jesus Loves Me" softly in your ear; I've sung that to you many times. I have trouble remembering birth dates, but there's no way I can forget yours. Halloween? Yes, your sister was born on Mother's Day, but that date can change. Halloween is always October 31st.

To think you're only 11 years old. You are sumpthin' else and definitely all boy. Davis, at the age of 11, you have displayed a ton of athletic talent. You are an outstanding soccer team player, a great distant runner, and even beat your dad in 5 Ks. I know your ultimate dream is to make it on the PGA tour, and you are truly gifted at golf. Heck, you've already scored a hole-in-one.

I hope all your dreams come true. As you grow, my hope is you experience all the venues available.

When I watch the movie Forrest Gump and hear that famous line, "I just felt like running…", I hafta ask, "Davis, what is it with you and running?" Not only are you fast, you have a motor that just won't slow down. At age 9, what did it feel like to beat your dad in a 5K? Never mind. I hope you never quit running. Your great grandfather, my dad, was FAST. He ran a 9.9 in the hundred-yard dash and that was without starting blocks and on a cinder track. I think you can equal or beat that. Keep it up.

If my dad, your great-grandpa, could have seen you run he would have said, "I bet he could break all my high school records. He's got some kinda speed." I have a newspaper from back in the late 1930s where people would write in asking about certain athletes. One reader wrote, "Whatever happened to Don Mills?" The editor replies, "Don Mills, the greatest track athlete Bremerton has ever produced, is now in the Army." Davis, I've seen it, you have the potential to make your great-grandpa proud.

Fishing? What's with you and BASS fishing? In a couple years, I hope I'm strong enough to take you on a road trip to Montana and introduce you to some "real" fishing. Come on now, you live on the water; get out there and practice fly casting with that rod I gave you. Be a kid. Try everything.

Right now, my fondest memory of you was when we skied Queens at Crystal Mountain. I had not skied in, let's say, 30+ years. You, Sophia, and I left Campbell Basin Lodge and started down "Queens". Sophia led off. After a bit, you guys got way ahead of me. Near the bottom of the run, I got hung up in a heavy drift and couldn't turn. Instead of going into the trees, I simply fell over. The two of you stopped about a hundred yards down the hill and waited.

Getting up for an old geezer is difficult and I was having a bit of a problem in the deep snow. You yelled up to me, "Popi, you ok?" Before I could answer, you had your skis off and were walking up the hill to help. "Davis, I'll make it.", but you kept coming. "No, no, I'm fine." I insisted. I finally got up, you turned back, and I skied down to the two of you. Once reunited, I said, "Davis, I was fine, you didn't need to walk up the hill." To that, you replied, "Popi, I would do anything for you." Buddy, you melted my heart. Davis, I love you.

Davis, one more thing (as there always is with Popi) the Lord has blessed you with such an outward expression of love like I have never seen before. And God has blessed you with this great gift: you are not afraid to speak to others about God. I've witnessed that from you. Never let that get away.

You have a tremendous witness for the truth.

Verses for you ~

John 3:16 For God so loved the world, that He gave His only begotten Son, that whoever believes in Him shall not perish, but have eternal life.

Joshua 1:9 Yes, be bold and strong! Banish fear and doubt! For remember, the Lord you God is with you wherever you go.

Conrad:

What can I say at this point? You barely utter "Daddy" and "Mommy", but I swear I heard you say "Popi" when Uncle Jim and I visited in the winter of 2020. I've seen the love in your spirit this past winter when you fell asleep in Uncle Jim's arms

I was so happy when I heard Susie, and Doug announce they were gonna have a baby. Your grandma and I had smiles all over our faces, "Doug's gonna be a father!" Oh, happy days! Popi's middle name is Conrad, and my grandfather's name was Conrad George Mills. When your mom and dad said they were naming you Conrad Gibbes Mills, I was tickled.

Grammy and I would have been at the hospital for your original due date, April 1, 2018, but you decided to come into this world early, March 20th, 2018. But we were so fortunate to celebrate your first Easter Sunrise Service, along with Grandma Susu and your mom and dad on top of Snowbird. Boy-oh-boy, it was Brrr-freezin'-cold, but God gave us a beautiful sunrise from what seemed like the top of the world. Held you in my arms and sang "Jesus Loves You" to you. Of course, you will not remember, but it meant a great deal to me.

Conrad, I've seen a video of you skiing, and at the time of this writing you're only 21months old? Trust me, I have shared that video clip with all my friends, even people I don't know. Be careful, it won't be long before you'll blow by mom and dad off the slopes. I think the Winter Olympics is in your future. But please, stay off the snowboard.

One not-so-fun memory. This last spring, while you, your dad, and mom were visiting Grandpa and Grandma, they left you with us and went on a "date night". Once you got going, I had a tough time keepin' up. You definitely have a set of wheels. Well, you slipped out of sight for a moment and I caught up as you swallowed a picture magnet off the refrigerator. I finally caught you the second time you ran around the dining room table. You slowed down because you started choking. That magnet was stuck in your throat. I grabbed you, turned you upside down, and shook you for all I was worth. Finally, the magnet dropped out. Oh my! A few minutes later, my knees turned to jelly. Conrad, I love you.

Conrad, it won't be long before you'll be able to read, and I want to leave you with the following:

Proverbs 17:6 Grandchildren are the crown of the aged and the glory of children is their fathers.

Psalms 119:105 (Living Bible) Your words are a flashlight to light the path ahead of me and keep me from stumbling.

First Day of School ~ Sophia 9th Davis 6th / Conrad Age 2

Sophia with Presidential Academic Achievement Award

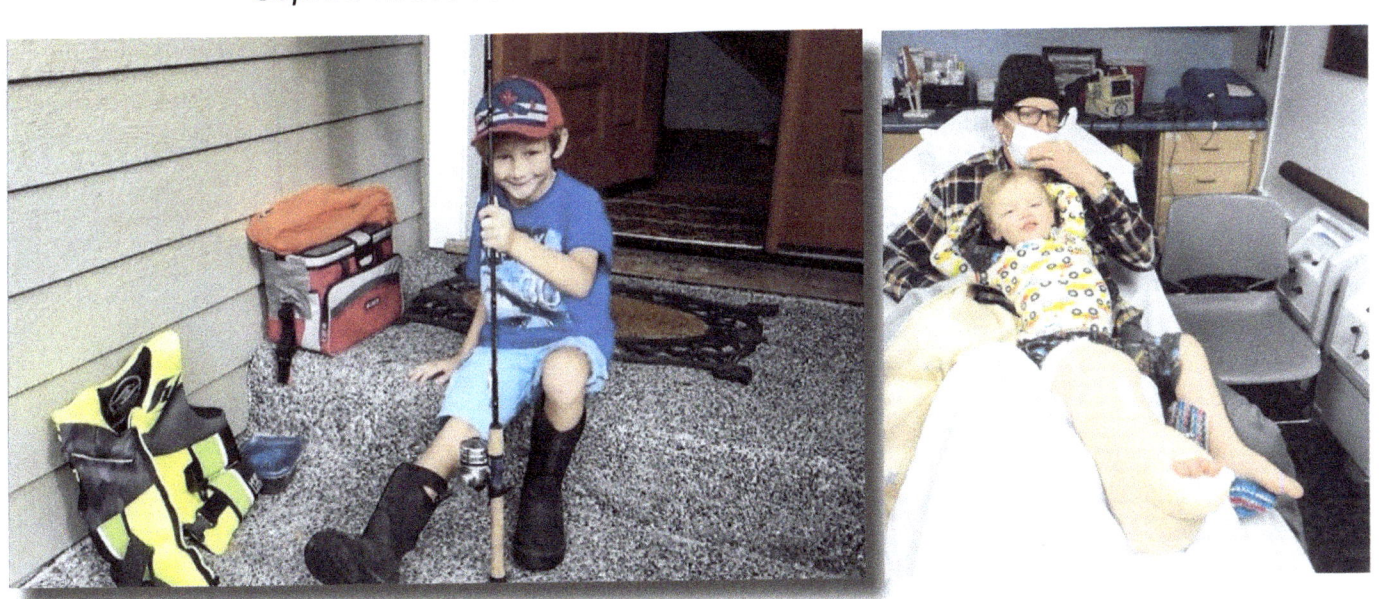

Left: Davis waiting for Popi to take him fishing.
Right: Conrad at age 2 with a broken leg from skiing.

Sophia: "Follow me, Popi, and make turns when I do."
Davis: "I'll do anything for you, Popi!"

Final Thoughts For Y'all

All my life I never knew who I was…

I wanted to be excellent athletically like Fred or Jim… that di'nt work (no talent).

I wanted to have a girlfriend like most around me… that di'nt work (fishing & hunting took all my time).

I wanted to be the best at SOMETHING… that di'nt work.

I tried to be "on the fringe" ~ not a punk, but sorta kinda naughty… that DEFINITELY di'nt work.

I tried the party scene, but that DEFINITELY di'nt work.

I even tried selling insurance. I was not aggressive "enuff," and networking wasn't developed yet… that di'nt work.

So, what I'm tryin' to say here is that this is all about Christ NOT LETTING me go 'til HE had His way in helping me be who He made me to be. Who I am is a child of God, created by Him for His good purposes (Ephesians 2:10) and while it's taken a while, I've learned His ways really Are the best! Please find this out for yourself Much sooner than I have….

KID LIFE, SCOUTING LIFE, YOUTH LIFE

Kid Life

Kid Life at Home & On Vacation

In the evening, we'd listen to the radio, play jacks, checkers, pick-up sticks, and Old Maid. Dad would always push the Old Maid slightly higher than all the other cards in his hand, and I would fall for his trickery every time.

I'd be lying if I could remember any of the programs, but Mom and Dad talked about "Amos and Andy" and "The Shadow". When we got our first television, a 10" screen mind you (measured diagonally), with a radio and record player, the folks bought a record album of the "Amos and Andy" radio show. My oh my, I can still remember Amos directing Andy on backing up a car:

"Come on back, come on back…" CRASH!

"Whoa."

Again, "Come on back, come on back…" CRASH!

"Whoa."

Finally, Andy got out of the car and said to Amos, "Uh, say, Amos, do you think you could get the 'Whoa' just a little ahead of the impact?" Funny stuff in those days.

I was prone to getting ear-aches, and I remember our doctor would make house calls. Yup, just call the Doc and he'd come over. No appointment necessary. Dentistry was totally different ~ to this very day, I am fearful of going to the dentist. Novocain was administered with a needle big enough for a horse's jaw and it HURT. Then he'd jamb your mouth full of cotton balls, hang a siphon tube off your lower jaw, and start drilling. Of course, in them days, the drills were not ultra-high-speed and the vibration would rattle your eyeballs.

Some of my fondest memories growing up are my National Park experiences. Our national parks were developed by conservationists like US presidents Teddy Roosevelt and Howard Taft, and others wanting to preserve nature, so all people could witness the unparalleled natural beauty of the United States. In the early '50s, President Dwight Eisenhower's administration took on an ambitious program, transforming this country's roads and highways, allowing people to access our parks. Before, only those able to hike for miles and camp in the backcountry had access.

Highways were under heavy constructions with gravel and dust everywhere and long lines of vehicles often waiting to be led through a "blast" area by the Pilot Car. While we waited for the pilot car, we would visit with people in line, and I'll never forget the canvas bag that hung on the front bumper of Dad's car. Radiators were not built by today's standards and that canvas bag, full of water, was the engine's reserve cooling system. Dad would take a large towel, cover the radiator cap allowing HOT steam out, and then fill the tank with water from the bag. One time he lost grip of the cap. It flew high into the air, and steam gushed out of the radiator like a mini Old Faithful. Of course, I thought it was funny, but was afraid to laugh out loud, and Dad would blurt out a few expletives. He thought I didn't hear. Anyhow, it was a great time in my life to see the bears and elk in Yellowstone National Park and stand beneath picturesque Yellowstone Falls. Wonderful!

Me and Santa, 1951 / 3rd Grade Navy Yard City Elementary School

My Pet

My dog is all black. He likes to hunt and he likes to follow me every where I go. I feed him every day. I pet him every day. My dog will eat anything. I like to take him for a walk, but my daddy does not want me to because he is too strong for me.

My dog's name is Coot and I love him very much. I try to teach him tricks, but he is too lazy.

David Mills

MY FIRST WRITINGS 3d GRADE

My First Essay

Mrs. Bandy

My fondest memories of growing up also included my babysitter, Mrs. Bandy.

She would pack my imaginary friend Bill and me a lunch and the "two" of us would spend a good deal of time fishing in Dad's rowboat, which was lying on the ground next to the dog kennel. Mrs. Bandy and I would play checkers, A LOT, but she would NEVER let me win. Later in life, when I took care of her yard, we'd play checkers.

I asked her, "When I was only 5 years old, why didn't you let me win once in a while?"

"How else were you to learn?" was her response.

People, you NEED to know this - back then, not everyone got a trophy - only the winners.

That's the America I grew up in.

There will be tough choices; that's just part of growing up, part of life. And, again, not everyone gets a trophy.

3 rules to live by:
(1) Do what's right. You know the difference between right and wrong. There ain't no such thing as situational ethics.
(2) Do your best.
(3) Show people you care, ABOUT THEM.

Ultimately, I don't believe in coincidences; God's hand is in everything. God's plan will always be more beautiful and greater than all of your disappointments.

Mrs. Bandy at our wedding. I was so blessed to have such a beautiful lady for a baby sitter. I know our paths will cross in Heaven.

Kite Flying
(and more on community)

Communities were so involved in youth activities; a local group sponsored a kite-flying contest. Kite flying, when I was young, was quite popular. On any given windy day there would be several boys on the field at the Westside Improvement Club, just having a good time, but eventually, a contest would break out to see who could get their kite the highest. The "box" kite was somewhat difficult to get airborne, so most of us had the standard "diamond" shaped kite. We'd lay our kite on the ground, lay out about 50-ft of string, and starting running into the wind to get the kite flying. Sometimes the wind made it a bit of a challenge to avoid all the power lines. If the wind was really strong, we would attach a tail made from rags, keeping the kite stable. Once in the air, you might need to "pump" the string to gain more altitude. Believe it or not, there was some science involved. We would even have special techniques on how to wind the string back on our stick. Some would simply wrap their line around a dowel in a big wad, which would always get tangled the next time out. Personally, I preferred the "figure eight" retrieve method... Whatever.

I will never forget the day of the "contest". A neighborhood mom took a group of us kids to the playground at Dewey Junior High in East Bremerton. Oh, that's another thing, neighbors looked after and cared for each other. Mom and Dad were working, and I wish I could remember the mom's name, but she cared enough to shuffle a bunch of us to the event. Anyhow, it was a bright sunny day. I had a new 10 cent diamond kite, with superman printed on the paper, a box of rags, if needed, and my string. There must have been a hundred kids or so at the field and for an 8-year-old, I was a bit intimidated. I was having trouble putting my kite together ~ come on, how hard could that have been? Two sticks that pivoted and attached top and bottom and both sides, but I was not doing all that well. Finally, a man came over and gave me a hand. Once assembled, he helped me lay out my string. I started running to get the thing airborne, but it would nose dive into the ground. I tried and tried and tried, but never got it flying. Guess what? I didn't even get a "participation" trophy.

That's the America I grew up in!

Another set of neighborhood volunteers were the moms who hosted the Good News Club. The Good News Club is a ministry of Child Evangelism Fellowship and primarily met in homes presenting Bible lessons, scripture memory, and playing games. I attended such a club, most notably at the home of Bill Rall who lived on B street. For 20+ years sisters Daisy and Violet Godwin were unsung heroes who organized clubs in schools and homes throughout Kitsap County. I don't believe they ever received the recognition they so richly deserved; they did it ALL for the glory of God!

At School

Paul Simon's 1973 song, "Kodachrome," with its now-famous line, "When I think back on all the crap I learned in high school, it's a wonder I can think at all…" definitely sums up MY elementary and high school education. In those early years, I had no clue about prepping for the future, I was simply in survival mode. Part of my lack of direction can be placed on a severe lack of self-esteem and an angry father.

I grew up with a dad who angrily demanded excellence, and if I fell short, I wasn't lifted up with encouraging words, I was verbally put down. I KNOW he loved me, but he didn't know how to parent, and of course, that stems from HIS home life. Mom was beautiful. She tried, but Dad was THE dominant figure, so you know how that goes.

I remember one year - all the local Pee Wee baseball teams were invited to Roosevelt Field for a jamboree. I was so excited just to be a part of the festivities. Before the games, a local pastor led all the teams in prayer. Instead of bowing my head and closing my eyes, like in church, I looked around the park, taking it all in. Dad was in the bleachers, and who do parents watch? Of course, their kids. When we got home, I was severely reprimanded for not bowing my head. Never dawned on me until this writing: Why wasn't he bowing HIS head? I now know God had a purpose in my life for what happened that day. Another character-building moment? You bet!

Anyway, in school, kindergarten through third grade came and went smoothly without incident. I really begin remembering most details of my life starting around the fourth grade. What a horrible year that was!

Navy Yard City was a great elementary school, but tucked between 3rd grade and 6th was the worst teacher I ever encountered. I can safely say I was NOT Mrs. McDonald's pet.

Fourth grade wasn't workin' out too good for me, not exactly sure why, probably because my attention was not in the classroom. Heck, I was only 9 years old and reading, writing, and 'rithmatic were not important. I did excel in recess, and when I got home, I had a pretty cool fort built in the vacant lot up the street. My report cards were indicative of my success, or lack thereof, but one day during a grammar session, I thought I had made a breakthrough. I learned the difference between the usage of the words "may" and "can". Actually, I was quite proud of myself and really wanted to share my newfound knowledge with Mom and Dad.

We were at the dinner table with a typical meal of hamburger, mashed potatoes, and some yucky vegetable, which I would generally gag on while trying to swallow. Most of the time, after chewing, I would try to hide it in my napkin, which rarely worked, and I would "hafta" sit at the table until I cleaned my plate or Mom got tired of me whimpering. Anyhow, dinner was goin' along just fine when Dad asked me, "Hey Dave, can I have some more mashed potatoes?" Ah, the opportunity I had hoped for. I adjusted my posture in the chair, and with a response full of my newfound knowledge, I proudly said, "I don't know, can you?"

POW! Dad backhanded me alongside my cheek, knocking me off the chair, and onto the floor. I started crying. Mom knew what had happened. She started crying, and through her tears explained to Dad, and then he started crying. He picked me up, said I'm sorry, but the damage had been done. I guess I can always blame Dad for flunking the 4th grade. Right? Nah!

I believe there's a purpose for everything along life's journey and I'm sure the Lord knew what He was doing. Scripture is very clear: Romans 8:28 All things work together for good to those who love the Lord. Looking back, I understand, but when you're 9 years old, those words don't resonate. So Yes, and I hate to admit it, I flunked the 4th grade.

Looking back, after all these years, I can see I just wasn't ready for the 5th grade, but when I got my year-ending report card and it said, REPEAT 4th GRADE, I was crushed. Not only was there the stigma of flunking a grade, but knowing when I got home it would be, "David, go cut a switch." I'd come back in the house, go to my bedroom, sit on the bed and say, "Dad, let's talk this over." Of course, we would talk, and Dad would listen, but I still would get a switchin'.

After the talk, he would always say, "This is gonna hurt me worse than it does you. Bend over." What a bunch of hooey that was ~ I never saw him cry.

As it turned out, Mrs. McDonald did me a tremendous favor. She was moved from Navy Yard City and replaced by Ron Hydorne. He and I got along wonderfully. We got new 5th and 6th-grade teachers, Mrs. Tell and Mrs. Wentworth, two of my all-time favorite teachers. Those three teachers helped me in ways I came to appreciate years later. They were the best.

Those two ladies, along with Mr. Hydorne, treated us like young adults. I was really starting to feel good about myself, actually doing my homework, and getting good report cards. No more crying over those stupid Flash Cards at the dinner table with Mom; I even took up playing the accordion.

Along comes the 7th grade with the "homeroom" concept. Guess who was my homeroom teacher? That's right, Mrs. McDonald from Navy Yard City, and she still had it in for me. During a classroom break, a few boys and I were standing in the hall; she was the hall monitor (we don't want kids running in the hall... sarcasm included). Typically, boys at that age will turn their attention to cars. Why? I guess it's in our DNA. Heck, we didn't even know about DNA in those days. Nonetheless, I asked Mrs. MacDonald which car was hers parked outside along the street. Oh my! Oh My! Did she become paranoid? You bet! I was immediately sent to the principal's office. She told Mr. Jacobsen, the principal, I was going to vandalize her car.

Hmmm? Another moment to be used later in life? You bet!

Eighth grade turned out fine. Ok. I had a girlfriend, and she was the only girlfriend I had all through Junior High and High School, but one NEVER forgets that first kiss or their "first love", do they? I know she was my only girlfriend all through high school because Dad teased me so harshly about girls, and in front of others, I was afraid to ask a girl on a date. Dad could never treat me like a young adult. More on that later.

Not sure what happened in High School, but the lack of self-esteem kicked in, and I was in survival mode. Fortunately, I had two GREAT friends in Jim Bennett and Fred Kegel. They didn't know it at the time, nor did I, but they were such a stabilizing influence. But I now realize it was after the Youth for Christ rally in Washington DC that those two were continually in my prayer life. Was I the perfect role model for them? Not even close, but the Lord has been at work in all of us.

Always Sumpthin' To Do

Elementary school years were actually a great time. Not a care in the world. Ride my bike, build forts in vacant lots, and sandlot ball games. As kids, we would never "hang out". There was always "sumpthin'" to do.

For instance, we lived at the corner of 13th & Naval next to Evergreen Cemetery for a while. It was a great playground, yes amongst the tombstones. There was a huge laurel hedge next to our yard, and Sharon Nobel and I had built our own little fort. One day we stole bread and milk off the neighbor's porch, took it to our hideaway and ate some, mostly wasted it all. Of course, Dad found out and, boy, did I get the switch for that one.

We always played cowboys and Indians. Mom had bought me a pair of cap-shooting, "pearl"-handled "six-shooters" and I was always the cowboy. Dennis Runnels, who was maybe 3 or 4 years older, was invariably the Indian. We were in Sharon's front yard that had a couple giant fir trees next to a path leading to the front door. I was off to one side and Dennis threw his spear at the tree; it glanced off, striking me in my left eye. I spent several nights at Harrison hospital, which at that time was on Marion Ave. Since then, I've been basically blind in that eye. More on that later, too!

Fishin'

Later on, when we lived in Navy Yard City, at the end of National Ave next to the train tracks was a long wooden pier. I believe it was left over from the logging era. Tug boats would tie alongside and transport logs to sawmills scattered all around Puget Sound. In our day, there was a gang of guys always fishin' off that pier. On low tide we would dig littleneck clams and piling worms and use them for bait. Most of us simply used a hand-line. We'd lay on the dock and feed our line through a large crack in the timbers. Poggies and rainbow perch were the number one catch, but once in a while we would catch a sea-run cutthroat. Whoever landed that fish would be king of the dock 'til someone else bested his catch.

My bike was the ultimate method to escape the neighborhood and get alone.

I used to ride my bike to a secret little stream that dumped into the head of the bay. The stream wasn't all that secret, there's only one in Gorst, but it was full of 8"-10" cutthroat and I had it all to myself.

My Bike and A Paper Route

During the 1950s and early 60's a lot of kids had paper routes.

Wait one second. Kids?

Let me digress.

Miss McDonald, my 3d grade teacher at Navy Yard City School, became obsessed with the word "kid". Now, I'm not sure she really worried about the political "in-correctness" of the word "kid" or if she was trying to expand our vocabulary. But in 1952, the word "kid" was reserved for a young goat, not young "kids" - children. We had to write sentences about our feelings on the word's usage, and she even invited Adele Ferguson, noted Bremerton Sun feature writer, to our class for interviews.

> **How silly, but that's the America I grew up in.**

Ok, back to reality and a paper route. Richard Strache, a neighbor boy, had gotten too old for his route and gave it to me. It was THE worst Bremerton Sun route anywhere. My good friend, classmate, and neighbor, Bob Reidhead, had the best. He could walk his route, and the customers never stiffed him.

I picked up my papers in a gas station at the bottom of Prebble; I believe I had 55-60 customers right across from the shipyard. That gas station was a dandy. Not sure any gas was ever pumped or any mechanical work done. Just 3 old geezers sitting by a wood stove and the owner, with his fat belly hanging over the counter, reading a newspaper. Not sure where he got the paper, but he wasn't one of my customers. I suspect he was too cheap to help the little kid.

Help out? Hah!

One day my bike tire was nearly flat, and I went to pump it up. Well, I wasn't being very careful and didn't notice the tire was starting to swell. Yup. With a loud POW, it blew up in my face. The blast of air nearly blinded me. Do you think any one of those three got up to help or even ask how I was doing? Nope. I ended up pushing my bike the entire route with my eyes watering all the while.

Anyhow, I picked up my papers at the gas station and delivered them all along the highway and out to Sherman Heights. It was a brutal route, and they were mostly transient customers, constantly skipping out of their bill and leaving me with the charge. Once a month I would collect. Often, I would hear, "Can you come back tomorrow?" When I did? They were gone. That was a regular occurrence.

I did have a few good customers. The Lighthouse Café was a great stop. I never made any money there, because I would generally stop and have a hot fudge sundae. I swear the owner never lost track and at the end of the month I owed her. I was a bit tight with my collections, especially if I wanted to buy something special.

For instance, I heard about the English 3-speed racer. I had to have one! Naturally the 3 gears were the ultimate selling point, but it also had saddlebags! I saved and saved and finally had enough ~ 60 dollars. Man, was I proud to have saved that much! One Saturday Mom took me to a bike shop just off Callow Ave and I bought it. I could not have been happier. The range for my trips just increased! It was my ticket to adventure.

I made a rack for my sleeping bag, bought a basket I hung on the handlebars for my tackle box, and rigged up a special latch for my fishing rod. When the weekend came, I took off. Blackjack Creek in Port Orchard, which, by the way, was full of cutthroat trout, the Union River in Belfair, and a couple times I found a great place to camp near the Tahuya River. Kitsap, Wildcat, and Mission lakes were also on my route. Not many homes on the lakes back then, so finding a place to fish from shore was easy.

So many trips. So much fun. Such freedom.

> That's the America I grew up in.

Baseball

I loved baseball. I remember my first practice with the West Bremerton Pee Wees. Francis Gaskill, Terry O'Neil, and I rode our bikes from National Ave to the Marion Ave school playgrounds. In high school, Terry was a three-sport athlete at West High, playing football, basketball, and baseball, excelling in all three. I have no idea whatever happened to Francis. He had a really cute sister, but that's another story.

Terry was a couple years older than me, but we really connected. He taught me how to catch, throw, and field grounders. In the vacant lot next to Francis's house, we worked on batting as well. The three of us would trade off pitching, catching, and batting, and of course it seemed like I always had to shag Terry's long blasts over the alley and into his backyard, but that was ok.

My first shot at organized baseball was on the C string. I still stay in touch with Bob Reidhead and Richard Barriger. Richard had a cute sister also, but again, that's another story. I played first base and batted 3rd in the lineup. I could hit just about any pitch thrown to me; of course, they were all fastballs.

After PeeWees, I hooked up with a Babe Ruth team - can't remember the team name or the coach. Bein' the youngest on the team, I got plenty of bench time, and my only play on the field would be during practice.

I do remember one very special game. We were at Roosevelt Field, now a parking lot for Olympic College, and I finally got in the game. I played centerfield the first half of the inning, caught a hard grounder, and made an excellent throw to Gary Gibbs, covering 2nd base for the third out of the inning. I was pumped. Then came the defining moment. It was my turn at the plate, and we had a real homeplate umpire calling balls and strikes. I picked out my favorite bat, walked to the plate, and dug in. I didn't have cleats like most did, just a crummy pair of Keds tennis shoes, not the hot Converse Allstars either. I made a couple practice swings like I knew what I was doing and waited for the pitch. HOLY COW! The ball was headed straight for my head. I hit the deck hard. Of course, you can guess what the Ump said - that's right, STRIKE ONE. I had never seen a curveball, EVER. I was so scared, I struck out, flinching on the next two pitches. Not sure what happened after that embarrassing moment in my sports career, but I do know it was THE last organized baseball game I ever played. I walked away from a sport I truly enjoyed. Should I blame the coaches for not teaching me what a curve looks like? Nah, just another one of life's building blocks.

Scouting Life

In the '50s, daily life pretty much centered around the neighborhood. Oh, once in a while I would ride my bike to Bremerton's outdoor city pool at Evergreen Park, but one time, some bullies stole all my clothes and I had to ride home in a wet swimsuit and peddle with no shoes. That was my last time at Evergreen, but that reminds me. In June, when school had let out, the city of Bremerton sponsored a free, learn-to-swim week at Wildcat Lake. I made one trip to Wildcat and that was it. You try swimming in Northwest lakes in June. It was COLD. One more swimming memory before I talk about the neighborhood. Dad decided to teach me how to swim… at the YMCA. That lasted one trip as well. If you know anything about the "Y", back in the 50's, men DID NOT wear swimming suits. Yup, one trip and that was it!

In my neighborhood, many activities were hosted by the stay at home moms. Richard Barriger's mom was a Cub Scout den mother. She helped me earn my Bobcat, Bear, and Wolf badges and got us young boys ready for Boy Scouts. Mrs. Barriger held weekly den meetings where we were required to wear our uniforms, but we were so proud to be in scouting, most of us would wear our uniform to school.

After Cub Scouts, I joined Pack 509 Boy Scouts with Donald Bennett as our scoutmaster. What a man he was. He often invited all of us to spend the weekend at his cabin on Wooten Lake. We'd fish, drop pots for crayfish, get merit badges for canoeing and orienteering, and spend time around the campfire. Good memories.

Every summer Don would recruit fathers to help chaperone week-long hiking trips. On one trip, we hiked up the Elwah River along the high divide and, I believe, ending up at Hurricane Ridge. Another time into Seven Lakes Basin, where we set up base camp at Morgenroth Lake, with side hikes into Hoh Lake, Long Lake, Lunch, and a couple others. There was a lake next to Morgenroth with no name. Don, our scoutmaster, decided we should give it a legit name. We found a flat piece of cedar and burned the name "Lake 509" into the wood. We held a little ceremony on the shoreline and lashed the board to a tree. Upon our return, Don registered the name with the park service. They must have trashed the request, because on the trail maps it's now called "No Name Lake". Oh well.

We had a great scout troop. Bruce Lent and my father went on several trips, along with other fathers. Gee, I wish I could list them all, but that's what happens as we slip into our "golden years". Golden? Whatever!

I especially remember Mike Rowley. He and I graduated from West High together and often were best of buds on scout trips. One time, to earn a merit badge, we had to hike into Sundown Lodge. My mother dropped us off at our starting point in Gorst. With full backpacks, we marched along the Old Belfair highway to the Bear Creek store. Up that long hill, past Tiger Lake, and then onto Gold Creek Road. Another mile or so and we arrived at Sundown. Part of the merit badge was that we had to pitch our tent and spend the night outdoors. The weather was threatening, so we pick a spot on a slight grade. Mike said, "In case it rains, we better trench around our tent." Oh, baby, was he right. That night it poured buckets. It was such a downpour; all the other scouts ran for cover in the lodge. Mike and I stayed dry as toast and were the only ones to EARN that merit badge.

At the trail head to 7 Lakes Basin. Two trips across the high divide with memories that cannot be erased. We attempted to fish all the lakes, but couldn't pull it off: Morgenroth, No Name, Hoh, Clear, and Lunch lakes.

Standing by the fire warming up, sleeping bags drying out on the rocks after a stormy night. Don Bennett in white sweatshirt our leader (troop 509).

Youth Life

Church

My life has revolved around my church family. I was 8 years old when I accepted Christ as my savior. Skeptics might say, "What does an 8-year-old know about acceptance?" Valid response, but the evening I made that decision, I KNEW it was real. It wasn't based on an emotional response - it was real; Christ entered my life at the Uncle Wynn rally.

Now I must confess, I have failed to follow Christ to my utmost.

Permit me to explain: I totally embrace the Christian concept of a personal relationship with Christ, but I have many "gods" before me. In the Bible, in the Gospel of Matthew, this truth is found, "You shall love the Lord your God with all your heart and with all your soul and with all your mind. This is the greatest and first commandment, and the second is like the first - you shall love your neighbor as yourself." (Matthew 22:37-39)

Oh brother, have I failed… on both counts.

I have worshiped fishing, hunting, my time alone, and all forms of selfish desires. I have felt and literally shown contempt for those who don't agree with my line of thinking. Not everyone, but more than I care to admit. Just today, today mind you, I saw a young man walking down the street with saggy britches and I mean SAGGY. I didn't look at him in any other way than contempt for his clothing. I had no idea where he was going or what he was thinking; it was all about MY idea on how he should appear.

God wants our whole heart. There's nothing inherently wrong with fishing and hunting, or enjoying the great outdoors, but loving it can lead to many forms of idolatry. When the love of "stuff" takes over, everything is seen through the eyes of your passion. God takes a backseat. Tony Carnes has said, "An idol is anyone or anything, other than God, that we allow to drive our lives. People and 'stuff' can never fill the longing God put in our heart for an intimate relationship with Him."

Think about this, if God isn't our first love, life will become an endless scramble to fill the emptiness we sense...

I was no angel

At Christmas, our group presented a Christmas play for the entire congregation. My memory slips on who was the director, and for the life of me, I have no idea why I was picked to play the angel proclaiming Christ's birth to the shepherds. I just as easily could have had a non-speaking part, but oh no. Didn't take all that long to get over being the angel, but when my costume included a white robe, halo, and wings Victoria Secret models would have been proud to wear, that was the last straw.

We must have put on a good program, or maybe not, but our director contacted the Bremerton Sun newspaper. They sent a feature writer to the church to take pictures and write a story. Pictures? Oh my! I was so embarrassed. Me? An angel and my face to appear in the Sun? Quite possibly, if I disguised my face, no one would know it was me. I had a "brilliant" plan. Just as the photographer was about to take the snapshot and said, "Smile", I puffed out my cheeks like a croaking bullfrog. Well, needless to say, that entire gambit failed. Monday morning at school, Jim Bennett had the laugh of his life, but worse than that, Dad saw the whole thing, and he let me know how "disappointed" he was.

Oh well, there would be further disappointment with which he would have to contend.

Sometimes Roy and Lola Hobaugh were counselors at Covenant Beach Bible Camp. On one occasion, I did something horrible, something I wish not to describe here, but Roy found out. Guess what he did? He put his arms around me, gave me a big hug and said, "David, I love you and so does Jesus." That was IT! No telling my parents. No telling the pastor. He didn't tell a soul. That is a moment in my life I will never forget.

Oh my, Roy and Lola were so instrumental in my formative years, as they were for others. At this very moment, I sat back, closed my eyes, and reflected on their influence. I didn't realize they had a "ministry". I just knew Roy and Lola were special people. But now it's oh so clear; they did all for the glory of God. They planted seeds of love within my soul. It has taken years for those seeds to find fertile ground and germinate, but Praise the Lord, here I am now!

Sword Drills and Bible Memory Verse

It was common in the '50s for traveling ministers to visit local churches and hold week-long crusades. The programs typically would be for the kids. There would be Awards for inviting the most people, learning Bible verses, and a "sword drill" competition. Sword drills were set up to teach kids how to use the Bible and where to find verses in the Bible fast. A few kids would be seated on the podium, the moderator would call out a book, chapter, and verse and say, "charge!". The first one to find the reference jumps up and shouts out the first few words of the text. Nobody, and I mean NOBODY, could beat Judy Bergquist. It was impossible.

But this year? I was gonna win Bible verse memorization. I had every scripture they used memorized forward, backward, and sideways. At home, I used the Bible Grandma gave me at Christmas. Grandma was good at that. I swear she gave me a Bible every Christmas and each one of my birthdays.

It was the final night of the crusade. Time to recite the verses. The judge started with an easy one. John 3:16. "Ah, no sweat."

"John 3:16 For God so loved the world that he gave his only begotten son that whosoever believeth in him shall not perish but have everlasting life. John 3:16."

The judge said, "I'll give you one more chance." I about died. One more chance?

What? Blow it on John 3:16?

Carefully, I said the verse EXACTLY like I learned from Grandma's Bible.

"John 3:16 For God so loved the world that he gave his only begotten son that whosoever believeth in him shall not perish but have everlasting life. John 3:16."

Then came the awful words that still ring in my ears, "I'm sorry, son. It's SHOULD not perish rather than SHALL not perish."

I was crushed. All that hard work. Tossed out on the most simple of all bible verses just due to differences in versions. But the worst part? Judy wins AGAIN!

Judy with older brother Bob & brother Don

(Judy is married to Greg Matzen & lives in Olympia, They have daughter, Julie, and a son, Bill; one granddaughter and one grandson. Brother Bob resides in New Hampshire and sadly younger brother Don passed away in 1996.)

Covenant Confirmation Class Circa 1957
Front Row L to R: Sharon Jessup, Trish McInich, me, Ruthie Nylund, Niki Guppy
Back Row L to R: Katie Albertson, Joyce Lind, Judy Bergquist, Pastor Emory Lindgren, Jo-anne Lindgren, Betty Nylund

Youth For Christ

During the '50s and '60s, Youth for Christ (YFC) was an active force all across the nation, especially in Kitsap County. YFC held a National Rally in Washington, DC and several kids from Kitsap County attended. There was a group from Poulsbo, John & Jerry Willson from the Bremerton Free Methodist church, David Danielson from First Presbyterian, Nadine Bergquist and I from the Covenant church (Mission Covenant then), and my lifelong friend, Phil Linden from Sylvan Way Baptist.

We rode a train from Seattle to Chicago and then on to Washington DC. What a trip. We slept in our seats; none of us could afford a berth. We played Rook, morning, noon, and night. I can't remember what or if we ate, but I'm sure we did.

Arriving in Chicago, we had but a few minutes to walk to the DC train connection, through ice and snow-covered streets. I can still remember the snow – it was covered with soot. First time I had ever seen BLACK snow.

We toured the US Capitol, Jefferson Memorial, Lincoln Memorial, Arlington National Cemetery, and many more. 'Twas the first time I had ever stayed in a motel. Billy Graham delivered the keynote address; it was awesome and inspiring.

That rally, and Billy Graham's keynote address, really moved me. I came home a changed, enthused, teenage young man with a heart full of love for family and friends. To this day, I still pray for a couple of my closest friends as a result of that trip.

YFC also sponsored a "preacher boy" contest. At the time, I hated the name; still do. Come on, Preacher Boy? On Friday nights, after the local HS football games, YFC would rally at First Presbyterian church. On the Friday night of this contest, the place was packed with kids from all around the county. Three of us addressed the crowd with a "mini-sermon". I did not win, but later was told by YFC leadership I should have been awarded the trip to compete at the national level, but they gave it to another, "because he came from a needy family." Scarred by this? Nah. Hmmm, life building? Not sure. I wasn't bitter; could have been, just took it in stride.

Left to right: me, Phil Linden, Jerry Willson

Legalism and Stupidity

Another scar or whatever: our church youth group spent the weekend camping at Lakeland Village, long before it was a golf course. The Anderson family, who owned property there, were members of our church. We had a great time, just being teenagers. Campfires, fishing in the ponds, and tent campin'. On Sunday morning, all us boys - ALL OF US BOYS - went to one of the ponds fishing. The next Sunday, Pastor Lindgren came directly into my Sunday school class, summoned me, and scolded ME just outside the classroom door because I took the boys fishing on a Sunday. Of course, all the kids could hear. Was I bitter? Could have been. It definitely hurt, and I was humiliated, but I simply took it in stride. Not sure it left a scar, but it was ANOTHER legalistic moment in my life.

A few weeks later, Dad told me how he "let the pastor have it" for bawlin' me out. Dad was tough on me. REALLY tough! When I did sumpthin' wrong, he would let me know it, but I felt so proud, because here was a time where he backed me up. Looking back, some 60 plus years later, that was a defining moment in my father's and my relationship. Oh, I still would get called on the carpet for messin' up, but things were different. That's when I knew Dad truly loved me.

This also might be a good time for me to address "legalism". I'm not a theologian, but allow me to put it in simplistic terms. When a church, or a person, embraces legalism it's all about do's and don'ts; what defines a person's Christianity is keeping all the rules. Personal performance is what mattered, and salvation was obtained by your behavior – and, if that were true, I failed miserably. (We all fail miserably, which is God's point in sending Christ to die for us.) Don't get me wrong - please, please understand. Leading a good moral life is something we all should work toward, but salvation comes from faith in Jesus Christ. Ephesians 2:8-9: For by GRACE are ye saved through faith and this is not from you, it is the gift of God.

If salvation is achievable through OUR efforts, if salvation is based on being good, that means the life, death, and resurrection of Jesus Christ is not sufficient to save us from our sin, and Christ died needlessly.

But in contrast to the legalism in our church, there was Roy and Lola Hobaugh. For me, it's almost impossible to say Roy or Lola singularly. They were such a beautiful team. Roy and Lola. They still hold a special place in my heart. They served our church youth group with an unconditional love that was unsurpassed. Many teenage boys were fascinated with cars. Roy had a '55 Ford station wagon with a unique set of dual mufflers. Howard Kubli and I would routinely come over to his house and wash his car just to hear him rattle off those pipes. He would invite us into the house, Lola would prepare lunch, and we would sit around the kitchen table talking about stuff. No lecturing, just stuff. It was a wonderful time.

We had so many kids attending our church, we needed a Sunday School bus, which was nearly full every Sunday. So many kids. So much fun together. We had a large group of high-caliber kids. As so often happens, I have a tendency to forget stuff, but let me take a stab at it.

Bob and Judy Bergquist: Bob went on to be a Covenant pastor. It's a shame we lose track of our friends we grew up with and only see them at funerals or weddings, but I believe Judy is a housewife and mother residing in Olympia. Tom Collins, another Covenant pastor. Ramona DeMellow became a highway patrolman in California, not sure what happened to her sister Cathy or brother Bill. Jim Jessup served in Viet Nam. My parents and I would pick up Dixie Meckler every Sunday, not sure of her whereabouts. Sandra Morrisey, Paul and Tom Kretz, David and Trisha McIninch. Betty Nylund and Howard Kubli ~ high school sweethearts; Howard and Betty got married in January 1966. Howard was such a good friend. He retired from the shipyard as a painter and passed away from mesothelioma. I still miss his friendship.

Weekly social gatherings, summer camp, and sometimes meetings with out-of-state Covenant groups. We put on Christmas skits; we even had a youth choir.

My singing and acting were awful. In the choir, Howard Kubli and I stood beside one another, and we both would just "mouth" the words. Did anyone else know? Eh.

And, of course, great as the group was, it wasn't perfect, either.

On my first ski trip I was asked if my clothes came from the Salvation Army. It was meant as a joke, but it hurt. I was ashamed. Growing up, I knew Mom and Dad weren't wealthy, but I never once thought we were poor. I had a loving family. Grandpas, Grandmas, Mom, Dad, and a slew of aunts and uncles. But that single comment, those misguided words, made me feel inadequate. We were no longer on a par with our neighbors. Did the Lord allow that to happen? Build character?

Another time in my life, as a young teen, I came face to face with a very racially insensitive comment about my appearance. I was well aware that Mills men had distinctive facial features, but no way did I give thought as to a racial component.

One evening, while with a group of boys and girls in the basement of our church, a fellow classmate said to me, "You really have nigger lips." Holy cow! All the kids stopped what they were doing, stopped what they were talking about, and stared at me, even the girls.

What do I do?

I did my best to ignore the stupidity, UTTER stupidity of that ignorant comment, but I just stood there, dumbfounded. The conversation shifted to something, I'm not sure what, but now, in that group of friends, I felt alone.

When I got home and was "really alone", with nothing but my own thoughts, I sat on my bed and wept. Why? "Why am I crying?" I don't ever remember "contemplating" anything growing up. I was just a kid, living for the moment. No thought for my future or anything else for that matter, but that comment stirred something within me, "Was I offended because I had 'black' lips? Was I offended because I thought of blacks differently? Am I a racist?" I never truly answered the question because the moment passed, as most things do for teens.

Yes. It was awful. Yes. He was a fool, but I believe God allowed that moment for this very reason:

I do not believe God is colorblind. We are different; we are individually handcrafted by God with different facial features, different skin colors. We all grew up experiencing different circumstances; we are unique in our own way with different ethnicity. Each of us needs to recognize that and look at the heart of a person.

For God sooooo loved the WORLD… John 3:16. Another building block?

Covenant Beach and Island Lake

Growing up in the local Covenant church was a major influence in my life. So many memories and countless friends contributed to the shaping of my life. The memories are eternal, but so many of the friends have faded from view.

One such memory was that of Vic Bergquist. I loved that man. He and Pastor Jennings came to visit me at St Joseph's hospital after my tragic auto accident. I will never forget Vic holding my hand and praying for my recovery.

Vic was a mainstay in our church and seemed to know just about everything we young kids did. Howard Kubli, Jim Jessup, and I would sneak out of church and walk down to Washington Narrows to watch the construction of the Warren Ave bridge. Of course, after church, he would gently ask about the bridge's progress. I'm not sure how he knew we were gone; I thought we were clever. Guess not.

At annual church functions, Vic would ALWAYS bring up the time Howard and I slipped away from church and went to Lake Washington to watch the hydroplane races. Our parents never figured it out, but he certainly did. Which brings me to Covenant Beach Bible Camp.

Covenant Beach Bible Camp was located on the waterfront, a bit North of Tacoma in Des Moines, about half a mile from the Spanish Castle Dance Hall.

The bible camp was established in 1931 by the North Pacific Conference of the Evangelical Covenant Church. Over the years, the church added cabins and outbuildings to the approximately 8-acre site. (The mess hall was designed by Marvel Johnson Blomdahl, a 20-year-old architecture student who became one of the first female graduates from the UW school of architecture.)

Our church typically would have a dozen or so kids attend camp. Church members would carpool us kids to camp, and I remember always wanting to ride with Bessie and Jessie Hyde because they always had the biggest and newest model car. Those sisters were heroes of mine. They never married, but boy did they love us kids.

Covenant Beach was a wonderful summer camp. Boys and girls from all over the Pacific NW would spend a week simply having a great time. Lots of crafts, swimming at the waterfront pool, exploring the seaside beach, nightly campfire programs with guest speakers, and a lot of singing.

So many Great memories from Covenant Beach
Back row L to R: Jim Jessup, me, Howard Kubli
Front row far right: Tom Kretz

My favorite craft during camp was carving a hydroplane out of a block of pine. Covenant Beach had a small creek meandering along the north side of the park and the day before camp was to end, a counselor lined up all the boats in the creek for a "race" to the saltwater. With most of the campers present, about 50 or 60 boats would be released, most painted to match colors of Miss Thriftway, Miss Bardahl, or Slo Mo - the real deal hydroplanes of the day. Once the hydroplane float started, half the boats would get hung up in creekside brush, others would swirl around endlessly in an eddy, and for whatever reason, some would even sink. Ok, here's where my memory STOPS. I "hafta" laugh. I have no idea if my boat ever made it to the finish line, and I have no recollection of an actual winner. Sorry.

Covenant Beach was sold and a new campground was formed. Circle C, near Leavenworth, Washington. I would have loved that camp - horseback riding and rodeo events. Fortunately, our boys, Doug and Derek, were able to attend. The only problem with Circle C? No swimming pool, and Leavenworth in the summer is H-O-T...HOT!

One summer Dalene and I picked the boys up from camp and on the way home decided to cool off in a roadside creek. Aaaahhhhhh, the water was cool and soooo refreshing, UNTIL we got out of the stream. Have you ever watched the movie "Stand By Me"? Yup, covered with leeches and some in places you don't talk about.

> **That's the America I grew up in.**

As a youth growing up in the local Covenant Church, our leaders put together so many functions for the kids. Betty Kubli recently reminded me of one such activity, which coincidentally would happen every year on her birthday, November 9th. We would travel to other Covenant churches in Washington and Oregon and meet with other high school kids. Would it surprise you if I remembered one such trip to Gresham, Oregon? Dad and I had just enough time to go hunt ducks near Belfair and make it back to church in time. And boy-oh-boy, what a duck shoot we had. A limit of Sprig drakes from my absolute favorite spot on Hood Canal – "the cove".

Another favorite activity for our church group was to spend a "long" weekend at Island Lake Bible Camp. Island Lake is now owned by CRISTA Camps, but in the late '50s and early '60s individual churches could rent the site for a weekend. Island Lake was great for swimming and fishing. We would have a fun time around the campfire, roasting hot dogs and marshmallows and making "smores". I never actually figured out how to keep the smore from making a giant mess. One of our favorite activities in the evening would be to sit around the fire and toss a stick in the fire, signifying our dedication to Christ.

> **More of the America I grew up in.**

Also, a couple of notes that should not be left out:

Lawrence Welk was an American accordionist, band leader, and hosted a weekly TV show "The Lawrence Welk Show" from circa 1950 to 1980. His style of music, to his many ADULT fans, became known as "champagne music" and he had a famous catchphrase, "wonderful wunnerful". My parents were glued to the TV every Saturday night just to watch Lawrence dance with Norma Zimmer, listen to Myron Floren, the "happy Norwegian", play his accordion, and you could hear a pin drop when Joe Feeney crooned "Danny Boy". As the show moved into the "modern age", my least favorite of all Mouseketeers, Bobby Burgess, was a dancing sensation. YUK! Of course, who can forget the Lemon sisters? Ooops. The Lennon sisters. They were America's sweethearts and I swear Peggy was every bit as cute as Annette. Ok, may not AS cute, but she was a teenage boy's idol.

Now you are probably asking, "David, where on earth are you taking us?"

Well, I'll tell ya.

Every Friday night after a HS football game, Jim Bennett and I would go to his house and record music. I hate to say this, but he still has most of the recordings. Jim would play the organ and I would act out as MC of various TV shows and sing. There are too many songs to mention here, but our favorite show to imitate was... drum roll... Lawrence Welk.

The Welk show, noted for its "champagne music" always had bubbles floating in the air behind the band. After my crude attempt singing "Danny Boy", I'd say in Lawrence Welk broken German accent, "turn off the bubble machine." We thought we were so funny.

Jim's organ was in the living room and his parent's bedroom was just across the hall. It wasn't 'til years later we found out we kept his parent awake with laughter over our charades.

Also, during the summer I would spend time with Jim at his folks' house on the North Shore of the canal. We would salmon fish in the morning at Bald Point or Hoodsport and water ski in the afternoon... what a life.

Now, THAT'S the America I grew up in!

WORKING LIFE/COLLEGE LIFE

Working Life

Summer of '61
(A Hobo's Life & Legal Lessons)

When my father graduated from high school in 1933, portions of this country were still feeling the effects of the Great Depression and jobs were extremely scarce, especially for a teenage lad with no job skills. Dad told me he actually looked for work (I'm not sure he was being totally truthful). Anyhow, he was without a job and typical in those days, once you graduated from high school it was time to leave home and make a life of your own.

In the early '30s, rail transportation was quite prevalent, as was the lure of crossing the country riding the rails as a means of escaping just to make a couple bucks. So, Dad and a good friend, Bob Langford, simply left home, hopped a freight car in Tacoma, and headed east. Dad told stories about living in hobo jungles, being rousted out of boxcars by the RR bull, finding menial paying jobs, and the dine and dash stories.

The depression era was a rough period worldwide and here in the United States. Hobo jungles were makeshift camps next to railroad tracks and close to a town. Often the hobos would sneak into town, commit petty theft, and eventually be rousted out of the camp by local police. "Railroad bulls" was a term for "railroad police," and they were employed to protect railroad properties, facilities, cargo, and passengers. Typically, the RR Bulls, as the name might imply, were tough and mean. They wanted no part of the transients and often beat them with billy clubs and sent them on their way.

Dad reluctantly shared numerous adventures about life on the rails (some of which I shall not repeat, unless forced). Eventually, the two vagabonds came home penniless and ended up joining the Army. Somehow his stories took up residence in me, and it wasn't 'til the summer of 1961 that I was able to live out my fantasies.

It was mid to late June, school was out, and the thought of riding that stinkin' bus to Bainbridge Island and another summer of pickin' strawberries or mowin' lawns was not sitting well, and summer doldrums had already settled in. Funny how kids are so anxious to get out of school and so anxious to return.

Now What?

Danny Johnson, son of Dad's best friend and fellow fireman Chris Johnson, and I were hangin' out, and he said, "Hey Mills, I heard there are tons of summer jobs in Eastern Washington, let's go." It never occurred to me how he knew, or even ask ANY questions, so I said, "Sounds great, let's do it."

The next thing I remember, Danny and I had our Trapper Nelson backpacks stuffed with a couple changes of clothes and a sleeping bag. No food. No money. I think I had 5 bucks and maybe a couple more, but nonetheless, we were ready to "hit the rails," as it were. One thing puzzles me to this very day: I have no idea if we got parental approval? No matter, we hitched a ride with his big brother Steve to Eastern Washington.

It didn't take long, but the next thing I recall, we were in Ellensburg, and we spent the night sleeping in a park. When we woke, Danny said, "Let's find the Farm Bureau; that's where we'll get a job." Again, how did Dan know these things? "Ok, let's go!"

The Washington Farm Bureau was formed in 1920 with the first offices in Walla Walla, Yakima, and Ellensburg. The primary purpose was to make the business of farming more profitable, to ensure rural citizens had good electrical and telephone access, and they assisted farmers in finding workers.

We found the local bureau, and a gal at the front window said, "You're in luck. There's a farm just outside of town and the gentleman needs a couple lads to buck hay and move irrigation pipe. Here's a map to his place." Unbelievable, first day away from home and we've got a job! We mended fence, bucked hay, moved irrigation pipe, and generally helped around the farm. We slept in a dilapidated bunkhouse, cooked our own chow (Hah! We heated cans of soup.) After a week, we were let go, packed our bags, walked out to the highway, and thumbed our way east.

The rest of that summer, we found work across the state. Everything from workin' in hay fields to harvesting wheat. We spent time in Ellensburg, Moses Lake, Quincy, Ritzville, and a few towns in between. In the '60s, there wasn't a Burger King or McDonalds, so we would buy some junk food from a grocery store, but mostly ate in small cafes.

We landed a job in Lind, Washington harvesting wheat. It's a shame most private farms have had to sell off to large corporations because the wheat harvest job was a picture of rural America. The entire crew slept in bunkhouses. We ate breakfast, lunch, and dinner at long banquet tables on the farmer's front lawn and meals were prepared by the farmer's wife with help from neighbor ladies. One family helping another and neighbors pitching in. Had I not spent a summer bummin' around the state, I never would have witnessed the true American Spirit.

During the harvest I drove a dump truck. I would pull up alongside the Caterpillar-pulled combine (self-propelled combines were for only the very wealthy farmer), the operator would dump wheat in the bed of my truck, and I would haul it to a grain elevator.

After wheat harvest was over, Danny and I (Or was it Danny Stroberger? Memory fails me on that one...) continued east and somehow ended up in Walla Walla. By now, we were pretty savvy and finding a job was a piece of cake. In the morning, we found the Farm Bureau, checked in, and after a bit a gal called us to the counter. "Boys, I have a great job for you two. Be back by 2 and the farmer will pick you up."

"Pick us up?" "That's right. Be here by 2."

Dan and I spent the rest of the day doing something that shall remain "in the vault", but made our way back to the Bureau by 1:30. (Dad always told me, "You're late if you're not 15 minutes early.")

The farmer arrived shortly before 2; we hopped in his car and drove to the: AIRPORT? That's right. The airport. The flight lasted no more than fifteen minutes. We bought groceries in Oro, Washington, and I have no idea of the rancher's name. (Dalene and I have made many trips to Walla Walla and the surrounding towns and can find no trace of the farm where we worked.)

We spent two weeks mending fence along a creek that ran through his property. A major railroad line ran adjacent to his property and it's possible for a rail car to throw off sparks and cause a brush fire. We spent hours control burning grass.

After the Oro, Washington job, we made our way back to Walla Walla and parted company. Dan Stroberger found a job in Milton-Freewater, Oregon in a pea factory and I headed home. I was never out of work for more than two days, got back home penniless, but much the wiser.

During my summer in Eastern Washington there were a number of events that shaped my life in a positive direction, but one encounter was a life-changing moment.

We were in Sprague, Washington and stopped at a local café for lunch. As we ate lunch, Dan and I came up with a not so brilliant idea: "dine and dash". Oh my. What came over me was not good, but it's a moment I will never forget. After eating, I slipped out of the café and made a mad dash down the street, turned a corner, and thought I had made it free! The city cop had headed me off and was standing by his car. "Son, get in."

I was scared to death. He lectured me 'til he was blue in the face, took me back to the café where I paid the tab, and then he said, "Son, back in the car." I thought to myself, "Oh no, oh no, I'm goin' to jail. Please no."

The cop lectured me for another 5 minutes, drove me to the edge of town, and said, "Don't ever do that again. Now get goin'."

Years later, I look back at that brief episode and realize that policeman had love in his heart. A love rarely witnessed.

THAT'S the America I grew up in.

I worked harvesting wheat, no self-propelled combines then.

Alaskan Fishing Life

The outdoors has always been a huge part of my life. Did I mention Dad christened me with a fly rod and a box of shotgun shells? Well, he did, and I've carried on that tradition with Douglas, Derek, and our grandchildren.

Dad was a fireman, which meant he always had a part-time job along with that. He drove the regional bookmobile and worked as a janitor at Olympic View grade school. Not only did he have part-time jobs and work a "24 hrs. on/48 hrs. off" shift, but there was plenty of time for fishing and hunting, and I always seemed to be with him.

During the summer months, Dad had a commercial salmon troll boat. He fished out of Neah Bay and on occasion I was his deckhand. What a thrill to fish all day and then spend the night, on anchor, in a protected cove. Meals were not much ~ something Mom had made at home and Dad would heat up on the Coleman camp stove, but I had a full belly and would fall asleep to the sound of waves slapping the bow of the boat.

It was the spring of 1963 and I would be graduating (by the skin of my teeth) from high school in June. Summer jobs were easy to find, but the lure of spending a summer on a fishing boat had captured my attention. So, one Saturday I caught the Bremerton to Seattle ferry, made my way to Fisherman's Wharf in Ballard, and started walking the docks. I was awestruck by the size of purse-seine boats, 60 to 70 feet long, (Dad's boat was 19') a huge cabin, a flying bridge, and rigging the like of which I'd never seen. It was quite intimidating! But not to be deterred, if I saw someone onboard a boat, I would introduce myself and ask if there was a job opening for the summer. The typical response was, "Have you ever worked on a purse-seiner?" Of course, I had to say, "No, but I'm willing to learn." Well, that wasn't working so well, and after several refusals, I learned to ask the skipper if he needed a deckhand.

Then I met Angelo Busanich. He was on the bridge of his boat, the Anne Marie. Boy, did he have a fisherman's look about him! I swear he had a few barnacles on his neck. He had a broad face and a short, snubbed nose with a ruddy complexion. When I shook his hand, mine got lost inside those "ham-hocks".

"Hi. My name is David Mills. I'm from Bremerton and was wondering if you might need a deckhand for the summer?"

"Have you ever worked on a purse seiner before?"

"No, but I'm willing to learn."

Don't be surprised what a firm handshake means to most.

"Well, tell ya what, starting next Saturday I 'hafta' hang a new seine. Be here by 8 o'clock, and you're hired. I'll start ya off at half a share, and we'll see how it goes."

I thought to myself, "Half a share? I don't care. I've got a job on a fishing boat, and I'm goin' to Alaska!"

"I've got a job!"

"I'm goin' to Alaska!"

Cloud nine? Nah. I was so far in the stratosphere that to this day today I don't remember one step from Ballard back to the ferry terminal.

I must confess, the night before graduation, Jim Bennett and I did a little painting on a certain train trestle near Belfair:

BOLD white letters ~ "MILLS AND BENNETT WEST '63"

{Editor's Note, included by the author's request: When I first read this part of the manuscript, I laughed out loud! "I know that sign! I saw it! And now I know the author personally!"

That "decoration" stayed there for Quite a while! When I was a kid ~ just old enough to begin reading well ~ my family was on a trip, heading south out of Bremerton. I'd been reading the road signs and asking my parents what they meant, so when we came to came to the "certain train trestle near Belfair" I read the sign there: "MILLS AND BENNETT WEST '63" and asked what that meant.

"It's graffiti from vandals." Mom replied with obvious disdain.

"Nah," Dad countered, obviously amused, "it's just some kids having fun and celebrating their graduation from high school. Mills and Bennett graduated from West High School, apparently in 1963."

My sister asked what graffiti was. There ensued a discussion from my parents about graffiti and vandalism, which finished with my dad saying that even though it was technically vandalism, he was impressed with the guts of Mills and Bennett to do the deed. He said it must have been quite a feat to get it accomplished!}

Graduation night was a blur. Our class had an all-night party at Kitsap Golf and Country Club, which was "ok", but so what!

I'm goin' to Alaska.

My seabag, with a few clothes and a sleepin' bag, was already packed, and the morning after graduation, I caught the ferry for Seattle. As I got off the ferry and headed toward Fisherman's wharf (totally on my own, mind you), I paused and looked back on a few of my adventures. I did so many things on my own. Looking back, I realize it was all in God's plan. I didn't know it at the time, because I was so wrapped up in my own desires, but His hand was in everything. I suspect that's the way it is for most of us. Right?

I had spent the previous summer bummin' around Eastern Washington finding jobs here 'n' there. Did my parents know where or what I was doing? Don't think so. I'm not sure if that's the way it was with most kids my age, or what? I haven't come to any conclusions. Sometimes I think my parents didn't care. Sometimes I think I was being taught some of life's lessons.

I just don't know. I do know they loved me, but... Oh well, it's one of those things that haunts me to this day. So be it.

There I was, trudging my way along Alaskan Way, headed to Fisherman's wharf, when a beat-up-lookin' pick-up truck pulled over and out of the window a shout:

"Hey, Mills!" It was Angelo. "You're walking to the boat? No ride from yer parents?"

Without much thought, I covered for them, "No, they both had to work."

That's when Angelo took a real likin' to me. He realized, no matter what, this kid's gonna get it done.

"Buds for life."

The entire crew was now assembled. All of us teenage boys: a nephew of Angelo's from Spokane, our cook from West Seattle, and another kid from Franklin High. We were to pick up our skiff driver in Ketchikan.

I wish I could get in touch with our crew, but when the season ended, we went our separate ways.

The next two weeks we spent hangin' a new seine, from the corks to the lead line. The trip to Ketchikan took several days. Through the Ballard Locks into Puget Sound, along the west coast of Whidbey Island, slippin' our way around the San Juan Islands, and then into the Straits of Georgia. What a wild ride that was. The straits are a bit unique in that most traffic goes north or south, and the swell and chop come from the west and pounded us broadside all night long. Worst weather I've ever been in but, I'm headed for Alaska!

Once through the straits, there still was plenty of open water, mostly protected by Vancouver Island. We passed by Campbell River and then, starin' us in the face, the infamous Seymour Narrows (Discovery Passage) and the southern entrance to the inside passage. Seymour Narrows was once considered the most dangerous stretch of water on the inside passage. Between 1850 and 1953, more than 100 ships struck one of the two mountainous rocks lying just beneath the surface. At low slack, the rocks were visible and careful navigation would get a ship past. For most of its length, the Narrows is only 820 yards wide with a current that can reach 15 knots when the tide is moving. The area would turn into a churning mass of water and a deadly whirlpool created by Ripple Rock with a slot on the east side so narrow you could literally touch the canyon wall.

In 1953, the BC government decided to blast Ripple Rock apart in what turned out to be the largest peacetime, non-nuclear explosion in the world. The blast was widely publicized and I can remember watching the explosion on television. So, when we approached the entrance to the narrows, I was completely caught up in the moment. Our boat, the Anne Marie, had a top speed of about 8 knots, so we drifted just off Campbell River waiting for slack tide. About half an hour before slack, we made our move and skirted the channel on the eastside, literally inches from the rocks on Quadra Island. Once into the passage, we passed by Port Hardy, Calvert Island, Bella Bella, Lady Douglas Island, a few more narrow passages, and Ketchikan was not far.

The journey through the narrows was awesome. There was an abundance of wildlife onshore, whales everywhere, and the occasional cruise ship passing by so close you would almost touch it. (That was scary, especially at night).

Prince Rupert, Duke Island, Metlakatla, and finally Ketchikan. We sat in port for what seemed like an eternity (one week) while the fleet negotiated a price on the fish with the canneries. Negotiations on this occasion – as is often the case with commercial fisherman – led to a strike. There wasn't a union, but the fisherman stuck together like glue and it would be very unhealthy, if you get my drift, for a fisherman to cross the "picket line". Once the strike ended, we headed due north, stopping to fish if we saw a lot of "jumpers", but our ultimate goal was the Icy Straits. Through the Wrangell Narrows, past Petersburg, past Juneau, and then the fishing grounds of Icy Straits, just off the tip of Glacier Bay National Park.

During the strike, we had plenty of time to experience the wild, and I mean wild, Ketchikan. During the late 1890s, Ketchikan was a mining center for gold and copper, but ultimately it was fishing and logging that allowed the town to grow. By 1936, 7 canneries were in operation, producing 1.5 million cases of salmon per year. Lumber was needed for new construction, salmon packing boxes, and with the advent of WWII, logging villages sprung up throughout the territory. Spruce was the dominant evergreen and was in high demand.

The town of Ketchikan consisted of Main Street, with its taverns and greasy spoon eateries; and, of course, with all the fisherman and loggers in the area, there had to be a red-light district (Creek Street).

Creek Street is a boardwalk built over Ketchikan Creek. Supposedly the brothels were outlawed circa 1954, but they appeared to be wide open in 1963.

Purse-Seine fishing is a method that uses a net, called a seine, that hangs vertically in the water with its bottom edge held down by a lead line and the top edge buoyed by corks. Once a school of fish is located, a skiff encircles the school, dragging the net off the main boat. After the school of fish is well within the stretched-out net, the skiff returns to the main boat with the net. The lead line is then pulled in, "pursing" the net closed on the bottom, preventing fish from escaping. The catch is harvested either by hauling the net onboard or bringing it alongside the main boat and dip netting the fish into the hold. In the '60s, fish were typically located by natural cues such as jumpers or large rafts of seabirds. Nowadays, fishermen rely on helicopters flying the coast and relaying information to the skippers.

At day's end, we would pull alongside a fish tender, unload our catch, scrub the boat and eat chow; of course, we ate A LOT of salmon.

More important than taking a shower which we never did until back in port, was the baking soda. Our cook always had a pot available to rub on our face and hands. The Man-of-War jellyfish seemed to be everywhere, and boy do they sting. Once chow was over, we'd hit the rack. Two hours' sleep was a luxury.

Fishery regulations would only allow 5 days of continuous fishing with two days off to ensure a pre-determined escapement of fish. Port was often miles and miles away; so often, instead of running back to port, we would set anchor in a cove and rest up for a couple days. During those times, we would drop a crab pot, fish for halibut with hand lines, and sometimes take the skiff to shore and explore the country.

Purse-seine fishing is not nearly as dangerous as crabbing, but there were times we experienced potential hazards. We had a killer whale get tangled in our net and nearly capsized the boat. We ended up losing the entire net, but fortunately, the cannery we dealt with had a new net ready, and we only lost a few days fishing. Another time the skiff got stuck in a turbulent riptide and had trouble returning. We lost a portion of that net, but the cannery bailed us out again.

Despite the hard work, lack of sleep, and salmon for chow morning, noon, and night, it truly was a magical time.

Oh! Did I fail to mention the pay? That I did.

Unlike the summer before, when I had bummed all over Eastern Washington and came home penniless, I left Alaska with what seemed like a fortune, I had a little over two thousand dollars in my pocket and felt pretty darn proud of myself. Afterall, Dad's annual salary was around nine thousand.

> **Now, THAT'S the America I grew up in.**

Jr. College and Logging

I barely made it out of high school, more than likely graduated in the bottom 10% of my class. There were times I felt like I had some "smarts", but those moments were all too fleeting. I could never commit to anything other than hunting and fishing, and boy was I committed!

I came up with a great formula, though! My grades were so poor I couldn't get into a major college (that turned out to be a blessing), so why not leave town, start fresh, and enroll at a junior college. Something was stirring within me; there was a spark to get off my duff and show what I thought I had. I'd commit to studying, get the GPA up, and get my references in line to get into a major University.

Yakima Valley Jr. College might be the ticket; it was inexpensive and not far from home.

My two best friends were enrolled at a university. Jim Bennett had been accepted to the University of Puget Sound in Tacoma and Fred Kegel to Washington State University in Pullman. Both were excellent students. After college, Jim would inherit Service Fuel Company from his father, and Fred was majoring in civil engineering.

I'll never forget Dad driving me to COLLEGE. I'm out of high school, have spent an entire summer "farm bumming" through central and eastern WA, have spent an entire summer fishing in Alaska, and he finally thinks it's time for the father and son talk about the "birds and the bees". I listened, but my oh my.

Well, Yakima Valley Junior College was NOT the answer. Far too many ducks, pheasants, and the Yakima River was phenomenal trout fishing.

So, it was back to Bremerton. Believe it or not, I was gonna give college one more shot, but before enrolling at Olympic JC, I got a letter from Jim. He said he landed us a job logging for Simpson Timber Company. We'd be choker setters and live in Grisdale. I knew nothing about setting chokers, much less about Grisdale.

I went to a nearby payphone – yup, a "payphone", no cell phones then. I called home, collect mind you, told Mom about working for Simpson. I asked her to send a few bucks so I could buy a pair of cork boots, denim jeans, suspenders, and a hickory shirt.

Ok, for my young readers, you'll hafta figure out what a hickory shirt is on your own, but I probably should explain what a "collect" phone call is all about.

Back in the early sixties, there was no such thing as cell phones, certainly not for the common folk. Kids weren't constantly carrying a phone/camera in hand, taking pictures, or "texting" friends 24-7. When we got together at a school function or a burger joint, we would actually make eye contact with one another and carry on a personal conversation. If someone said something funny, we would laugh, no such thing as LOL. If another person started getting a little too personal, we would say something like, "whoa, that's enough", no such thing as TMI. Now, if I was out of town and wanted to call Mom or Dad, I didn't have a cell phone in my hip pocket. Later on, when I moved to Yakima and I couldn't afford a rotary dial phone in my crummy basement apartment, I had to find a "payphone" (again, you'll hafta figure what a payphone is on your own) drop a dime in the slot, dial "0" for the operator, and talk to a real person on the end of the line.

"Operator, please call 360- XXX-XXXX and ask if they will pay for a call from David Mills."

Or some families set it up like this, "Operator, please call (insert phone #) and ask if they will pay for a call from YouCanPickMeUpNow. The family would refuse the call, but they got the message, and Ma Bell didn't get her dime.

That's the America I grew up in.

Okay, back to Jim and the summer job… Fred spent the summer working on a survey crew for WSU as part of his schooling. Jim could have worked for his father at Service Fuel driving an oil truck, but felt the lure of the woods. For me, I was thankful to have a job. Any job!

Jim always had a chainsaw in his hand and loved cutting down trees. I remember one Saturday afternoon! Allen Bergquist, a member of the church I grew up in, heard Jim and I were working for Simpson and asked if we'd like to drop a tree in his backyard. We had been setting chokers for a couple weeks and jumped at the chance.

Allen grew up in Hoquiam and had spent time working in the woods, so he knew what was goin' on. Allen always had time for the boys in our church and could not have been a better mentor.

When we got to his house, and he pointed out the tree, we both thought, "Oh my, no way!" It was a 60'-70' tall fir tight against his fence, with a landing area about 5 ft wide. No problem, right? Not true. There was a telephone pole and power lines next to the top, and a steep bank down to Lower Marine Drive.

Allen was a master. He walked us through the entire process. How to measure the height of the tree, the angle of undercut required, and exactly how to make the final cut. Jim did the undercut, which is the most critical part, and I dropped the tree. It laid along the 5ft. strip perfectly, not a hint of rolling to the road below.

The Bergquist Brothers: Hank, Roy, Allen, Carl & Vic. They owned "Kitsap Radio & Appliance Store" on Callow Ave and attended the Covenant Church where I grew up. I could not have asked for better mentors! And how they could sing! But what is is with "old people"?

They tell the same stories over and over! I can't tell you the number of times Vic would tell the story how Howard Kubli & I sneaked out of the church and went to the hydroplane races. Of course, the story changed with each telling. All the brothers have passed on to be with the Lord except Carl and wife Betty Mae and they reside at Crista Shores in Silverdale.

But back to the story, Jim and I first reported to Simpson's main office in Shelton, filling out the necessary paperwork. Then we drove to Grisdale, checked in, were assigned to a 4-man cabin, and got our gear ready for the next morning.

Grisdale was a logging town in Grays Harbor County, Washington. Today nothing remains of the town except for a few foundations and rusty, worthless logging equipment. Grisdale was the last company-owned logging camp in the lower 48 states.

The town opened in 1946, complete with a two-room school, a mess hall, and company store. It was built on the concept of "sustained yield" logging practices, instead of cut and run like that of many cheap here-today-gone-tomorrow operations.

There were 52 single-family homes built - all exactly alike and painted white with Kelley green trim. Recreation included weekly films, bowling, dances, and a camp newspaper.

Single loggers were housed in 4-man cabins built along a raised boardwalk that led to a community shower, the mess hall, and to the main yard. The camp was shut down fully in 1986 and totally leveled in 1988.

Simpson Logging had become successful by constructing a network of RRs from Shelton westward. Every few miles along the tracks a numbered mobile logging camp was set up, ready to move logs to the mill in Shelton. By 1945 loggers had reached the high country of the south Olympics. Camp Grisdale was then formed and it was a place to attract the loggers and their families.

It was given a name, rather than a number, and was named after brothers J. William (1874-1968) and George M. (1872-1929) Grisdale, nephews to founder Sol G. Simpson.

Grisdale became a timber transfer station where logs came off the surrounding hillside, were transported by logging trucks, put on to flatbed rail cars, then hauled to Shelton.

Jim and I are so fortunate to have been a part of Northwest logging history.

My first day of the job bordered on overwhelming. After breakfast of steak and eggs and just about every breakfast food you could want, we boarded crew buses in the transfer yard and headed into the hills. The crew consisted of 4 choker setters, a whistle punk, riggin' slinger, hook tender, chaser, and yarder operator. When we arrived at our show, we walked up a steep, narrow trail to an area the crew had shut down the night before. Being the rookie on the crew, I had to pack twin 10 gal. fire-fighting water tanks to the haul back block; it seemed like 5 miles, but probably was about 500 plus yards. Steel choker cable ran back and forth from the landing through a 100 lb. block, and sparks from the steel could have caused a fire. Heaven forbid!

My first time on the hill was in a High Lead operation, which is a method of cable logging using a spar tree, yarder, and a loader. It is accomplished with two cables and two winches, or cable drums. The main line extends out from one winch, while a second, usually lighter line, called the haul back, extends out from the other winch to a tail block, or pulley, at the rear end of the logging site, passing through it, and then connects with the main line. Butt rigging is installed where the two lines join and logs are hooked to the butt rigging using chokers. The procedure is to wind up the main line and the logs are pulled to the landing. The spar tree elevates both lines off the ground, enabling logs to be pulled free of obstructions.

My first day was tough. When the rigging arrived, we'd scramble down the hill to the logs we were to choke, often falling over small logs or being slapped on the legs and arms from the brush. Once choked, run back up the hill.

Run down the hill. Choke the log. Run back up the hill. Run down, run back all day long. Of course, we'd take a 45 min break for lunch. A sandwich from the mess hall, water, and a piece of fruit. Water was from a community canvas bag. It didn't matter: rain or shine, we ate lunch in the woods. If it was hot, you were constantly swatting those nasty, biting, horse flies. If it rained, your sandwiches got soggy.

After about two weeks, we were tougher than nails, lean and mean. After evening chow, we'd head to the Wynoochie River and fish for cutthroat trout or summer run steelhead.

On weekends we headed home and would go salmon fishing at Hazel Point or Sekiu. Quite often, we would take my little brother. If we went to Sekiu, we'd hide Jim in the boat to save the 10-cent passenger fee when we crossed the Hood Canal Bridge. Actually, we didn't need to save 10 cents; we just felt the need to beat the toll-taker out of a dime. When summer was over and school about to resume, Jim returned to UPS and I went back to Olympic and my life was about to take a 180-degree turn. (See the Family Life section.)

I'm not sure if I ever had dreams or aspirations. Oh, I gave some passing thoughts to becoming an oceanographer or in the Forest Service or Department of game or... I have always doubted myself. I never gave myself a chance. Was that God's plan for me? I believe God knows what choices we will make. I also believe God has been with me all ways, laying choices at my feet, saying, "David, try this, I'll be with you." Oh, I heard. I resisted. I cannot blame my lack of trust on some of the critical comments directed my way because there were just as many positive experiences.

"Picnic" lunch on the landing.
What you don't see are them dang horse flies taking a bite from any exposed skin.
I loved logging, but I am soooo glad Dalene said, "No!"

Fall 1964 ~ Summer '65

I was now living at home with little direction in my life, so I decided to enroll at Olympic Junior College. I truly felt like I should be doing something, but I still had no goals and no vision for the future. Hunt, fish, and hang out. That was my life. Oh, I was involved in my local church ~ probably out of respect for my parents.

My first class that year was Geology. When I entered the classroom, I noticed the back of a girl sitting in the front seat, and the desk directly behind her was empty. As if by some cosmic force, I was drawn directly to that chair. We didn't speak for the first couple of days, but then it happened - somebody had thrown a box of soap in the campus fountain, we began to talk, and "that's all she wrote."

We became inseparable. After a few coke dates at the student union building and a Halloween party at her apartment, I invited her to church and a family dinner at my folk's house afterward. Mom and Dad took an immediate liking to her ~ how could a person not? Dad's first word to Dalene after being introduced, "So this is the chicken farmer's daughter you've been talking about?" I was so embarrassed, but not Dalene. She took it as a compliment.

At first, we were just a couple, but it became so obvious that God brought us together. No question about it.

Still, though, my focus on education was in the tank. Hunt and fish. Fish and hunt. This is still what I was most truly committed to... as illustrated here:

The winter of '64 was extremely cold with record levels of snow. The temperature dropped so low and the snow was so deep schools shut down, including Olympic College.

Let's see, stay home and study?

Nope! I asked Dalene if she would like to go duck hunting with me. I cannot believe she actually said yes.

I loaded Dad's pick-up truck with our duck boat, decoys, and my yellow lab Rip sat in the cab along with Dalene and me. I had Dalene so bundled up she barely could move: one of Dad's heavy mackinaw sweaters, gloves, rain slicker, waders, and the classic Jones duck hat. Oh, for a picture of that!

When we arrived at the Skok flats it was near blizzard conditions, but that did not slow me down. We launched the boat, rowed across the river, built a blind behind a log, set the decoys, and hunkered down. It was a beautiful duck day. Gray skies, snowing, blowing, and the bay was full of white caps.

It didn't take long.

"Dalene, mark. Here they come."

I made a couple calls and three mallards set their wings straight for my spread. It couldn't have been better and I dumped a dandy drake. I set Rip for the retrieve and said, "FETCH!" He tip-toed into the water and refused. Poor ol' Rip. He was covered with snow and ice. I rubbed him down, removing most of the snow and ice. I hopped in the boat, retrieved the bird, headed back to the blind, picked up the dekes, and made our way back to the truck. Oh ya. That was Dalene's last duck hunt.

School resumed after the weather broke. My interest in book-work remained the same, neutral, but Dalene stuck with me. I now know it was God's hand that kept us together.

On Valentine's Day, 1965 I gave Dalene a pearl ring and asked her to "go steady".

Spring brought the end of the school year. I returned to Grisdale for the summer and Dalene found a job working for Budget Finance in Tacoma.

I got promoted from choker setter to hook tender to chaser and a loader. It was one of the first jobs where I truly excelled. Oh ya, there were plenty of heart-pounding moments. One time I got caught in the "bite" of a road change. When the yarder on the landing tightened the line, it came sweeping across the brush. I dropped to the ground next to a stump and felt the wire come way too close. I've had root wads roll down the hill, coming far too close for comfort. None of that phased me; I loved logging.

Dalene would pick me up on Fridays and we would spend the weekend with her folks at their house or with my parents. We spent a lot of time salmon fishing at Hazel Point and Sekiu. My brother was 10, and he and Dalene bonded like brother and sister. To this day, Jim considers Dalene his big sister. What a blessing.

One Friday evening, Dalene was waiting to pick me up after work. I limped off the crew bus; it was just a swollen ankle, no "biggy". When I got in the car, I asked her, "Dalene, would you like to be a logger's wife?" I was dead serious (no pun intended). Without hesitation, her word rang clear, "NO!" and it was the BEST "NO!" of our lives.

I continued with Simpson throughout the Fall. When the snow made logging in the hills too dangerous for all the vehicles, Simpson shut down and I never returned.

USMC

And then it happened ~ Uncle Sam came calling. My draft status changed from exempt for schooling to 1A, and I realized the draft was right around the corner. The Army seemed too big. Living in Bremerton, the Navy was out of the question. So, I decided to join the Marines ~ "The Few, the Proud, the Marines". (Their recruiting slogan of the day.)

I went to the local recruitment center and made a serious commitment to serve my country. I love the United States of America and it just felt like the right thing to do. Looking back, I know God had HIS hand in my decision. There was some physical testing, and I could have become exempt because I'm basically blind in my left eye… Instead, I memorized the eye chart and passed with 20-20 in both eyes.

I had two weeks before leaving for boot camp and boy, did I make the most of it.

Salmon fishing every day.

I was engaged to Dalene at the time, but I'll save that for another story. (See the section "Married Life/Family Life/Grands Life")

We, my fellow recruits and I, boarded a flight out of SeaTac and arrived in San Diego late at night. There was a white "school" bus waiting to pick up a large contingent of recruits. The Marine rep was wonderful. "Ok, guys, follow me." Those were the last civil words I heard for quite some time.

When we arrived at Marine Corps Recruit Depot, this big nasty Marine boarded our bus, screaming and yelling every obscenity known to man. When I got off the bus and planted my feet on those yellow footprints, I thought to myself, "Mills, keep your %$#&ing mouth shut, do what you're told, and become the best damn Marine you can."

The verbal yelling and screaming were an attempt to immediately disassociate us from our previous environment and comfy mentality, and to shock and disorient us, so the Marine corps could put us where they wanted us ~ mentally and emotionally off-balance and receptive to instruction.

I actually was shocked and disoriented. The USMC apparently knew what they were about here. It was the first step in turning young men into "Lean Mean Fighting Machines".

Boot camp was torture for some, those unable to follow directions....
Some recruits fought back and others were able to focus inward and overcome. I didn't have any trouble. I believe my 3 months on a salmon purse-seine boat in Alaska, two years as a logger, and being raised by parents that survived the depression, provided a solid foundation. Those were tough jobs and not for the pampered.

For the first time in my life, I excelled in the classroom. I was the top recruit in my platoon and graduated from boot camp with a meritorious promotion to PFC.

You did not smile!

The Rifle Range ~ BRASS

During basic training, recruits spend two weeks on the rifle range. The first week was total "dry fire". Holy Cow. After 3 days, it was soooo boring. We practiced every position over and over until the body would slip into each position with ease: prone, kneeling, sitting, and off-hand.

And I will never forget BRASS. Every position. Every target.

Breathe (inhale/exhale slowly), Relax (easy now), Aim (put the bead on the black), Slack (take up the slack in the trigger), and Squeeze (every time the bead crossed over the black squeeze a bit and you never know when the weapon fires)

Time spent on the range was very stress-free. Because…

A Marine and his weapon were, well, you know…

After a week of dry fire, we headed to the range for live fire.

The live-fire range was spectacular. Targets that stretched seemingly for miles left and right. I will never forget the first time I laid in the prone position and looked at the target 500 meters away. The bullseye looked like an aspirin tablet.

BRASS. A hit! Dead center. Holy Cow! BRASS does work!

Live fire was great. Excellent windage and elevation notes put me in a groove, and I was on a roll.

Two days remained: Pre-Qual and Qualification Day.

To become a Marine, you had to qualify with your rifle, and there were achievement medals to be earned. Basic Marksman, the "toilet seat". Sharpshooter, a beautiful medal resembling an iron cross, and Expert, crossed rifles over what I believe are oak leaves.

Pre-qual Day was totally stress free. I was recognized in front of the entire company with a near-perfect score. In boot camp, a recruit is not allowed to be cocky, but deep down I felt un-touchable. Then came Qual Day. OH MY!!

The first round was 150 meters "off-hand," and I was so nervous I totally missed the entire target several times. I was shaking so bad I could not hold the rifle steady and was staring at not qualifying. Of course, my drill instructor witnessed the entire debacle. Now a normal person would think the drill instructor would come to me before the next round, give me a warm pep talk, "Come on, Mills, settle down, you'll pull it out." but oh no, not in the Marine Corps. He got in my face with a vengeance, calling me every name in the book. Had he known the term "Cougin' it", he would have laid that on me as well.

Well, his verbal beat-down worked because after my opening volley, I hit every bullseye and ended up qualifying as Sharpshooter.

WHEW!!!!

The Marine Corps was one of the very best things that ever happened to me.

I fulfilled my enlistment, returned to college, made up all those nasty F's, D's, and incompletes, and eventually graduated on the Dean's list from the University of Puget Sound. What a trip!

Yes, I finally discovered what I had in me – put there by God – and I learned how to focus and work hard to achieve a goal.

But I know I owe it all to my Lord and Savior, Jesus Christ.

Officiating

There's an old saying, "Those that can't do – teach, and those that can't play - officiate." I loved being part of a game I never was good at in my youth. I wish my basketball officiating skills matched that of football. With all humility, I was an excellent football official, but a horrible basketball ref. In all fairness, I remember a couple top-ranked basketball officials - Ron Burley and Joe Frank Guerrero - that could not "hang" on the football field. Frank often asked me, "Mills, you are the best football official in the association. What happens to you on the basketball court?" I had no answer.

All officials start at the bottom with Pee Wees, where every mom and dad only watch their son, thinking he's the second coming of sliced bread, and coaches think they are another Vince Lombardi. On to Junior High and JV ball, where talent starts to shine and coaches have a clue. Once an official is rated by the association as capable enough to advance, high school varsity is next. The speed and talent increase with each level of ball.

Speed? Talent? Hard-hitting? I will never forget doing a Friday night HS varsity game and the following Saturday working an Olympic Jr. College football game. What a transition. I can only imagine the difference between college and pro.

Oh, I had my gaff or two over the years, but in a twenty-year career I was elected president of our association a couple times, was the training coordinator, voted referee of the year several times, and officiated many high school playoff games. Don't ever ask South Kitsap's Joe Bloomquist about the South vs. Puyallup semi-final. We all know it wasn't my fault, but I feel guilty nonetheless. After the game, all hell broke loose in the officials' locker room, but that was much too late.

I have a very good friend who was an outstanding athlete. Had it not been for multiple injuries, who knows how far he could have gone. I once asked him if he felt any regret, and to his credit, he emphatically answered, "I never look back." I'm not that strong and there isn't a high school game I watch where I think back, "I cost south Kitsap a state championship." Of course, I didn't but that one game, that one "no call", haunts me to this very day.

I will always treasure the camaraderie within our association and will never forget Dick Todd, "Old Man" Welling, and Gerry Almy (God rest their souls), Kevin Mayo, Terry Welling, and Kitsap County Sheriff Jim Rye, who by the way, never took the state test on his own, he would hand it off to me. Dick Terry, the best secretary we ever had, Gary Eaton, and so many others. Most have gone their separate ways; a reunion would be fun. My ONLY regret was that Rodger Richards didn't get me started earlier.

That's the America I grew up in.

L to R: Bill Von Essen, Steve Green, Dick Dexter, memory fade, me, and memory fade

Working Life Epilogue

I have had so many careers, failed or otherwise. During college, I found work as a bartender at The Top of The Ocean in Tacoma. It has since burned down. I worked at the Cedar Inn on 6th Ave in Tacoma. One week the Cleveland Browns were preparing for an exhibition game against the 49ers; they were giants of men and drank us out of beer every day for a week.

I also tried selling insurance, but was horrible; if the client said "No", ok, fine with me. Good insurance agents don't hear "no". I built foundations for spec-house contractors. After gaining some experience, I bought a few lots and started building custom homes on my own. I really enjoyed the work and the freedom associated with being in private practice, but it all came crashing down. In 1977, Jimmy Carter was elected president; interest rates soared to 24%. I was unable to borrow money on just my name, so I ended up in the shipyard.

I worked in the Design Division at Puget Sound Naval Shipyard, working primarily on submarines. I really enjoyed the work when I could step on the deck plates, consult with the mechanic, and sign off changes to his blueprint without "upstairs" wringing their collective hands. But with the advent of computers, which were supposed to save paper (quite the opposite occurred), I became increasingly miserable and retired immediately on my sixtieth birthday in 2004. I will never regret THAT decision.

HUNTING & FISHING LIFE

Hunting Life

Trout fishing, duck and pheasant hunting were my dad's passion. Being a fireman ~ with the "24 on/48 off" shift ~ was ideal for an outdoorsman. On weekends, Dad would often take me to Toppenish for pheasants. If I couldn't go with him, I could hardly wait for his return because he would always bring me my favorite candy bar, the Idaho Spud. He also had time to get to know every good duck hunting location along the canal and would take me with him on weekends. We would hunt the "Skok" (Skokomish River) at the south end of the canal, Belfair Flats on the south, and a few sneaky places in between. During the '50s and '60s, a private gun club, which we called "Nalley's", leased several acres on the West side of the river. The land was diked, and the club planted barley to attract birds, and boy-oh-boy did it attract. Thousands of migratory waterfowl wintered in the area, which provided great hunting for the club and across the river, on public land, good shooting was also available. The public land was so popular on opening day we arrived at the flats around midnight, even though legal shooting time wasn't till noon, just to get a good blind.

Further south, near Belfair, Dad had discovered a couple spots with a lot of birds that eventually turned out to be Fred, Jim, and my favorite haunts - the "cove" and the "spit". Mostly widgeon, but also many sprig, a few mallard, and later in the season, the crème de la crème of birds in the Pacific Northwest... brant.

When I reached 14, it was legal to hunt without adult supervision. I could hardly wait for duck season. Mom would drive and drop me off. Dad taught me valuable lessons on gun safety, so there was no worry on their part. I would have my shotgun, shells, Dad's dog, a sack of decoys, and I always had a thermos of tomato soup. I knew how to call ducks, without a store-bought call, and I felt like Huck Finn.

I also had a couple "watchful eyes" in my neighborhood. Walt Bush and Jerry Fairbanks were the local game wardens. Jerry lived directly across the street and Walt one block up National Ave. I spent several days on patrol with both of them. I was never along when any arrests were made, but they gave me the grand tour of the "oak patch". Those were good times. I always wondered why neither one of them tried to recruit me. I now realize God had other plans for me. Walt Bush "pinched" Fred and me one evening ~ shooting "after hours" at a stinking widgeon hen. We were taken to the firehall in Belfair, stood before the judge, and issued a fine. I can't remember if our parents were called or how we paid the fine, but Fred and I agree, we didn't shoot after hours. It was close. Yes, it was getting dark, but still legal. We believe Walt wanted to teach us a valuable lesson. Did It work? Let's put it this way, we were much more careful.

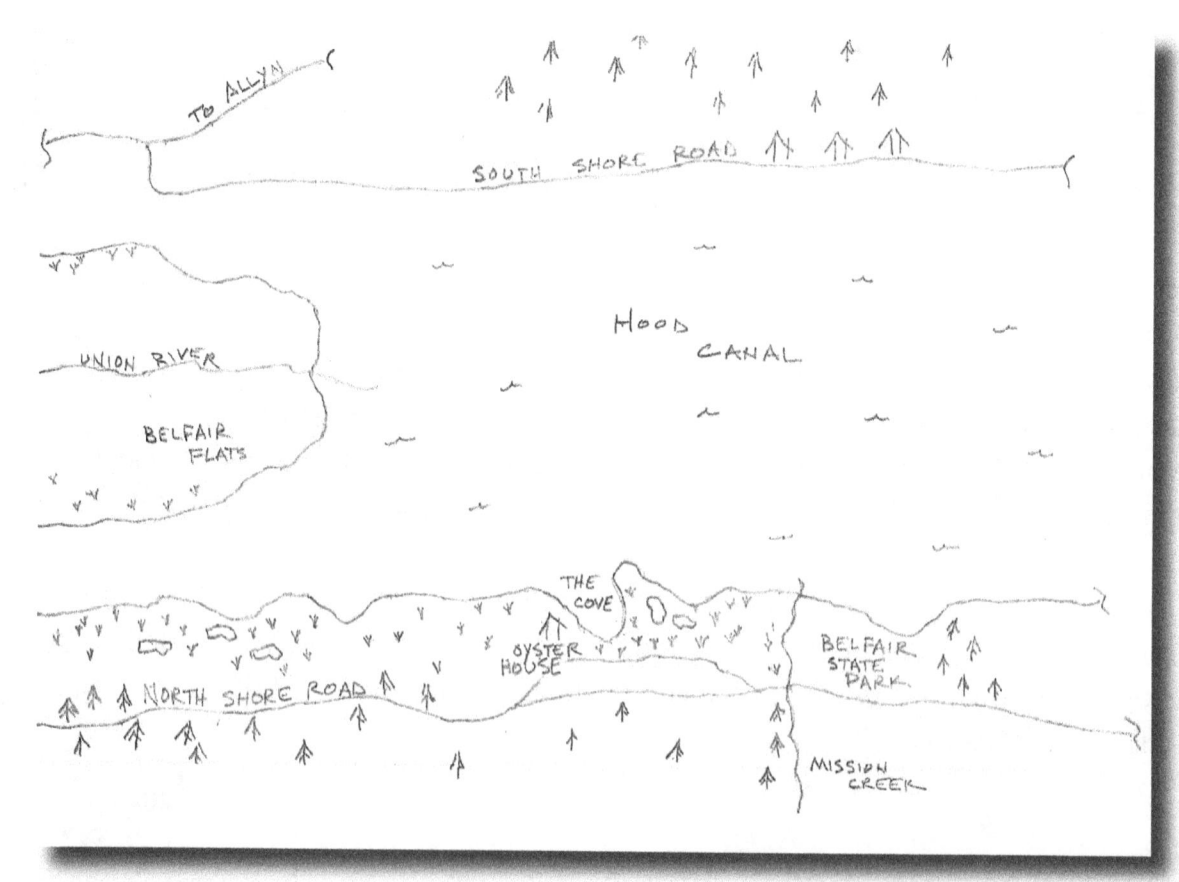

The Cove: OH, how the Sprig loved the cove. Shot my first Sprig drake in 1958. Dad and I limited on 14 Sprig and 3 Brant. At low tide a gravel spit formed and the Brant came in to "gravel-up". One eve Kegel got a Canadian Lesser goose and we both got "pinched".

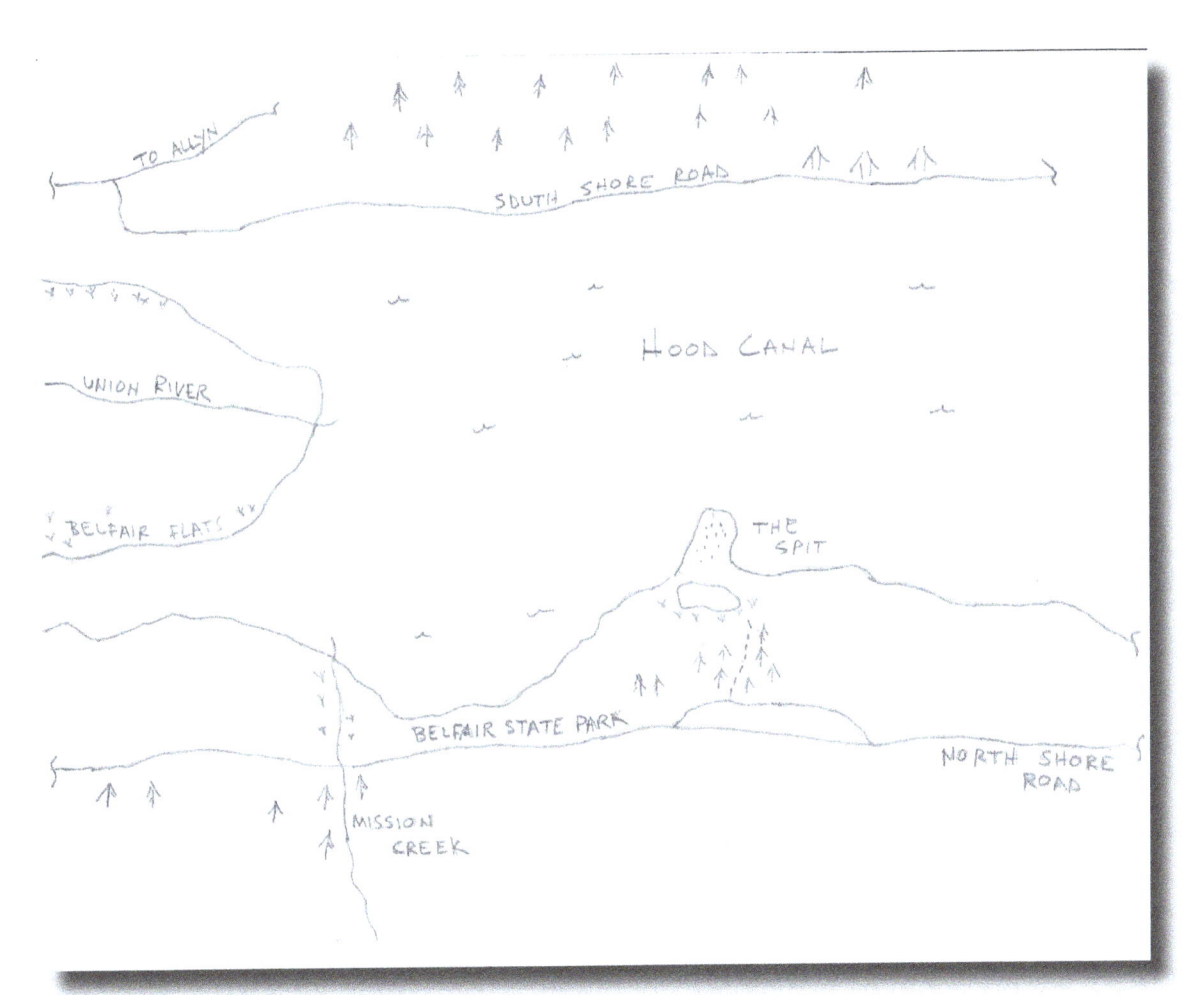

The Spit: so many stories, so little time. My dad and Dick Strickland shot there a couple a times and both agreed to leave it for "the boys" (Fred, Jim & me). "Thanks, you two." It was a natural for decoying Widgeon and Mallard. At low tide the Brant would decoy without a care. There wasn't a better spot on Hood Canal. One memory lingers to this very day: the sound of a chain saw (you had to be there).

Stormy Night at Camp 5

I grew up surrounded by a great cast of characters from the Bremerton Fire Department, many of whom had a real passion for the outdoors. As I became old enough to "hold my own", a few of them invited me to tag along when they went out.

I was invited to spend the weekend deer hunting with Dick O'Connor near the Wynoochee River. Dick and "French" Francoeur, yes, another fireman, had a beautiful camp set up on Simpson Timber Company's vacated Camp 5 at the foothills of the Olympic Mountains. They had a portable Quonset hut complete with bunk beds, dinner table, shelving for canned goods, a wood-burning stove, and near the front door a section to remove muddy boots and hang wet clothes.

If you've lived in the Pacific Northwest longer than 6 months, you know the Olympics are a rain forest and can get pounded by nasty windy-and-wet weather. This trip was no exception.

It was November 1960-sumpthin and we left Bremerton early in the morning, arriving at "Camp 5" as daylight was breaking, and it was one heck of a storm. Dick thought all this wind and rain would keep the deer moving and we should have a good chance at seein' sumpthin'. Let me tell ya, the woods were definitely stirred up, but the deer must have really been hunkered down, 'cause we didn't see a track all day. Dick was hardcore. Once in the woods, he would stay right up to the last hour of light and this day was no exception. The wind and rain never let up and when we returned to camp we were soaked to the bone. Gore-Tex had not yet been made available to the average hunter.

The others in our group were already in camp and Frenchy, chief cook and self-appointed leader of the clan (no banjo music please), had a meal prepared, which was kept warm on the woodstove.

Dinner was over, dishes washed and put away, and the boys were sitting around the table having a nightcap—a Manhattan being the drink of choice. Nothing but class for these guys.

The storm was relentless and the sound of the rain pounding on the tin roof was nearly deafening, but with that wood stove, it was oh so comfy. Camp 5 was situated just off the main gravel road, so visitors often would stop by and chew the fat, so it was no surprise to hear a knock on the door. It was a fellow hunter. He was invited in, shared a drink with the group, and we swapped stories for the better part of an hour.

You could sense a bit of uneasiness in the stranger's demeanor and it became obvious he was hoping to get an invite to spend the night in the hut. Frenchy, who typically led most conversations, was about to offer up an invite, and that's when the stranger blew his chance.

"You guys sure have a great set-up. I have a pretty nice travel trailer, but my wife won't let me take it hunting."

Ooops! The conversation went stone cold silent. The stranger squirmed in his chair, waiting for an invite. Crickets!

He took one last stab at it, "Wow, listen to that wind and rain. Sure is nasty out there." Total Silence.

Turns out he spent part of that night curled up in the back seat of his car. When we woke up in the morning, he was nowhere to be found. Someone said they heard him leave around 2am.

That's the America I grew up in.

The Good Ol' Days

So often we glamorize the past. The "good ole days" always seem better than they were, but for the most part, times were pretty darn good growing up. I think it's quite natural to block out negative events, much less share them. Although hunting and fishing today doesn't even come close to what we had in the '50s, '60s, and '70s. There were plenty of times we got skunked. I remember one day with Fred and Jim hunting at the "spit". It was a beautiful bluebird day, not a riffle on the water, not a duck in the air. Our decoys sat motionless in the pond and by mid-morning we could hear a chainsaw fire up from across the canal.

When we could hear a saw running, we knew the day was gonna be a bust. On one particular day, we were so bored; when the occasional seagull flew by we would practice following its flight with our shotguns. Then it happened. Someone, and I will not say who, fired and a seagull dropped stone dead near our blind. When the bird landed, a dozen other gulls starting circling, a sure indication there was a dead bird on the ground. What now?!? I quickly got out of the blind, gathered the bird, and covered it with seaweed. Oh, were we lucky. Half an hour later, Walt Bush showed up. He asked how we were doing, checked our licenses, chatted a while, and left. Whew! Do you really want to know the culprit? Fred and I know exactly who shot, but Jim's memory has faded to the point he doesn't even remember being there. Ok, just kidding. Jim's memory is juuuust fine, sorta; I threw that out there to add some suspicion....

Yes, there was a private gun club at the Skok, but the three of us pretty much had our own private club at the south end of the canal. We had the cove and the spit. Rarely would we see another hunter along that shoreline.

During the early '60s, Belfair State Park was under construction. Its adjacent flats attracted quite a few migratory birds, but with all the bull-dozers operating in the park, creating a disturbance, the ducks sought a quieter refuge and what they thought would be a safer hangout. The "cove" was a small inlet adjacent to a commercial oyster plant and a hot spot for Brant and sprig (pintails). The "spit", as we called it, was adjacent to Belfair State Park. On low tide, a firm sandy beach would become exposed, attracting brant. At high tide, a couple ponds would form, ideal for decoying ducks... oh the good times there.

Columbus Day Storm

The Columbus Day Storm that pounded the West Coast of Canada and the Pacific Northwest on October 12, 1962 ranks among the most intense to strike the region since the "Great Gale" and snowstorm on January 9, 1880. It hit Bremerton full-throttle on Friday night, immediately after the opening kickoff between West High School and Stadium High School. It was a windstorm with winds of 100+mph and was linked to 46 deaths and nearly 250 million dollars in damage. More importantly, as far as I was concerned, it hit the day before the opening of duck season.

My father and Chris Johnson were in Eastern Washington for the opening of pheasant season and didn't even know what happened at home. A group of Bremerton firemen were in British Columbia on a moose hunt; they reported the woods turned upside down and moose were running everywhere. The four had been hoping to bag a moose a piece, but there was a liberal limit of 2 moose per hunter and they came home with 7 moose. Fred, Jim, and I had planned opening up on the Skok, but the South Shore of Hood Canal was blocked with downed trees all the way from Belfair to Union.

That night, I couldn't get home from the high school because of downed trees and power lines and spent the night at Jim's house. The next day, the three of us hunted "the spit" near Belfair State Park. We knew it wouldn't be any good, too early in the season for migratory birds in the lower canal, but what the heck, we HAD to go somewhere. The next day, the roads were cleared and we headed for the Skok. We figured it would be crowded, opening day usually was, so we met at the "launch" site around 3 in the morning. There was no "real" place to launch the pram, just a wide spot in the road and a steep bank down to the water. When we arrived, we were shocked! No other rigs! "We're the ONLY ones here?" It was a good thing we were alone. We dumped the boats in the water and loaded our gear. "Where are the guns?" Oh my! Jim left them on the front porch. I'm not saying he broke any speed limits, but that round trip from the Skok to Bremerton and back took a mere 45 minutes.

The tide was pretty low, so we had to drag our boat upriver for about a quarter-mile. Once to the main branch of the river, we were able to float downstream to our favorite spot alongside a large cedar log that had been buried in the mud for nearly half a century. All the while we were pushing birds up as we sloshed along in the river. We gathered driftwood and marsh grass, built a blind next to the log, set our decoys, and waited for daylight. The weather wasn't promising ~ no breeze, at all. Friday's storm used up a months' worth of wind, but we sat back waiting for something to happen. It didn't take all that long. Around 9am, someone opened the box and every bird on Hood Canal got out. Usually, the canal has a predominant number of widgeon, but this day? It was flock after flock of mallard.

It was a sunny day, with broken black and purple clouds making the colors on the mallards oh so beautiful. Even with the bluebird weather, the ducks were more than eager to settle in our decoy spread. There were so many birds we picked out nothing but the drakes, except for one mallard hen, more on that later. Fred seemed to always have a hot hand with the gun and at one point made a spectacular shot, knocking down a triple on mallard drakes. I could generally hold my own, and we gave Jim the nickname "claimer". No explanation needed?

Fred would never hunt without his trusty bird dog, Trixie, and I must say, there was no finer duck and pheasant dog than Trix, but you would NEVER suspect it. Trix was a salt 'n' pepper English Cocker Spaniel, no more than 16" tall, but with a heart bigger than any dog I've ever seen. One day, the three of us were hunting the spit and it was a GREAT duck day. Rain coming down sideways and a strong 15 to 20 mph wind. Trix was havin' a ball, retrieving ducks all morning. Most of the birds we shot would land in a pond on the lee side of the spit, but one of us shot a bird that came down on the windward side. The canal was a froth, with waves of 3 feet high pounding the beach. Trixie ran out of the blind to retrieve the bird, but was unable to get a good mark on the downed bird. She ran back and forth, looking for an opening through the waves, but the surf was too much. Finally, that dog stood on its hind legs, hopped up and down, spotted the bird, and swam out to make the retrieve. We lost sight of Trix for a couple of minutes until she returned with a fat mallard. The three of us stood there in awe. One of the greatest retrieves I ever witnessed. The weather was much, much tamer the day after the Columbus Day storm, but Trixie still amazed us with her heart.

Back to the one mallard hen and the "claimer". Our bag limit was 21 birds, and we needed one more bird. Fred had put his gun away and it was up to Jim or me to end the day. Here they come. Oh no. Two mallard hens, we had 20 drakes. Oh well. The birds set up oh so perfect. Jim jumped up and shot, not a feather; I shot a microsecond after he did, so it was obvious I knocked it down. Jim yelled, "I got it! I got it!" "No way, Jim." Trixie was in the boat, so I waded out for the retrieve. Oh My! It had jewelry on its leg. My first banded duck. I think I'll save the rest of the story for another time. Let me finish with this, it was THE greatest duck shoot the three of us ever had.

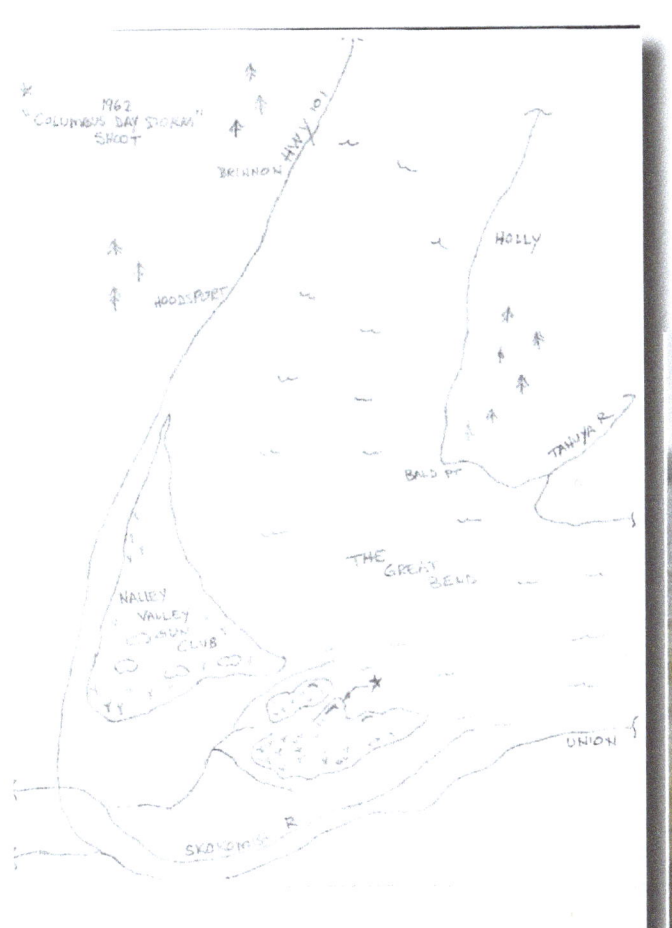

Rip, a sack of decoys, guns, and two hunters. Over-loaded? Nah! Hoodsport and the Olympics in the background. plenty of memories to share. One I will never forget with Bill Nylund and a flock of "cans", ok, Canvasback.

The T's

Duck season would end sometime in early January and then it was time for brant. The brant is a small coastal goose and not much bigger than a nice mallard drake. Back in the '60s, there was a large population that would migrate from Alaska, Northern Canada, and the Arctic. They would spend the winter all along the shores of Hood Canal, attracted to the gravel beaches and eelgrass beds. They were a delicacy at the dinner table.

I'm not sure why, but Fred and Jim were always in a bit of friendly competition with me when it came to hunting brant. Everything else? We were as thick as thieves. On a low tide, brant would come to a spit, picking out small bits of gravel for their craw. They were fun to hunt because they were one of the easiest birds to decoy. I would set up on a gravel beach surrounded by two or three dozen silhouettes. I got my share of birds, but it would have been much easier if I had a few floaters. One Monday at school, Jim and Fred told me about the fantastic brant hunt they had over the weekend. They kept saying it was because of the T's, but would not elaborate. Trust me, I continued to ask, but all season long they bagged more birds than I did and never failed to rub it in, "Hey Mills, it's the T's; we crossed the T's." It wasn't until two years later that they shared their "secret". I will NEVER forgive them, but I will NOT give up THEIR secret.

While writing about the T's and the "competition" between Fred, Jim, and me, I remember its origin. Oh, it goes a long way back. I also remember how we became best of friends, but first let me share the battle. We were in the eighth grade, and intramural basketball pitted one homeroom against the other. The games were pretty intense and officiated by junior high teachers with little referee experience. My homeroom faced Fred and Jim's during the regular season and we won the game. During the game, I had to guard Fred. I had limited basketball skills; he was a superior athlete, so I took extreme measures to keep him from scoring. Let's face it, I was a "banger". Truth be known, I should have fouled out in the first half.

As it turned out, we had to play one another for the 8th-grade championship, and rumor around the locker room was that Fred planned on working me over. It was a hard-fought game, nothing bitter, just a rough battle. Fred got the better of me, and they won the championship.

We next met in Chuck Semancik's 9th grade Washington State History class. We sat beside one another, started talking about hunting and fishing, and we've been best of friends ever since. Didn't hurt that Chuck loved salmon fishing and would often share in the conversation. Strange that an 8th basketball game found its way to the duck flats, but

That's the America I grew up in.

The Pigeon Tree
(and how Jim became a "claimer")

Band-tailed pigeons are typically a migratory bird that nest in old-growth timber during the spring and summer months in the Pacific Northwest then migrate in the fall to central California and parts of Nevada. Like other doves and pigeons, they are entirely vegetarian. They eat grain seeds and wild berries (especially elderberries and madrona berries). Eating a pigeon is as American as apple pie. The flavor is ever so slightly gamey, but in my opinion, one of the best tasting game birds other than a ruffed grouse. After feeding, they seek out gravel beaches picking up small stones to grind the food in their craw. Their call is a soft "coo", and they fly pretty fast (unless they are about to land in a snag).

Enter the hunter. If you can't find a grove of elderberry bushes in the hills, the next best thing is to locate a beach the birds frequent. The birds will land in a snag, survey the area, then drop to the shore and pick up gravel. Hunters position themselves around the snag, waiting for a flight of birds, typically 5 and 6 at a time. Once the morning flight has subsided, the birds would send out a scout from high in the hills. It would land in the snag, sit there for a while, and if undisturbed another flock would decoy to the scout. It didn't take long for us to figure that out. We would have a good morning shoot, things would die down (no pun intended); then here comes the scout, we remain hidden, and before long we'd have more shots. You might ask, "What happened to the scout?" Ahhhh. While Fred and I took aim at birds on the wing, Jim would blast the bird sitting motionless in the tree. After several times doing that, we just decided to call him a "claimer". Jim, you KNOW I love you. Don't ya?

George and the Bottle

Once O'Sullivan Dam was completed, creating The Pot Holes Reservoir, and finished backing up Crab Creek that flowed out of Moses Lake, the creek seeped through the sand dunes and created a myriad of ponds of all different shapes and sizes. In the '50s and '60s, even private gun clubs could not have experienced better shooting. It was a duck hunting mecca...

George Nobel was a good friend of the family. Dad and George became acquainted in the late '40s when we were next-door neighbors living on Naval Ave. I can't recall George ever having a "9 to 5" job, but he was always working. Doing something. He always had a welding torch in his hand, or he was under his truck wrenching. I do remember he always had a truckload of oysters in the backyard. It wasn't 'til later I learned George owned a lot of waterfront along the south shore of Hood Canal, rich with clams and oysters. He would gather truckloads, sell them to local restaurants and if any remained, he would park his rig at the bottom of Prebble St. near the shipyard and sell to the shipyard workers.

George and I were good hunting buddies and even better friends. He loved chasing pheasants with his German Shorthair; I preferred being in a duck blind. Once in a while he would join me in the blind, but normally after a morning shoot; I would go with him in the afternoon. His dog was a joy to watch. When that dog slammed on point, she was rock solid.

It was early November and I was standing on a hill, just east of the power lines that crossed Crab Creek. George and I had parked his camper, and my heart grew heavy thinking back when Dad and I pitched two umbrella tents on that exact location ~ one tent for sleeping, the other for cooking and drying off foul weather gear. The time we built a duck blind from bleached-out driftwood came to mind as well. When the creek was at flood stage, the high water washed a ton of wood suitable for building a blind. We called that pond "the boneyard". If you kept your eyes fixed on the lights off a grain elevator fifteen miles off in the distance, it was only a 15-minute walk, but that rarely happened, and that walk typically turned into a 25-to-30 minute hike.

Now back to this story...

It was the second week of November, prime time for the "northerns" to show up. My dad and Elling Simonsen, both Bremerton City firemen, had just returned from Moses Lake and reported the "northerns" had definitely shown up. So, George and I headed out.

The drive to Moses Lake typically took 3-4 hours, depending on pass conditions, but not with George. DID NOT matter what the conditions were like. He always drove 5mph UNDER the speed limit forcing cars to pass. Oh ya, they would blast their horn. Didn't faze him. When they did pass, he'd slow down, not wanting to tailgate. Our four-hour trip took 7 hrs. I ain't makin' that up. Once parked at a Public Access just off the frontage road, I climbed into bed - 3am comes mighty early.

The next morning, I set out for the "boneyard" packing my shotgun, a box of shells, and a couple dozen decoys wedged in a gunny sack. I missed a few of my landmarks, wandered around a bit, but finally found the blind. Good thing I left the camper at 3:30 because a couple other hunters came by my blind. It wasn't really hard to find a good pocket of water, away from another hunter, that attracted birds and they kept going, and I never saw or heard from them the rest of the day.

It was still very dark. Too early to wade out and set decoys, so I poured a cup of tomato soup and listened to the whistle of wings overhead and the splash of birds landing on the water. One more cup of soup while I listened to a lone mallard hen calling in the distance. I listened intently and would call back, using a practiced method my dad taught me, without a store-bought call. The dark sky was starting to break; time to set my decoys.

The wind was hard against my back, perfect for decoying ducks, and I had a great shoot. When I had a limit, I sat for a while and called to passing birds to work on my calling. The morning flight was dying down; I picked up my decoys. Knowing I was coming back in the morning, I hid the sack behind some sagebrush, put my ducks on a strap, and headed back to the camper. George was not back from his hunt. I had a can of beef stew and took a snooze.

George returned with a couple birds. I skinned 'em, cut 'em up, and he prepped them for the skillet. Fred Kegel was a sophomore at WSU (Go Cougs) and made the trip from Pullman, arriving just in time for dinner, and a good meal it was: pheasant, with the drippings, boiled potatoes (skins on) and fresh corn on the cob.

After the meal and the dishes were washed and put away, the three of us sat down for a "night-cap". George pulled out a bottle of Crown Royal and pulled the cork. Stories of his life and past hunting trips started pouring as much as the "Crown". George had a way of telling a story that "roped us in". We were so captured by how he used vivid details to make the stories visual we just sat and listened. At one point, George reached for the bottle, and when he pulled the cork, it fell to the floor; he stared at it for a moment, looked up, poured himself another drink, and more stories flowed.

That happened 55 years ago. I can't recall much about the hunt Fred and I had at the "boneyard" (neither can Freddy), but we will never forget George and the bottle.

> That's part of the America I grew up in.

*My dad rearranging the decoys.
Of course, a duck hunter is always watching the sky for birds.*

Point Defiance in Moses Lake?

It was Howard Kubli's first duck hunt circa 1980. CIRCA? What a great way to cover up for not being able to remember, what should be, a significant date.

Opening day of duck and goose hunting on the Pacific Flyway is generally the 2nd Saturday in October. Also, there's quite a population of local birds, mostly mallard, which makes for good shooting. Don't expect to show up opening morning, wander around the dunes, and find a place to set up. There have been years when I thought half of King County was on the flats.

Dad and I had opened up in the sand dunes for several years and knew the routine. Pop was getting on in years, so Howard and I decided to take the lead. We arrived long before daylight on the Friday before opening, drove out Sand Dunes Road, and stopped at the Public Access parking lot by the first flumes. We were in luck. The parking lot was empty. No hunting rigs. The flumes are large, man-made culverts on the Southwest corner of Moses Lake and were part of a massive reclamation project in the 1950s.

Howard and I waited 'til daylight, taking our time loading the pram with several dozen decoys, enough for two separate blinds, hedges trimmers to cut willows for blind camo, and fishing rods. Oh ya! Lots of spiny ray fish and some large rainbow trout have found their way into most of the deeper ponds. It was gonna take more than one trip for all our gear, so we left the sleeping bags, guns, and other "stuff" in the truck.

Well, forgive me. I failed to mention Rocket? Fred Kegel's yellow lab? Dad still had Sadie, a black lab he trained who won many ribbons at field trial events. I was without a dog, and Fred loaned me his dog for the weekend. I had hunted over Rocket many times, so he and I were familiar with one another. Duck hunting is not the same without a dog beside you in the blind. It's a joy to watch the dog's eyes follow birds in the sky, and the times when you're about to nod off, the dog comes to attention, ears perk up, and you awake to duck cupped and about to land.

We drifted down Crab Creek, wound around a couple sand islands, drug the boat over a large beaver dam, which I had never seen before, and found the spot where Dad and I had shot the year before. The water was much higher than in years past. Didn't dawn on me it was due to the newly constructed beaver dam. MUCH more on that later.

Once over the dam, a pond opened up surrounded by willows. Perfect spot for Dad and Warner. Off to the right, a narrow channel led to another pond about a hundred yards away. Just where Howard and I wanted to roost.

We unloaded the decoys. While I stayed back gathering sagebrush and cutting willow branches for the blinds, Howard motored back to the access, getting the rest of our gear.

When he returned, I continued with the blinds and Howard collected driftwood, cut willow branches, gathered sagebrush, and built a sweet lean-to for the night's "sleep". Once everything was set up, we sat back in the warm desert sand, had a lukewarm beer, and did a little fishing. We caught a few small bass, bluegill, trout, and wrestled with large carp. I'm not sure how Howard happened to have a deck of cards, but he taught me how to play crib. We didn't have a crib board and kept score with twigs in the sand.

It was a beautiful evening, not a cloud in the sky, and the light pollution from Moses Lake didn't seem to make any difference. The sky was so full of stars it felt like you could reach out and touch the Big Dipper.

It was getting a bit chilly, so we climbed in our bags, laid there for a while listening to ducks splash into our pond, and finally we nodded off. Minute by minute that warm desert sand got colder and colder, and I kept getting closer and closer to Rocket. At one point, it got so cold I dragged Rocket into my bag and snuggled up to him. He didn't seem to mind, and it certainly was a blessing to me. I was never so thankful for a rising sun.

Dad and Warner showed up around 8am. Legal shooting time wasn't 'til 12 noon, and there were several groups of hunters wandering the dunes, looking for a pond to set up on. The four of us sat in one of the blinds drooling over decoying mallards while Dad & Warner told stories about their tour of duty in the Army. The two met at Scofield Barracks in Hawaii and instantly became good pals. Warner was the "un-official" All Army light-weight boxing champ. Dad was Warner's second and told how "Champ", Dad's nickname for Warner, would stalk an opponent in the ring, shuffle like Joe Louis, and when he landed a punch - and it usually only took one - it was lights out. Uncle Warner, how I addressed Warner, was the most humble, kindest man you could meet. You would never suspect he was All-Army unless you took a glimpse of his hands. I swear, big as dinner plates they were.

It was approaching noon, and we went to our separated blinds. It was about 11:45, and it sounded like a war zone over the flats. So much for a noon opening. Dad and Warner waited 'til legal shooting time, and then it was nothin', but singles and doubles, constantly circling their spread - a couple calls and they dropped right on in.

Howard and I were getting only the occasional. It got so bad Uncle Warner walked our way and shouted out, "Hey you two, come down here and shoot with us." The invite came several times, but we were determined to make a go of it at our spot.

Dad and Warner were having such a good shoot, someone crept up about 20 yards behind their blind and when birds circled behind them, he would jump up and take a shot. This happened maaaaybe three times. After the fourth, Dad had enough and walked behind the blind, found the guy crouching behind some sagebrush and said, "Hey fella, that's about enough. Go find your own pond." The guy must have thought he was gonna bluff my old man; he puffed out his chest and said, "I'm a sheriff from King County; nobody tells me what to do." Good thing Dad aged over the years, and with a classic come-back which will remain in the annals of Don Mills hunting and fishing stories, Dad said, "I don't care if you're Wyatt Earp. Take a hike!!" Shall I say the "sheriff" left with tail tucked between his legs?

Uncle Warner and Dad limited by 2 o'clock and headed back to their trailer parked at the flume. Sheepishly, Howard and I looked at each other. Didn't take long. Only two words were muttered, "Let's go."

We finished the day in Dad's blind and hung the nickname on our spot, Point Defiance.

My dad and Warner Coffman limited in a couple hours. Sadie was the best dog Dad ever owned.

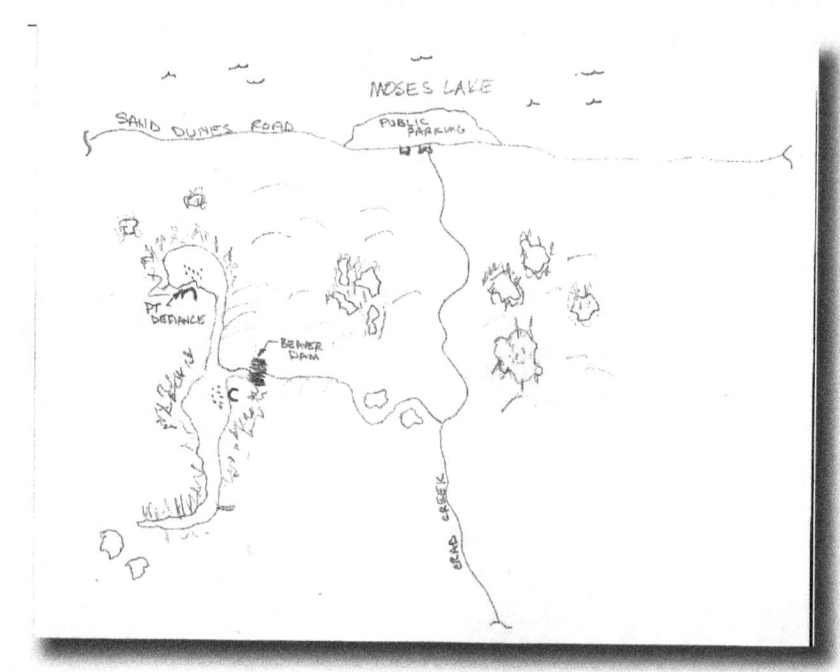

Point Defiance

A Confrontation, A Duck Call, and A Calling

North America is divided into Four Flyways: Pacific, Central, Mississippi, and Atlantic. Each Fall, when the weather up North turns harsh, millions of waterfowl migrate south in search of food and warm weather. The Pacific Flyway stretches North to South from the Arctic, the entirety of Alaska, portions of Russia, the Canadian provinces of British Columbia, Alberta, and Saskatchewan to the southernmost points of Mexico. It spans the entire West coast of the United States east to the Rocky Mountains.

Through trial and error over years of hunting, my father learned that the 2nd week in November marks the arrival of Northern ducks and geese in the Columbia Basin, a lesson he taught me well. With the advancement in weather forecasting, I was able to track conditions in Canada, making a better decision on when to spend time in the Potholes.

It was the end of October; the weather was starting to turn cold in the Northern provinces, and I knew the Moses Lake Basin would soon be full of birds. Dad would schedule his vacation around that 2nd week; I was a little more flexible and could take time off much easier.

I called Howard Kubli and Bill Nyland to see if they were available and let me tell ya, it didn't take much arm twisting.

OK, time for confessional. Actually, in the Fall, I would quite often have to take sick leave, with a case of "migratory bird flu". I had similar ailments in the Spring associated with the "Idaho trout syndrome", and in the summer months I would be afflicted with "salmon fever". When I retired from the shipyard, I had ZERO sick leave on the books. Do you think my boss ever figured it out? No matter.

When I was quite young to hunting, Dad taught me another valuable lesson when it came to hunting, "If you want the best spot on the flats, you BETTER get there early." You might think "early" means a couple hours before legal shooting time.

NOPE!

I learned what "early" meant from my father. In the fifties and sixties, opening day legal shooting time commenced at 12 noon. When we would "open up" on the Skok, we left home at MIDNIGHT! We launched our pram around 1am, rowed across the flats to our spot. If the tide was high, it was an easy row. If the tide was out, we had to drag across the mud. We never checked the tide; we left at midnight, that was it. We would get to the spot we liked, build a blind out of driftwood and marsh grass, and there we sat for the next NINE hours. Other hunters started showing up around 6am, but we had the spot.

I knew we had to be on the water no later than 4am. The night before we had all our gear organized and lunches made. In the morning, all we had to do was make a pot of coffee (tomato soup for me) and get rollin'. Breakfast could come later.

We left Pier 4 campground just a touch after 3am, drove the I-90 frontage road west to the first Public Access. When we arrived at the parking spot there was a truck camper rig with an empty boat trailer attached.

"Oh-oh, we're in trouble. Let's keep quiet and get to the pond as fast as we can." In utter silence, we took the boat out of the truck, loaded it with decoys, guns, and foul weather gear, and slid it down the sandy embankment to the big water. In the pitch black, we rowed across the pond and searched a bit for the hidden creek. The creek was surrounded by marsh grass, cattails, and a few willow trees. It was difficult to find in the daylight and much tougher in the dark, but I had a solid bead on its location. The creek was very shallow, so we had to drag the boat about a hundred yards to the open water.

Once through the creek, Howard and Bill walked the remaining 50 yds to the blind, and I rowed across the pond. It was a beautiful duck blind made from bleached driftwood, tight on all sides, to hide any movement from decoying birds, but just big enough for 3 guys to sit comfortably.

I pulled the boat onto the sandy beach, grabbed some gear to stow in the blind. When I stepped into the blind, my heart sunk into my stomach. "Hey guys, there's a sack of decoys in here." My first thought was another hunter in the area. I walked around yelling, "Hello? Is there anyone here? Hello?" After a few minutes of that, I still didn't know what to do.

Bill took a closer look at the bag, "Hey Moocher, this bag is covered with ice. I'll bet those guys in the parking lot brought it out last night." (Moocher was a nick-name given to me in years past because when I sport fished for salmon I liked to "Drift Mooch")

It's illegal to secure a blind overnight, and I said, "You're right; this spot is ours now."

We ditched our boat in some tall reeds and swamp grass, tossed our decoys in the pond, set "their" bag outside the blind, and sat back sippin' coffee and listening to the sound of birds overhead. We talked about what to do when "those guys" showed up. We knew we were in the right, but ya never know what can happen.

Around 5:30 we heard some voices coming up the creek. As they got closer, we could see flashes of light bouncing off the reeds, and the voices were getting more distinct. Our eyes were adjusted to the darkness, and we saw a hunter emerge from the reeds draggin' his boat. Once fully in the pond, his flashlight scanned across the water and abruptly stopped on our spread.

In a not so gentle voice, we heard the "leader" shout to his buddies, "Uh oh, we're F...ED!"

I knew words were gonna be spoken, so I told Howie and Bill, "Don't say nuthin'; I'll take care of this."

As they rowed across the pond mumbling and whispering, I thought back to my dad and his run-in with "Wyatt Earp".

They pulled up alongside the blind, got out of their boat and sauntered up the slight incline all bold-like.

Now Bill is 6'4", I'm no slouch, and Howie fears nothing.

The spokesman for the group walked up to me and with a voice trying to intimidate said, "Well, BOYS, we've got a perplexing situation here."

I looked him square in the face and said, "I don't see any problem at all. This is our spot and nuthins' gonna make us move."

He turned to his buddies, talked for a couple seconds and came back with, "We brought our bag out earlier and this is our second trip."

I sorta chuckled and said, "Sorry, pal. Nice try, but when we pulled in here, your bag was covered with ice. You brought it out last night; it's illegal to save a blind like that, and you know it."

A few more expletives and off they went, tails between their legs, and we stood next to the shore with knees that felt like jelly. We were 100% in the right, but ya never like to have a situation like that.

WHEW!!

Over the years, my dad and I had our own special name for beaver ponds and duck hunting spots. Beaver ponds like "Ole Weedy", "Dead Pine", and "Three Tree Pond" and Potholes like the "Bone Yard", "Pile of Rocks", and "Warner's Point" were epic.

One evening, Bill and I were camped out looking out over the dunes. The sky aflame with orange and red, the setting sun casting shadows over the dunes. That low sun gleaming on the reeds and sagebrush with a gold hue, oh so majestic… Broken clouds painted black, blue, and silver hanging over it all. The sunset glistened off this one pond such that we said it should be on the cover of "Field and Stream", and forever after was called "Field and Stream".

(I digress… it breaks my heart and brings me to tears that Howard can't share so many memories with me, but I KNOW he's in heaven with the Lord.)

Field and Stream Pond was quite unique. Typically, hunters want to set a spread of decoys in front of them, with the wind at their back, 'cause ducks and geese always decoy INTO the wind. This pond, with the prevailing wind in the hunter's face, was the exact opposite. As birds would circle the pond, checking out the spread, they would disappear behind the blind, and all of a sudden, you'd look up and there they were, straight above your decoys, and then drop down like they were in an elevator shaft. They had no idea we were there. It just wasn't fair.

Ok. Not true. It WAS fair.

So often the birds have every advantage, but on Field and Stream, we owned 'em.

The day started out a bit slow. We picked out the few greenheads that decoyed, passed on the mallard hens, the gadwall, and had fun watching teal dart in and out of the decoys. Then something changed. Nothing was flying. Not a single bird in the air, then Bill noticed high on the hill dust swirling about. The wind picked up and before you know it, the sky was full of birds, and they poured into our pond recklessly. Half a dozen birds locked up, circled behind us, and dropped down the shaft. We dumped 3 fat greenheads. They all had the bright orange feet. Yup. The northerns were "in".

The wind blew, the ducks flew, and we shot like the devil for an hour or two.

Off in the distance, a flock of birds circled another hunter's pond. We watched them drop in. Boom! Boom! Boom! The entire flock escaped.

Bill looked at me and said, "Ok, Moocher. You think you're so good with a duck call. Let's see ya call them in."

Accepting the challenge, I layed on my call and did the best "hail" call I could muster. One more "hail" call, and those birds made a 90-degree turn and headed straight for our pond, circled one time, and dropped in. It was so incredible, we let them sit in the decoys. One by one, they took off, leaving one lone mallard hen. We jumped up and down, trying to get her to leave. But oh no, there she sat. Needing one bird for our limit, I finally told Howard, "I'm gonna step out of the blind, make her flush, and you take it." With my gun in hand, I rose up, stepped out of the blind, the bird jumped up and POW!

Guess who shot the bird? Let's put it this way, Howard was not that quick on the draw. We picked up our gear and headed back to the truck.

When everything was put away, Bill suggested goin' to George and havin' lunch at Martha's Inn.

Martha's Inn and Café are as much a part of the Columbia basin as Quincy or Moses Lake. Farmers, stuck in the middle of nowhere, needed a local stop for supplies and the towns of Quincy and Moses Lake were a bit too far from home.

In the beginning, three men met in Quincy and talked about the necessity for another town in Grant County. To make a long story short, an entrepreneur, Charlie Brown, invested his own money to buy 339 acres of deserted farm buildings and sagebrush. A man with the Bureau of Reclamation asked Charlie what he was going to name his town and went on to say, "Why doesn't somebody get smart and name a town after our first president?" Charlie followed his advice, and his town became George, Washington.

The town was dedicated on July 4, 1957 with the then-governor Albert Rosellini in attendance. The first business the Browns started was Martha's Inn and Café, which quickly became a stopping place for truckers, farmers, and hunters. Let me tell ya, they had GREAT cherry pie. Get it? Cherry pie?

Howard, Bill, and I found a booth, sat down and ordered a cold beer. Never mind that Bill was not yet 21; we won't go there.

While eating our lunch Bill said, "Guys, I've spent a lot of time hunting and fishing with you two, and I really value your opinions. The Holy Spirit has laid on my heart to go into the ministry. What do ya think?"

For the life of me, I have NO idea how I responded. Howard has passed away, so I can't ask him, but many years later, Bill came to me and said, "Moocher, you were instrumental in my CALL to become a minister."

You never know what you say or how your actions will affect another person's life decisions. It might be an overworked saying, but God DOES work in mysterious ways.

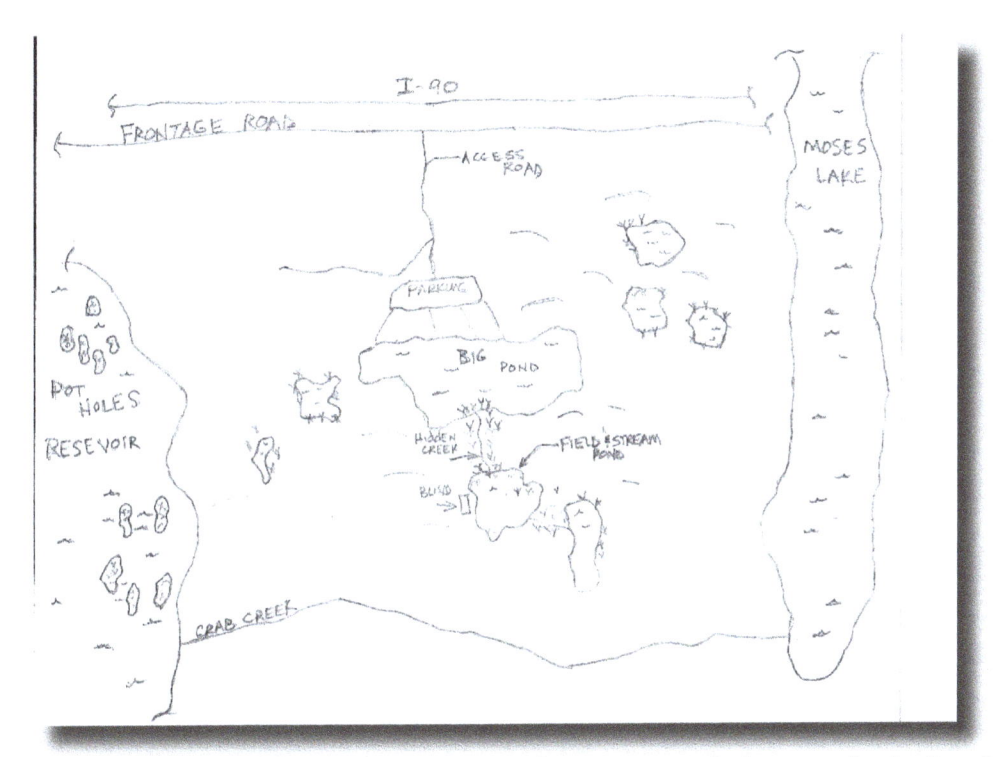

The Field & Stream pond: with a setting sun and the myriad of colors bouncing off the water and spreading a golden hue on the reeds, there was no more beautiful duck hunting spot in the world. Field & Stream mag should have put it on their cover.

Fred and Barb, David and Dalene

The year was 1970. Dalene was 7 months pregnant with our first child. Now one would think that was our main focus. Yes, it was. We had a mobile hanging above the crib, a changing table, and I was practicing how to... well, you know. BUT, the weather in Yakima was ideal for duck hunting and a trip HAD to be made. Most of the fields along the Yakima River were ankle-deep in water which makes for perfect mallard habitat.

I was working at Fircrest Golf and Country Club and had made friends with a member who had a private club just outside Toppenish. He knew I hunted ducks and asked if I'd like to hunt his club. I told him my friend and I were headed that way this weekend, and he said, "Stop on by Sunday, and we'll set up you and your bud." We worked out the details; I got directions and immediately called Kegel, telling him the good news. A private club. What could be better?

Private clubs typically only shoot on Wednesdays and weekends. The off-days allow birds a bit of rest.

I knew of a couple fields along the river that might produce. After all, when I was going to college in Yakima, I wasn't going to college.

Fred's dad had an 8' Alaskan "pop-up" camper. We packed our gear and the four of us, Fred, Barb, Dalene, and I headed out Friday right after work.

We made it to Yakima in the early evening, had dinner at the Arctic Circle Drive-In, continued on through Union Gap, past Harrah, down Branch Road, and found a wide spot just off Brownstown Road. While the gals were inside attempting to figure out sleeping arrangements, Fred and I stayed outside. The night air was alive with the sounds of mallards. "I think we're in a good spot."

It was getting late, we wanted to be in the field before daybreak, so we went back inside to see what the gals had set up. Fred and Barb would sleep in the bunk above the cab. Dalene turned the table into a bed, of sorts. It was barely big enough for one average-sized person, maybe, much less Dalene and me. I'm well above average height, and at the time you could have set a dinner plate on Dalene's swollen belly.

Thankfully daylight was about to break because I had a sleepless night filled with mallards dropping into our spread and contending with Dalene's, well, "fat" belly, so Fred and I grabbed the decoys and sloshed our way, in ankle-deep water, along a flooded ditch toward some trees. We found a likely-looking small pond surrounded by a thick grove of willows, put out a spread of decoys, and it didn't take long.

Oh, what a shoot! Mostly singles and doubles, but the occasional flock of five or six dropped into "our" spread. The sun was out just enough where you had no problem pickin' out the drakes.

The ditch we walked along in the semi-dark had now swollen to nearly calf-deep. With our limit of mallard, our pace back to the camper was quite a bit slower. That's when we saw the sign: NO TRESPASSING.

Yes, we picked up the pace out of there.

Dalene and Barb had a case of "camper fever" and decided to take a hike and join us in the field. Barb had boots, Dalene none, so she piggybacked Dalene across a flooded creek. They laughed, and we laughed to see such a seriously pregnant gal being carried across a swollen creek piggyback.

After breakfast, we drove into Harrah to visit Jim Hurt, a farmer friend my dad and I had known for years. We had hunted Jim's fields for pheasant, duck, and doves. Dad would park his trailer behind a stack of hay bales away from the road; it was like having our own private club.

We talked a bit. Jim shared the latest gossip in the valley and then invited us to dinner. After dinner, he took us under the house to his "wine cellar". Jim had about 50 acres of grapes and took great pride in his "juice". We sat in that wine cellar for a couple hours (the gals left after 15 minutes) tasting wine from every gallon jug. Need I go further? Let's just say, from that day forward, Jim - rest his soul- called me "Wino Joe" ... not sure if I slept in the cellar or made it back to the camper, but I will say, Dalene had the bed all to herself.

The next morning, with a few "clouds in my coffee", we headed for Toppenish. We met Gordy and drove to his club. It was a beautiful piece of water, a few willows scattered about, and 5 or 6 duck blinds along one edge of the pond. Fred and I were just happy to be there. Neither of us had ever shot at a private club, but typically the best blinds are reserved for the most senior member and so on down the line. Gordy put us in the least desirable spot, but it didn't matter to us; we were just happy to have been invited. When we got to our blind, a sack of decoys was laying inside and we tossed 'em out. After the storm the day before, it was your typical bluebird weather, which is to be expected, and no one got much shooting. Fred and I said, "Let's head back to Jim's place, and maybe we'll get in on an evening shoot." We thanked our host for the hunt and headed back to Harrah.

We got the Hurt's place just as the sun was setting and sat in the stubble cornfield behind his house. My oh my, it was wave after wave of birds, all mallard.

I still have that mental picture of a single mallard hen leading a couple hundred birds in a cyclone manner closer and closer to the corn. It was an amazing sight. We shot our limit of birds (ok, maybe a few more than...), said our thanks to Jim, and headed back to Tacoma.

*Who said "Ya need a private club to have a great shoot?"
That's the America I grew up in.*

Crab Creek

Douglas was a senior in HS and I took him and his buddy, Mark Olsen, on a duck hunt in Eastern Wash. We had set up our blind on a small "seeps" pond just off Crab Creek.

Seeps ponds were formed throughout the sand dunes all along Crab Creek when O'Sullivan Dam was completed in 1949. O'Sullivan is one of the largest earth-filled dams in the United States, located south of Moses Lake, and is on Crab Creek. The 28,00-acre Potholes Reservoir formed by the dam collects return flows from all irrigation in the upper portion of the project, for reuse in the southern portion, and was built as part of the Columbia Basin Project. The project was initially to assist farmers with irrigation; however, the formation of lakes and ponds created a mecca for hunters, fishermen, and campers. Potholes Reservoir is loaded with trout, bass, and walleye pike. The large body of water, and surrounding ponds, provide a resting spot for migrating ducks and geese.

In the late '50s, the full effect of damming the creek provided what could be described as the best hunting in the world. I started hunting the sand dunes, which is open to the public, with my father in 1959 and I often heard Dad say, "No private gun club could have better shooting." And he was right. Today, what with the changes in surrounding agriculture and the formation of private gun clubs, the sands dunes have fallen off dramatically. I'm so glad I got to share that part of my life with my father and pass it on to my boys.

So, back to this hunt with Douglas and Mark.

The day's hunt was over, and boy what a day we had! The morning started off a bit slow, but a stiff breeze came up around 9, driving the rafting ducks off O'Sullivan, and they just poured into our decoys. We shot a limit of mallards and got 3 large Canadian honkers. We loaded the duck pram with two sacks of decoys, 21 ducks, and three geese. I drug the boat through a narrow channel out to the main portion of Crab Creek. Once there, our dog and the three of us hopped in and motored upstream to where we had parked the truck. About 100 yds. from the "take-out," I slowed the motor way too fast, which drug my wake up and over the stern. The water poured in so fast, dumping all of us in the river, I had no time to direct the boat to shore. The ducks and geese, along with our decoys, floated downstream. Mark was in big trouble, waders full of water and goin' under. Doug started to swim after him, but fortunately the creek was shallow, and Mark was able to get his footing, and we all made it to the bank. All of us safe, only by the grace of God.

We were able to grab a line off the boat and drag it to shore and start bailing the water out. We laid out soppin' wet coats on some sagebrush to dry, shell bags, lunch buckets, but there were no guns. All three guns... GONE! We knew the exact spot where we capsized and Mark said, "I've got a SCUBA license. Maybe we could find some tanks in Moses Lake?" Now Moses Lake ain't the SCUBA diving capital of the world, so chances would be mighty slim to find some gear. By now, it was late in the afternoon, not a lot of daylight remained.

I remained at the spot we dumped the boat for a reference, and the boys got in the truck and sped off to town. About an hour later, I see my truck speeding down the gravel road; the boys jumped out with a wet suit and two air tanks. Mark suited up and dove in; not ten seconds later, the muzzle of my gun poked the surface, then Doug's. Mark's gun was a Christmas present from his dad, and this was the first time he had ever used it. He went down, came back with nothing, checked his bearings. Up again with nothing. It was now nearly pitch black and his tank nearly out of air. Time for one more dive. Mark was under longer than previous dives, and then... oh my... another muzzle poked the surface. WHEW!

We returned the SCUBA gear, rented a motel room, and dried out. The next day, Fred Kegel showed up to hunt with us. He helped locate our decoys and guess what... the four of us hunted that day. The only thing we lost was Dalene's camera, and she DID NOT want me to take it on a hunting trip, especially in the sandy dunes. I never heard the end of losing her camera... but

That's the America I grew up in.

Fishing Life

Seven Lakes Basin

Of all the hikes we took as scouts ~ Flap Jack Lakes, Upper and Lower Lena, and many more ~ Seven Lakes Basin was my favorite. Olympic National Park was somewhat of a well-kept secret back in the '60s. No more. Now reservations are required for overnight camping. The view of Mount Olympus and the Hoh River headwaters was breathtaking. One summer, David McIninch and I decided to hike into the basin. Fish was to be our main staple, and we left home with minimal provisions. Oh, we had the essentials: rod, reel, and tackle, along with some Melba Toast, powdered milk, pancake mix, and dried eggs, but we weren't the best of planners.

We got a late start our first day and spent the night in a shelter at Deer Lake and continued on the next morning into the basin. We had a great time and caught a lot of trout, but our spartan menu got to us, and with a brief threat of bad weather, we decided to head home after only three nights on the lake. The gas tank on his mother's car was nearly empty, so we pooled our funds. David figured how much we needed to get home and we ended up with one dime to our name. One dime TOTAL and we were HUNGRY. What can you get for a DIME? We bought THE biggest candy bar available, and that was our meal home. What candy bar? It's still my favorite, but they ain't nearly as big and cost a lot more than a dime nowadays ~ PayDay.

*It's a shame how we can lose contact with friends.
I haven't seen Dave since high school.*

His mother's car? Before I forget, that's an interesting story. Ok, I forget many of the dates, but here goes ~ it was circa 1965. Dalene and I were dating, going steady, and maybe even engaged. Whatever. David Mc had left home and was living in Oregon. Bessie, his mother, and I attended the same church, and she put out the word her house needed painting. So, Dalene and I volunteered. She owned a one-story house on the corner of 12th and Callow, and it took us maybe three or four days to complete the job. We didn't expect anything for our effort, but Bessie came to us and said, "I just can't drive anymore, and I want you to have my car for the work you've done." Holy Cow! We were totally surprised, didn't think it was fair, but she insisted. It was a 1948 Chev four-door sedan. We loved it.

But! Oh yeah, it happened. Dalene and I drove to Point Defiance to pick up some fresh herring for a salmon trip the next day. (Imagine THAT, an event centered on fishing...) On the way home, while driving along Pearl Street, a car made a left turn in front of us, and I was not able to stop. That beautiful '48 Chev was totaled. The driver was cited for reckless driving, but to make matters worse, he was uninsured and in the Navy. We were able to contact his commanding officer, but that was fruitless. "Oh, we have no jurisdiction over such an incident, and besides, we don't want to damage his career." Oh well, life goes on. After that, Dalene got a job with Budget Finance and bought her first car. A four-door Rambler Classic. That was OUR first car.

Captain Puget and Elling Simonsen

In 1957, KOMO TV held auditions for a children's show to be called The Captain Puget Show. Don McCune won the role and was forever known as Captain Puget. He sang songs about the Pacific Northwest (some he learned from Ivar Haglund, who founded "Ivar's restaurants) as well as taking kids on short filmed adventures around the northwest. The show evolved into the series Exploration Northwest, which began in 1960. It was not a children's program, but appealed to the entire family, consisting of adventures filmed in Alaska, British Columbia, Washington, Oregon, Idaho, and Montana. In 1970, Don married his biggest fan, Linda Street, who had been writing fan letters since 1962. They were married on Rialto Beach near LaPush, Washington and she became the mother of his three children, Zane, Clint, and Grace. Don was a devout Lutheran and died of pancreatic cancer in 1993. Captain Puget will always be a part of my America.

Elling Simonsen passed away July 12th, 1994. The Bremerton Sun's Seabury Blair, Jr. wrote about Elling's career with the Sun, which began in 1992 after retiring from the Bremerton Fire Department.

 As a child, Elling immigrated with his family from Hilleshamn, Norway taking up residence in Portland, Oregon, later moving to Puyallup, Washington. Elling told me about the first time he ever saw an orange. He said it smelled so good, and he took a bite without peeling it. I wish I knew more about his childhood.

Elling was drafted into the Navy and then joined the Bremerton Fire Department in 1945, where he met my father, and the two became great hunting and fishing partners.

In my opinion, Elling was the best outdoor writer the Sun has ever had, or will have for that matter. His talent as a writer brought him a friendship with Bremerton Mayor Glen Jarstad's brother, John. The two pioneered hunting and fishing shows on Channel 13, which led Elling to become friends with Don McCune of "Exploration Northwest".

There are hundreds of beaver ponds scattered across Kitsap and Mason counties loaded with native cutthroat trout. Some of the ponds were known by fly anglers: Mays Ranch Pond, Three Fingers, Blacksmith Pond, and Erickson Lake Pond, but there were many others tucked away from fisherman unwilling to spend the time scouting. It took a lot of driving the backwoods and burnin' up a significant amount of shoe leather to find that hidden gem. Once you did, you kept it hush-hush. Those ponds didn't have a name attached, so when Grandpa George and my dad found a pond, they would tag it based on the landscape. There was Dead Pine, Ole Weedy, 3 Stone Pond, and others.

Most of the ponds were surrounded by brush, making access by a rowboat nearly impossible. Dick O'Connor, another Bremerton fireman, often used a canoe. Even that was difficult to transport and move around a pond silently, and he came up with, quite possibly, the first-ever float tube. Boy, did we blow that one! Who would have thunk?

Dick's idea was to criss-cross straps, creating a seat, and then lash them to a large truck tire. A person would wear chest waders, straddle the straps, dangle their legs in the water and kick their feet like a duck. I'm tellin' ya, it worked great except for two MAJOR problems. First, after about three trips in the "tube", the straps wore holes in the waders. Second, after ONE trip your inner thighs were so chaffed, it took a week to recover. Eventually, Dad and Dick designed a canvas seat which worked great.

*My dad looking for another rise in "Dead Pine Pond"
and yes, that's our home made float tube.*

The ponds were a fly-fisherman's heaven, and trout grew large and fat. Ok, our waters don't come close to the "blue ribbon" rivers and streams in Idaho and Montana, but they were in our backyard. The Callibaetis mayfly was the predominant food source and my dad, a master at tying trout flies, developed several patterns attributed to his name: Don's Buck, and the teal and red, to name a couple.

Elling, with his contact in the Washington Department of Fisheries, helped get many of the ponds stocked. Once the department decided a pond would not dry up in the summer heat, they would contact Elling to set up a time and place to introduce fish to a newly discovered pond. Boy, did we try and keep that a secret. But, for all his pluses, I must say, Elling was not good with anything hush-hush; he flourished in the notoriety department.

Opening Day for trout fishing was fast upon us; Elling invited Don McCune to film an adventure on a pond my grandpa and Dad discovered. Yes, Elling helped with the stocking of that pond, but the three of them promised to keep it a secret for "at least" a couple years. Well, that lasted only one year.

Dad was not invited on the shoot and for years after his legs were chapped. (Get it?) So, Dad and I, with his Army buddy, Warner Coffman, opened up on a pond not far from where Elling was fishing. Dad, Warner, and I had a banner day. Like clockwork, the Callibaetis hatch erupted at 11am and it was lights out.

A few days later, Dad contacted Elling to find out how the filming went. I believe the word from Elling was "skunked"? Weeks later, the show aired, and Don McCune did a masterful job talking about the trout fishery in our area. The net result? There's a line in one of my favorite movies that sums it up: "And that's all she wrote!"

> **That's the America I grew up in.**

A further note on beaver ponds ~

Population growth throughout Kitsap and Mason County has "destroyed" so much of our pristine forests, rivers, lakes, and ponds. There have always been cabins on many of the local lakes, but now people have sought refuge from city life and are building their dream homes where once there was just a get-away for the outdoorsman. I can't begin to cite all the examples, but I have a couple that come to mind.

"Three Fingers" - one of the first ponds I ever fished. To get there, you traveled on an old, deeply rutted logging road and a narrow tree-lined trail to the water. Dad and I would fish from a canoe and take turns paddling. No homes. No cabins. Solitude. My dad would roll over in his grave if he could see "Three Fingers" today. I'm sorry, but that once beautiful "lake" and prime forest is surrounded by homes.

Dad and Elling Simonsen found two ponds across the road from Square Lake. They contacted Fish and Wildlife and assisted in planting native cutthroat. It didn't take long before those ponds produced large trout. No homes, no cabins, and CERTAINLY no golf course. Now, that once pristine beaver pond is Trophy Lakes Golf and Casting. "Casting"? Give me a break!" (sarcasm notwithstanding)

Typical catch of cutthroat from a local beaver pond w/ Bremerton fireman Dick O'Connor

Hot Shots

In 1939 my dad completed a four-year hitch in the US Army. Got married September 14, 1941 to Gail Maxine Talich. Mom and Dad loved to say, "Dad got married the same day he was born." Ok, a bit of family humor goes a long way. World War II was being fought on two continents; Dad was bouncing around from job to job, and a dear, dear friend, Chris Johnson, who incidentally led Mom and Dad to their Christian faith in Christ, talked him into joining the Bremerton City Fire Department.

What a job that turned out to become. Not a better job could be had for someone with only a high school education and who loved to hunt and fish. It wasn't the highest paying "blue-collar" job available, but a shift of 24 on and 48 off allowed firemen to seek part-time employment. Oh, did I not mention? In the Fall, when the wind blew, you'd find Dad on the duck flats. In Summer and Spring, he'd be fishing somewhere. Ok.

As I said in the "Stormy Night at Camp 5", I grew up surrounded by a great cast of characters from the fire department, many of whom had a real passion for the outdoors. As I became old enough to "hold my own", a few of them invited me to tag along when they went out. I had a memorable summer once as a deckhand for Roy Swan on his salmon troll boat, fishing out of Neah Bay. Elling Simonsen and I spent some time in the beaver ponds, but it was the salmon fishing trips I remember most. We would drop anchor off Point No Point, and he taught me the art of cutting and rigging up a spinner from a whole herring. I never quite got the hang of it. Try as I might, he'd end up cutting one for me and hook it up. That was some fun times, catching salmon, in the salt, while on anchor.

Dick O'Connor, another fireman and close friend of my father, took me on several hunting trips when I was in my teens. We became such good friends; when I became an adult, it was as if we were "joined at the hip". Many duck hunting trips to Moses Lake, coupled with a pheasant hunt over his German Shorthaired pointer "Reecy". What a dog she was. I swear she only went on point over a rooster. Ok, maybe a hen or two, now and then. We floated every river on the Olympic Peninsula, but back then, we considered the Skokomish River our favorite.

On one "Skok" steelhead trip, I borrowed a drift boat from Jeff Wentworth. (Jeff and I became friends when he worked at Kitsap Sport Shop, and it didn't hurt when he found out his mother was my 6th-grade teacher at Navy Yard City School. Living in a small town does have some advantages.) Dick and I launched at Vance Creek and planned to take out at the Highway 101 bridge. Fishing that day was not good; maybe a strike or two, and that was it.

We were getting close to the take-out and I noticed Jeff had left a couple Hot Shots in the tray alongside the rower's seat. Hot Shots were pretty new to steelhead fishing, and I said to Dick, "Say, here's a couple of those plugs I've been reading about; let's give 'em a try." Dick tied one to the end of his line and stripped off about 30 feet. I positioned the point along a nice seam, took NO MORE than a dozen strokes with the oars and POW! FISH ON! We land a bright 7# buck. Dick got the plug back in the water and this time stripped off EXACTLY 30 feet of line. Again, and I swear, trust me, I took no more than half a dozen pulls on the oars, and it was FISH ON! The VERY next day, I went to Kitsap Sport Shop, told Jeff the story, and ended up filling my tackle box with just about every color on the shelf.

That's the America I grew up in.

Hot Shots and misc plugs

Hood Canal Was Our Playground

Growing up in the '50s and early '60s, very few people owned their own boat; so, Hood Canal boathouses with rental boats stretched from Foulweather Bluff to Seabeck to Brinnon and Bald Point. There were others, but my memory has faded, juuuust a bit.

Dad always had a pram, which we used in lakes and for duck hunting. Dad didn't own a pick-up truck, and I'll never forget how he would jam the bow end of the boat in the trunk of the family car with the stern sticking out the back. It's hard to believe it never snapped in half. When I think about it, not many people in the 40s and early 50s had pick-ups. It was not uncommon to see hunters headed home with a deer draped across the hood of a four-door sedan. Quite often, Dad and I would fish Bald Point out of his homemade pram. (And I must say, it was the ugliest pram you've ever seen. After countless trips being drug over rocks and nasty oyster beds, there wasn't a seam that didn't leak. There were no fiberglass kits available to repairs, so Dad painted the seams with tar. Black, ugly tar. It was an embarrassment, but guess what? It didn't leak!) We would park alongside the road, slide the boat down a steep embankment, and drag it across the oyster beds. We started fishing long before daylight. Dad didn't have an outboard and would row slowly in no more than 30 to 40 feet of water, using a cut plug herring with no more than 1/2 oz mooching lead. The bite typically lasted until 8am; if you hadn't caught by then, you might as well hang it up. We caught quite a few blackmouth in the 8-to-10 pound range, nothing large, but what a battle in an 8ft pram.

The 4th of July was always a special family day. Dad would borrow an outboard motor from a fellow fireman, rent a boat at Bald Point or Seabeck, and take Mom and me fishing. After the morning bite, we would dig clams, search the beach for crab hiding in the bull kelp, and have a picnic. One year, Dad rented a boat at Manchester and we fished near the lighthouse. We weren't having much luck, a few rock cod and a ton of sand sharks (dogfish). All of it was exciting for an 8-year-old. Toward the end of the morning, I hooked a fish and it acted like another stinking dogfish. But soon I knew this was different because the leader didn't get cut in the first few seconds of the battle. I think Dad was kidding, but he said, "Aw, let me cut the line; it's just a dogfish." "No! No! I think it's a salmon". Sure enough, the line finally screamed off the reel, and a few minutes later, I landed an 11-lb Chinook. Biggest fish of the day at the boathouse, and I didn't realize there was a small derby for those who rented a boat. I won $5, which was more than my monthly allowance.

Once Fred Kegel, Jim Bennett, and I got our driver's licenses, it was non-stop fishing and hunting. The "canal" was our playground. Our parents never worried about us. My dad was a city fireman, Fred's dad a school principal, and Jim's dad owned Service Fuel Company. We knew watchful eyes were everywhere, not that it really mattered because we had the ultimate respect for the property of others and never got into any trouble. Ok, I confess, we "may" have shot too many ducks or caught a few too many fish, but that was it.

Over time, we learned many valuable lessons on how to "drift mooch", mostly by trial and error, but a lot of our savvy came from watching icons Harvey Quy and Ernie Kabelac. Proper cutting of bait, line control, depth of water where fish typically "held", but THE number one lesson, which most people never quite figured out… there WILL be a "bite" at some point during the tide. So many times, we would be at Hazel Point, along with a dozen or two other boats before daylight, using a flashlight to cut our bait. There were times when the bite was just as the sun hit the water, but quite often, not a strike, not even a scratched bait for hours. Slowly, fishermen would get impatient and leave, but at some point, a bite would come on, and we'd limit in half an hour. That's the way salmon react. It was true THEN and remains true today.

We loved fishing Hazel Point, Pleasant Harbor, WaWa Point, and Jackson Cove. We knew where, when, and how. Hood Canal was rich with salmon, and plenty of ling and rock cod, if you knew where to find 'em. When weather was nasty and the Canal too rough, we would fish the protected waters around Bremerton. Rocky Point, the Warren Ave bridge, 140 hole, tennis courts, Battle Point across from Brownsville, and Point White. It was mostly wintertime blackmouth fishing. True cod came into those waters in the winter to spawn, and the population was off the chart. Commercial fishing wiped that out.

We had great mentors being able to fish around Kabelac & Quy; we would mimic their every move. How they held their rod, how they let out and retrieved line, and how they used their motor to maintain proper line angle. We also got valuable info from another local legend, Vern Jones, owner of Ted's Lunch. In later years, I had the privilege to fish with all three. Vern taught me the ropes fishing the "beach" at Westport, and Ernie and Harv were often guests in my boat at Port Townsend and Point Defiance.

During mid-to-late Spring, massive amounts of herring entered the canal to spawn. The pilings at Seabeck Marina would be covered with milt and the rocks in Jackson Cove would be white with spawn. Fishing was phenomenal. Plenty of fish in the 10, 12, and 18-pound range and many much larger. I never caught anything larger than mid-teens. It was pretty much a "hush-hush" thing for several years, just the locals knew about it, but the word finally got out. Some guy caught a 39 pounder in Jackson Cove, went directly to the newspaper, had his picture published, and the next Spring, the crowds started to show. Didn't take long before commercial herring fisherman found out about the huge run of herring, "And that's all she wrote."

Left: Bennett and me from Bald Point,

Right: Fred Kegel and Chuck Semancik from Hazel Point

From left to right: Vern Jones, Chuck Semancik, Fred Kegel and Jim Jones

Westport and Kelpers

The Chehalis River bar at the entrance to Grays Harbor, sitting between the towns of Westport, Washington on the south and Ocean Shores to the north, can be extremely intimidating. The Grays Harbor bar is VERY dangerous. The experienced fishermen plan their trips to avoid crossing during peak out-going tides. I have crossed the bar when it was as smooth as Kitsap Lake and when I was surrounded by nothing but green water, and it takes great skill navigating your boat through an approaching breaker.

Westport was the premier Chinook fishery on the Washington coast. Access to the ocean was primarily from Westport, with a few anglers launching at Ocean Shores.

There are many components to its demise: foreign fleets off our coast, unfavorable ocean conditions, salmon ranching pens, river net fisheries, and the least of which would be over-harvesting by the sport fishermen. Each user group wants to hang the blame on the other. I won't get into the political aspect of Washington's salmon decline here; I will save that for another time. But I will say, all fishermen have been impacted to the point that Westport, once called The Salmon Capital of the World, is now a ghost town compared to the heyday of the '50s, '60s, and '70s.

In November 1972, courts banned the use of sport-fishing gear for commercial salmon fishing. In the '60s and early '70s, the number of "kelpers" grew to approximately 1500 license holders. Some people believe the larger commercial salmon boat, "long-polers", with their active lobby group, were able to stop the small boats from using sport gear. Purely anecdotal on my part, but I believe the larger boats were jealous of the kelper because we could fish the shallows for Chinook. They could not, due to the large number of land mines (crab pots), which were difficult to fish around even for small boats.

Most Kelpers were sport fishers who enjoyed salmon fishing and were looking to sell their catch to a licensed buyer to pay for gas, bait, and make a few bucks. Some were very serious and used commercial salmon fishing to augment their full-time jobs, most notably, school teachers who had the summer months free from the classroom. Either way, serious or not, like-minded fishermen would band together and create their own mini fleet. I loved salmon fishing and was able to purchase a boat suitable for fishing the Washington coastline, and eventually became part of a group of guys that would stick together. On the water, we communicated using CB radios and would give ourselves a "handle". Quite often, fishermen would name their boat for a girlfriend or a lifestyle. I fished with Spring Skier, Whale Bird, Bandito, Freddy K, Landlubber, Dog Fish, Bar Hopper, Limb Lopper, Frog, and others. I named my boat Moocher.

We were called Kelpers because we fished close to the shore and the kelp beds, typically in 30 to 60 feet of water. Kelp is a type of large brown seaweed that grows in the shallows, often described as an underwater forest. Baitfish such as herring and anchovies could hide there from predators that cruised along the beds seeking a meal. Kelpers were hoping the salmon's last meal would be their cut-plug herring.

I made many lasting friendships from my time on the water and carry fond memories of my time at Westport. I started taking Derek with me when he was about 6 or 7 years. Douglas had a problem with the "Westport Flu" and stayed away. Our mini fleet called Derek "the little moocher". The top of his head was barely visible above the gunnel, but he would help land fish, bait hooks, and clean the boat. The instant we tied up the boat after a long day of fishing, you could always find him slipping around the pilings catching poggies or perch. But the best times were our trips home after a weekend of fishing. He would fall asleep on my lap, and I would have to carry him to bed once we arrived home. Oh my!

Steelhead, Salmon, and Boldt

Before the infamous Judge Boldt decision, Hood Canal streams were loaded with salmon and steelhead. On February 12, 1974, Judge George Boldt issued a historic ruling reaffirming the rights of Washington's Indian tribes to fish in accustomed places. The Boldt decision allocated 50% of the annual catch to treaty tribes. Western Washington tribes had been assured the right to fish as usual at accustomed grounds and stations by Federal treaties signed in 1854. But during the next 50 years, the Indians were forced out by Euro-American immigrants who used modern technology and much larger boats to intercept migrating fish. The campaign to reassert Indian fishing rights began in 1964 with fish-ins on the Puyallup River, led by Billy Frank. Eventually, tribes sued the Federal government. Finally, Judge Boldt ruled that the historic treaties made by the government gave Indians the right to fish. Further he ruled, it was not up to the state to tell the tribes how to manage something that had always belonged to them. AND THIS IS THE BIGGIE, Judge Boldt ORDERED the state to take action to LIMIT fishing by non-Indians. It didn't take long after the Boldt decision that many small streams along Puget Sound and Hood Canal were nearly void of migratory fish.

During the late '50s and '60s, I spent countless hours fishing for steelhead on streams that entered Hood Canal, and I learned my skills from Dad's Army buddy, Warner Coffman. We didn't have level-wind casting reels, and I hated spinning reels, so Warner got me to use a single action Pflueger Medalist fly reel and a stripping basket. On the small canal streams, long casts were not required. Flip it under that overhanging pile of brush or along a mossy log. No leader, the hook was tied directly to the end of my main line, and I used a split shot for a weight. I would ride my bike to the Union River and fish all day, but when I got a driver's license, I spent time on the Dewatto and Skok; I never cared for the Tahuya, even though, for some reason, it had much larger fish.

It just didn't fit my style.

A personal diatribe:

I believe the Boldt decision was more about rectifying supposed past injustices and was made with little regard for the non-tribal fisherman. Yes, the Indians' share of the salmon fishery had dwindled to a meager 5% of the total harvest, but when Boldt ruled it was not up to the state to tell tribes how to manage the resource, it gave them license to fish without any regard to the future. Year after year, most tribes, not all (the Quinault tribe and a smattering of other tribes are the exceptions) would purse-sein at the mouth of a river and then if any fish were remaining, would stretch nets across the entire width of a river. Think about it.

I once served on the Washington State Salmon Enhancement Advisory Board; I realize many factors have led to the depletion of our salmon runs. I have seen first-hand the loss and degradation of salmon habitat. I also know ocean conditions and foreign fishing fleets have had a major impact, but don't be fooled by the Northwest Indian Fisheries Commission's propaganda. Tribes may "monitor" the catch, but where do they send their report? A tribal Commission? Think about that one for a moment. Then there are groups believing the only way to rebuild salmon stocks is by eliminating all hatchery programs and rebuilding by allowing "wild" fish a chance to spawn naturally. WILD STOCK? SPAWN NATURALLY? HAH! How can that possibly happen when nets are stretched across a river bank to bank. The Washington State Department of Fish and Wildlife have their hands tied. They've given it their best shot, but have lost every court case. It's up to the tribes to enhance our fishery, and I don't see that happening. Casinos and fireworks stands have made them extremely wealthy, and they really don't care about salmon. "Oh, salmon are part of our cultural identity and spirituality." Hoooey! If that TRULY were the case, what are they doing to protect their way of life?

One final vent

Indian reservation gambling generates more income than Atlantic City and Las Vegas combined. In 2009 this totaled $26.5 billion in revenue. Where does the money go? I've traveled through several reservations, and conditions have been cited as "comparable to Third World." (May 5th, 2004 Gallup poll). If you don't accept the Gallup poll assessment, look for yourself; I have seen the living conditions first hand. They are deplorable! Four to eight out of ten adults are unemployed (2005 BIA American Indian Population & Labor Force Report). Right here in the "Good ol' US of A" we have an example of how socialism has failed its people. No need to look at Argentina or Cuba; it's right under our noses. Indians have free health care and free access to education. Those who don't have jobs subsist on entitlements that provide basic food. Where are their leaders? There must be someone, someone willing to rise from the ranks and restore the once-proud Native American...

My editor tells me that more recently, there have been changes, at least in our local tribes. The next generation has come into power as tribal elders and leaders. They have been expanding their economic base beyond casinos and fireworks stands, developing construction companies and other businesses. Along with these, they have been developing training programs of many kinds, along with rehab programs for substance abuse. As with all complex situations, it's an uphill battle; and you can lead a horse to water but can't make it drink. Changing the effects of generations of poverty and the despair/depression that comes with that is an uphill battle. Yet a start has been made in many places, and it's something to pray over.

Ok, there. I've said my piece.

Warner Coffman. My dad and Warner met while in the army at Schofield barracks in Hawaii. Warner was All-Army middle weight boxing champ and Dad was his cornerman. "Uncle" Warner (Champ) taught me how to steelhead fish on the Puyallup River.

With Ted Hauschel from Pt. Dalco. Ted and I have hundreds of stories that shall remain locked in the "vault."

Howard Kubli & me with a nice catch from Possession Bar.

Northwest Outdoors (northwestoutdors.com)

During the mid to late '60s, the Pacific Northwest had many outdoor fishing and hunting shows on local television. It was all about salmon, steelhead, and trout (NO BASS fishing, thank you), and the hunting shows featured mainly migratory waterfowl and pheasant.

Don McCune's (Captain Puget) "Exploration Northwest" was the family's favorite, not so much for the fishing, but he was such a wonderful, down-to-earth host and traveled all around the NW. It was such a good "outdoor" show Mom even liked it.

There was "Gadabout Gaddis the Flying Fisherman". He said, "Fishing is more than just catching fish; it's soaking up nature and all its marvelous wonders." Roscoe Vernon Gaddis was a rep for the Shakespeare fishing tackle company and got the nickname "Gadabout" due to his wanderlust. He had a remarkable folksy style and passed away in 1986 at the age of 90.

Larry Schoenborn's "Fishing the West" was one of the best on TV. He and his wife, Ethel, owned Larry's Sport Center in Oregon City, which led to him hosting more than 300 segments that aired across the United States and were carried internationally from Britain to Japan. One day, while steelhead fishing on the Humptulips River with good friend Roy Harvey, we were fortunate enough to meet Larry. He was a true gentleman and took time, during his filming, to shoot the breeze with us. He passed away at age 72 after an extended battle with cancer.

One GREAT show (just my opinion, because Dad and I made a few cameo appearances) was Elling Simonsen's fishing and hunting program on Channel 13, hosted by John Jarstad, but on top of my list was Jim Conway's "The Outdoor Sportsman". Jim guided around the Portland area, traveled all over the Pacific NW, and hosted a classic fishing program. I have no idea how I remember that it aired Thursday nights on KOMO (CH. 4). I can still see him cooking a lunch right next to the river, and him saying, "Let's get down the creek." And he used to say, "All I need to catch steelhead is an Okie drifter or a Sammy Special." Jim made you feel like you were the one holding the rod and would set the hook. It saddens me to find out he had cancer and took his own life.

Those outdoor programs were so much fun to watch! In the early '70s, Fred Kegel and I often talked about putting together our own outdoor show. Heck, we were pretty good hunters and fishermen and thought all you had to do would be "point and shoot", and there you have it, a successful TV program. But reality set in. We barely could afford the trips we did take, much less go out and buy cameras, and on top of that, we knew nothing about filming or editing. So, it was nothing more than a pipe dream and finally died on the "cutting room floor" of a duck blind.

The outdoor shows I grew up with laid dormant in the back of my mind for many, many years. It wasn't 'til Derek opened his hunting and fishing store, "Baystreet Outfitters" in Port Orchard, and I met Willie Toth, that the "dream" came to fruition.

Willie, an accredited Jeweler, worked at "Rings and Things" in downtown Port Orchard and often frequented Derek's store. He was an accomplished fly tyer and he and I became good friends. We spent time fly fishing from the beach at Point No Point for Coho; we both enjoyed fly fishing Cady Lake, and I took him into a couple secluded beaver ponds. Willie was a solid still water fisherman, but never fished "moving water", so I showed him how to fish a few rivers and streams. I also took him to a few beaches in Hood Canal and Puget Sound, introducing him to fishing for sea run cutthroat. Willie and I were, and are, different as night and day, but when we were on the water, we "clicked" like "peas and carrots".

Dalene and I were on a mini-vacation to British Columbia. One evening, after a round of golf and dinner, I watched a couple locals report on fishing hot spots in the area.

BING! A light flashed in my mind! I immediately called Willie, told him what I was watching, and said, "Hey, why don't we put together our own local fishing report show? You've got the cameras and a sweet studio; I think we could come up with a great program."

And then it happened.

Willie said, "Let's go one better; we'll put together our own fishing show. Heck with just reporting. I know how much you've talked about past programs; I think we can do it. Wha'cha think?" I immediately bought into the idea and said, "Let's call it Northwest Outdoors." Willie told me he would have to check into the legality of the name; a couple days later, he called and said, "Northwest Outdoors is ours!"

And that's how our television career was born. It only took 40+ years of inactivity on my part, Derek's fishing store, and a jeweler from Northern California to bring it all about. At first, we thought a good fishing show needed to show a lot of fish being caught, but it didn't take us long to realize we needed quality, not just numbers. Show a nice cast to a rising trout, the take, a good hook set, strong runs, a dandy fish in the net, and then a smooth release. We hooked and landed far more fish that didn't make the final cut than those we showed on air. We wanted people to experience as much as possible from their living room - every aspect of fishing in our great NW outdoors. Things were goin' fairly smooth, then Willie came up with an added dimension to our show. Not only did we talk about where, when, and how to catch fish, but we needed to show what flies we used. Willie was an excellent fly tyer, so we had a segment where he tied a specific fly pattern we were using, and the show was now complete.

We traveled from our home waters around Kitsap and Mason County to British Columbia, into Idaho, Oregon, and Montana. Our goal was to have a show the entire family could enjoy. For several years, we filmed the Kitsap Poggie Club's Opening Day, for young kids, at the Gorst fish hatchery. We looked forward to that event every year, especially watching little girls with big smiles on their faces, reeling in trout on a Barbie Doll fishing pole.

We were featured on Bremerton Community Access Television with our own weekly time slot and won several awards. With some herculean effort on our part, there was a good chance we could have become syndicated, but Willie's job forced him to move out of town, and we parted company.

The two of us must have had quite an audience because we were often stopped in stores with people asking, "Aren't you the guys on that fishing show?" We both enjoyed the notoriety. There even was an incident with the Bremerton Police. Yup. Them.

One New Year's Eve, Dalene and I were driving home from a party at a friend's house. As I crossed the Warren Avenue bridge and turned up Sheridan Ave, I noticed "rollers" blinkin' behind my truck. Didn't matter that I had NOT had a drink all night, TRUTH, nary a one, but I said to Dalene, "Oh no, we're bein' stopped by the cops." I pulled off the road, stopped, rolled down my window, and waited for the inevitable. The policeman carefully came to my door and said, "Let me see your license and proof of insurance." Dalene was fumbling through the glove box for the insurance card as I handed him my driver's license. He took one look at the picture on my license, shined his flashlight in my face and said, "Hey, you're that guy on television that catches all those cutthroat. Our family loves your show. Have you been out lately?" I shared some info with him, and he said, "Be careful on your way home. Keep up the good work."

Now, THAT'S the America I grew up in.

Some Final Memories (maybe)

Dad and I had a favorite stretch of water on the Henry's Fork of the Snake River, about a mile downstream from our campsite. For some reason, it produced an evening hatch of mayflies that would make a fly fisherman's hand tremble with excitement. One particular evening, Dad and I left camp around 5pm ignoring the numerous rises along the way, knowing we would be casting to hundreds of trout gorging themselves on the spinner fall, and we did not want to miss one second of the feeding frenzy. Along the way, we saw a moose, knee-deep in the river with its head fully submerged. After a few seconds, a cow moose lifted her head out of the water, mouth full of aquatic vegetation. Once that was chewed and swallowed, her head went underwater again; moments later, she came back with another mouth full of grass. It was an amazing sight, and we could have watched for hours, but we didn't want to miss one moment of the hatch.

Once we got to "our" bend in the river, we sat on the bank not saying a word, each of us dreaming about hangin' one fish after another. As the summer sun began to cool, the most prolific dance started. First, the nymphs emerge from beneath the surface and shoot into the air almost immediately. Then clouds of mayflies filled the air. The flies mated, their life span completed, and the spinners fell on the river so thick they would even cover us with the spent flies. It was a fantastic spectacle. Hundreds of trout were feasting on the emergers, the duns, and the spinners. We made hundreds of casts with an equal number of refusals, but that's not the point. There are times in your life so indelible they never fade away.

~~~~~~~

I will never forget Doug and I leaving home at midnight, headed for Eastern Washington. I was told thousands of geese were working a stubble field just east of Royal City. We located the field, and in the dark, we walked around and found tons of goose droppings. This had to be the right spot. It took us the better part of an hour to set our spread and ready ourselves for the flight. We knew there would be snow on the ground, so we had "borrowed" a couple of Mom's white bed sheets for camouflage. Daylight broke and we could hear geese heading our direction. Oh, baby! We're gonna have a great shoot. But as luck would have it, flock after flock of birds would land in a field less than half a mile from us. We got one mallard hen and no geese, but that's not the point. Another memory I will never forget.

Ok, I need to share one more. Derek and I spent the night sleeping on my boat in the Westport boat haven. Of course, the harbor was full of sea lions, and their barking lasted long into the night before I was able to doze off. The rumble of the charter boats leaving the basin meant it was time to head out. We had a bowl of cold cereal, untied the boat, and made our way out of the harbor. As I approached the south jetty, I could see white water stretching all the way to the north jetty. The ebb tide was so strong and came on us so fast, I had no chance to turn back. I fought to keep the boat headed directly into the oncoming breakers, and then it happened. A wave some 10' to 12' broke over the top of our boat. All I could see was green water in front of me and on both sides. I looked at Derek and said, "Derek, we need to put on our life jackets. I think we're in trouble." We did, and I continued westward, and finally made it across the bar. Amazingly, the ocean was flat calm, but my knees were knockin' until we had our first salmon in the boat. I don't remember what kind of day we had fishing, but that's not the point. Another memory I will never let go.

I still have a ton of hunting and fishing adventures to pass on, and many friends that shared in those experiences. Time simply doesn't permit stories like Joe Bloomquist and our "midnight ride" hauling out two bull elk. Or Dennis Gregg and our scrape with the law along the Marion Drain. It was difficult to leave out one of the greatest shotgunners in Jack Strickland, and my dad and our duck hunt in the "bone yard". Andy Skobel, a good friend from Fircrest Golf and Country Club, and our trips to the Cispus River. How could I not talk about Al Showalter, former KBRO Disc Jockey and Olympic Savings & Loan manager, and our many salmon trips to Hazel point, especially the Bangor Salmon Derby? There were so many steelhead trips on the Peninsula with Roy Harvey, Marv Novak, and Jay Weatherall. And so many more trips with Douglas and Derek when they were young, and Fred and Jim, but for now, those stories will be told around the dinner table.

Summing It Up ~ Courtesy of Bill Nylund

The customary time of release for cultured fish from most salmon hatcheries is about the time when wild stocks in watersheds reach the peak of out migration seaward. The exact time of release may vary due to floods, water temps, and uncontrolled diseases. It was essentially a need to respond to the declining sports angler harvest in Puget Sound that led to the development of delayed salmon releases; that is, extending the artificial rearing periods beyond the normal time of release or migration.

The saltwater catch of salmon by the sport fisherman in Puget Sound reached a peak in 1957, when anglers harvested 208,000 chinook. Within 12 years the catch of chinook declined to a quarter of the 1957 peak.

Let me say, by all anecdotal evidence, the delayed release program was a huge success making winter time blackmouth (immature chinook) fishing phenomenal.

That being said, I was saving a winter time salmon fishing adventure for another occasion, but Bill Nylund would not allow it.

Let me have Bill tell the story:

We were fishing Point No Point and thanks to the delayed release of chinook salmon, the bite was so hot we couldn't quit. There was a family nearby that never had so much as a strike, so we gave them a few fish so we could continue. That was also the day you grabbed your rod to set the hook and it slipped out of your hands and fell into the water. You dove in for the rod - were able to grab it with your left hand while your right hand had a death grip on the gunnel and your toes stuck somehow in the motor well. I grabbed your belt so you didn't fall completely out of the boat. When you were coming up for air, I could see you had caught your glasses with your teeth. You were soaked from the waist up, your whole torso had been in the water. All you said was, "I lost the fish."

It was winter, we were in 120' of water, and you dove in to save a stinking fishing rod!

That's Mills for ya.

Thanks Bill. And yes, that's the America I grew up in.

OTHER OUTDOOR LIFE

Trailer Life

We Bought a Trailer

Dalene and I wanted to upgrade from our 8' truck camper to a travel trailer. When our boys were young, we did a lot of camping using the truck camper, and would often pitch a tent for a bit more room and another place to sleep if the boys invited friends. Now, the boys were pretty much "out of the house" and we decided to look for a travel trailer.

In the spring of 2006, Howard and Betty Kubli suggested we go to Arizona, watch some Spring baseball, and shop for a trailer in the Phoenix area. Sounded like a great idea.

While in Tempe, we watched baseball, enjoyed the warm weather, and did A LOT of shopping, but found nothing that tickled our fancy or fit within our budget, so we headed home.

We were in no hurry to get back to Bremerton and decided to take I-15 north rather than I-5 and visit Douglas in Salt Lake.

We were a few miles north of St. George, Utah, and were about to pass someone pulling a travel trailer.

WHOA! There's a "For Sale" in the rear window. We dropped back and gave it the "once over".

"Looks nice."

I pulled up alongside, trying to guess the length, then dropped back again.

Dalene asked, "I wonder if it has any slide-outs?" So, I pulled up alongside in the passing lane, AGAIN, saw that it did; then dropped back and crept close to the shoulder to see that side of the rig.

One more question, "I wonder what kind of truck they have pulling it?" Again, into the passing lane I went, "Wow, it's the exact same truck as ours." Yes, we dropped back one more time, to get the phone number in the rear window.

I must confess, this was a convenient time for a cell phone.

Dalene dialed the number and before she could say anything, the person on the receiving end said, "Are you the ones that have been looking at our trailer?" Dalene chuckled and said, "Yes, we are and we'd like to take a look."

At the next off-ramp, they pulled over. We loved the trailer; it was exactly what we were looking for. We made a handshake deal right there alongside the freeway.

Once in Salt Lake, we went to the bank, paid them off, had our truck wired accordingly, and went our separate ways. They were returning to Wasilla, Alaska and, of course, we to Bremerton. The beauty of the deal? They left us EVERYTHING!

All the dishes, silverware, cooking utensils, pots and pans, bedding, TV, and a pantry full of canned goods. Only in America.

Giltner, Nebraska and the Talich Life

As I said back in the Family Life Section on Mother, not long after watching "The Grapes of Wrath" for the umpteenth time, I felt the need to connect with my mother's hometown of Giltner, Nebraska. Dalene and I discussed our itinerary and how to go about it. Should we simply fly to Omaha, rent a car, and drive to Giltner? But not knowing if there would be accommodations along the way and besides, we owned a fully equipped travel trailer, we opted for:

ROAD TRIP!

As it turns out, we could not have made a better choice!

We left Bremerton in mid-March after ensuring mountain passes were free of snow and weather conditions were favorable. Living our entire lives on the west coast and mainly in the Northwest, we gave not an ounce of thought to the bane of the prairie states ~ TORNADO!

We packed our rig with the absolute necessities for any road trip: television, golf clubs, AND fishing gear! Of course, we filled the cupboards with groceries, but that was a mere afterthought.

And, of course, we had announced our plans to the three sisters, so our first stop was to visit Aunt Norma in Moses Lake. Then we headed southward, crossing the Columbia River near Hood River, Oregon and winding our way through central Oregon ~ stopping to play a bit of golf and cast a fly in a remote stream. Eventually, we intersected with I-5 and made it to Los Angeles. When I tell you pulling a 30' travel trailer through the heart of LA is nerve-wracking, that's a gross understatement!

We spent a couple days with Aunt Charlotte and Uncle Fred, and we all shared a common excitement over the destination of this trip. Neither Dalene nor I had ever traveled the highways east of Utah, so we had decided to make the most of it. If we played close attention to our route, we might make Augusta, Georgia in time for the "Masters". Of course, we considered that really as a mere pipe dream.

From LA, we traveled east through Arizona, New Mexico, across the panhandle of Oklahoma, through Arkansas, Mississippi, Alabama, and WaaLaa (Voila!) ~ we did reach Augusta in time to watch a couple rounds of the tournament!

After the Masters, we spent Easter Sunday at a church in, "I have no idea where we were America", but what a blessing! Dalene and I were met at the front door by a sweet elderly lady. She asked where we were from and if we were planning to move to the area. We told her about our journey to connect with my mother's past, and she understood. Then without hesitation, as if she could see into my soul, she asked, "I feel you need me to pray for someone." Holy Cow! How did she know I had been praying for a young man who had fallen into deep depression? We sat for a bit and prayed together. She promised to pray for my friend, and no doubt she did. Oh, how I wish I could talk to her now. That young man is still in need of prayer, but his life is so much better now. After Easter Sunday, we were now on a mission to reach Giltner. We headed north through Tennessee, Missouri, a portion of Iowa, and westward to the Nebraska state line.

Giltner is a town with a population of about 300 people, located approximately 15 miles south of I-80 between McCool Junction and Doniphan. (Ok, I stuck that in just to be a smart-alec, knowing full well no one knows those towns.) Dalene and I were still a day's drive from Giltner and spent the night at a small roadside rest area, where we talked about a few of the places we visited. We will always cherish those moments, the good AND the sad.

The panhandle of Oklahoma was eerie with all the abandoned homes and stark landscape. We stopped in a small town for dinner and met the high school graduating class: 7 kids (4 boys and 3 girls). We also had a very near miss with a tornado. We walked a boardwalk through an Arkansas swamp to see the initial point from which the land survey began for the Louisiana purchase. Driving along a remote stretch of road in rural Mississippi, we stopped to talk with a man fishing from a bridge. Oh, the stories he relayed about living in the South!

We talked about our time in Tupelo, Mississippi where we visited the Elvis Presley museum; and the short drive to Memphis, Tennessee, and our time on the legendary Beale Street. Having a curb-side lunch at BB King's Blues Club and sitting at Handy Park listening to blues musicians. But now, we were a day's drive from Giltner. We had no idea what to expect, and we left everything in God's hands.

W pulled into town around 6pm. The streets were empty of any cars, no pedestrians along the sidewalk, no movement anywhere, but we had the distinct feeling we were the center attraction. There was no RV park, so we parked alongside a picnic table in the city park, and ~ what seemed like right out of a Hollywood movie ~ a young boy, all alone, was shooting hoops at a tattered backboard.

In the morning, we talked about where we might meet a few locals who could share a bit of Giltner history. The choice was obvious, "Let's go to the local café; surely there must be a few guys having their morning coffee." Actually, the choice of cafes was rather an easy one; there was only one cafe. No "Family Pancake House", no "Denny's". With a bit of trepidation, we walked in and sat in the corner. In the middle of the room was a round table with 8 men having coffee. Never fearful of striking up a conversation, I approached the men and explained who we were.

One of the men said, "We've been talking about you all morning. Nobody stops in Giltner." Sure enough, the eyes WERE watching as we had pulled in the night before. I explained more about who we were and the nature of our visit.

One man stood up and said, "Holy cow, I'm a Talich!"

The ice was broken.

We talked about Giltner history, the dust bowl era, the economy, the weather ~ you name it, we talked about it. I explained how my mother moved from Nebraska to Idaho and eventually ended up in Bremerton. The men truly enjoyed our stories.

Another man actually stood up from the table and said, "You're in luck. I'm the superintendent of the school district. Would you like to visit the high school your mother attended?"

OH MY! What an answer to prayer. Our dreams were being fulfilled.

The gentleman took us to the high school where we walked the hall ~ yes, hall singular.

"Would you like to see pictures of all the high school graduating classes?"

Any idea what we said?

On our way to a vestibule with all the class pictures, we passed through the gymnasium. OH MY! A page right out of the movie *Hoosiers*.

We walked across the gym floor, past the raised stage to a small alcove with all the senior pictures. We scrolled through the years, noting a Talich in just about every class, and then a picture of Aunt Charlotte appeared. Instantly tears came to my eyes.

We called Aunt Charlotte, Aunt Norma, and finally Mother to tell them what we had found. We all wept with joy ~ our mission was complete!

That's the America I grew up in.

Skiing Life

My First Trip Skiing

It was the winter of my freshman year in high school, and skiing was quite popular. Teachers Kent Heathershaw and David Hicks put together an active mountaineering and ski club. I didn't have any equipment, but there was a huge warehouse sale coming up in Seattle, sponsored by "Ski Bonkers"; so I saved a few bucks from my paper route and mowing of lawns. I knew nothing about picking out skis or bindings, so fellow classmates Joe Munson and Bill Rawl tagged along. Joe found a pair of Stein Ericksons and said, "Let's see if they're the right size." He stood the skis vertical against my chest, had me extend my arm, and if my fingertips curled over the tips, that would be perfect. I reached high and barely got my fingers over the top. "Yep, just right." (Looking back, it's a wonder I was able to ski on those giant boards. 7' 2"? I still spend time on the slopes and have a pair that are 190cm, 74", and they're so smooth.) In 1959 that's just the way it was. I spent all my money on the skis, cable bindings, and poles; Mom and Dad bought me a pair of ski boots (leather, ankle-high, and lace-up) from Kitsap Sport Shop on Callow Ave. I was set, except for a jacket and ski pants. Mom bought me that - looked fine to me, but what did I know.

I was pretty good friends with another classmate, Jay Ullin. His family spent a lot of time mountaineering and skiing. His brother Gary climbed some of the tallest peaks in the world. McKinley, Everest, and K-2 were among his conquests. His father, Chet, was instrumental in promoting scouting in Kitsap County. Jay was an accomplished skier. We were in a few classes together and often talked outdoor stuff, and one time he invited me skiing. I told him it would be my first trip, but that was fine with him, and I was thrilled just to be able to ski with that caliber of skier. We took the Bremerton to Seattle Ferry, were picked up by a friend, and went to Snoqualmie Summit. He taught me the snowplow and wedge christie (stem) turns. I was so-so, but had a great time.

On the way home he asked, "Where did you get your ski clothes? From the Salvation Army?" I was embarrassed beyond words, and quite possibly, that's where Mom bought my clothes.

Jay was one of the nicest kids in school, just wasn't thinkin'; wasn't trying to be mean, but that was the first and only time I ever skied with Jay. Jay's comment was not meant to be mean, but I felt a sense of rejection and simply slipped back into the security of my usual world: my family life, my church life. It wasn't intentional; that's just what happened. Oh well, another building block that shaped who I am. To God be the glory that I did not allow it to fester, and yes, that's PART of the America I grew up in.

 ***See the end of Family Life – Letters to my grandchildren for more (and happier) skiing anecdotes!

Outdoor Gear and Clothing Then vs. Now

Today's outdoorsmen are so lucky. I wish for one year, heck, just one wet stormy day, they would have to wear the clothing their forefathers wore. Before the invention of waterproof Gore-Tex rain gear, we had canvas "slickers" lined with a thin layer of rubber that kept you dry from rain, but would sweat so bad, after a couple hours you were soaked from the inside. Synthetic fabrics, with their heat retention and wicking properties, were not available to the average guy. So, we wore wool underwear (which itched like crazy) or cotton long johns, and all they were good for was to provide a barrier between your skin and the heavy, itchy, green wool pants.

Socks? Yes, we had wool, which wasn't bad, but nowadays you can buy SEALSKINZ, which are waterproof. Waterproof socks? Cold proof? Unbelievable. Years ago, my feet would get oh so cold. I tried everything. Multilayers didn't work. I even tried Mom's nylons under the wool. The thinking was that friction between the wool and nylon would create warmth. HAH! Didn't work. At day's end, you had to peel off your clothes, and your skin looked like a prune, but that's all we had. Oh, did I fail to mention chest waders? Bulky, solid rubber, and if they lasted more than one year, you found a bargain. Now we have breathable waders. Waders can breathe? Come on!

Shotgun shells were paper and would swell up like a balloon, with just a slight bit of moisture. We tried everything to keep them dry, nothing worked. You didn't dare go duck hunting without a ramrod. You literally had to force a round in the chamber, and after every shot you needed to use a ramrod to force out the spent shell. I grew up using a side-by-side shotgun, but those with pump-action or semi-auto shotguns were often limited to one round. Then some company from Japan introduced shot shells with a thin layer of plastic, covering the paper, but that absorbed moisture worse than plain ole paper. But that's all we had.

Cat gut for fishing leader -now we have "low viz fluorocarbon".

My first fishing rod was a metal, tapered, telescoping fly rod that extended to 9 ft. Then came split bamboo, followed by glass, and then the holy grail, graphite. I treasure my dad's beautiful Phillipson split bamboo fly rod and fish with it once a year out of respect for the past.

It's often been said, "Like most hunters and fishermen of modest means, I have more shotguns and flyrods than I can afford, and certainly more than I need, but there was always one more that I wanted." My rod room will always have a spot for another.

That's the America I grew up in.

Dahlia Life

How I Got Started Into Dahlias

I entered kindergarten in 1949. I don't remember if there was any teaching going on, but I do remember playing with the big blocks, cookies and milk, recess, and nap time with my blanket. Naval Avenue School was only 3 blocks from our house, so I walked to school. Yes, at 5 years old I walked to school. It was a different world in the late 40's and there was no fear of being abducted. The United States was coming out of rough times economically. During World War II there was gas and food rationing, and most families had a hard time making "ends" meet. After the war, jobs were plentiful, so most parents worked. I was fortunate to have Mrs. Bandy as my babysitter. I loved her like my own grandmother, but let me tell ya, she wasn't afraid to use the paddle. I have a vivid memory walking home one day from school. I believe I was in kindergarten or maybe 1st grade, doesn't matter. I couldn't get home fast enough and "held it" as long as I could, but didn't make it and she caught me widdling my way up the sidewalk. Yah. I got the wooden spoon across my behind. Not fair, but...oh well.

I transferred to National Avenue School starting in the 3d grade and really enjoyed school. I believe school was harder in the 50's. Teachers were very strict, corporal punishment was commonplace and there was no appeal against the system. There were many methods of punishment. Sitting in a corner facing the wall wearing a dunce cap. Removal from the class room and standing in the hall or having to stay in the classroom during recess and writing, "I will not chew gum in class" a hundred times on the blackboard.

During the 1950's there was a "cold war" between the US and USSR and a great threat of nuclear war. In the Pacific Northwest, because of the Naval base in Bremerton, nuclear "fallout" tests were conducted in the classroom and students were required to go through a fake atomic bomb attack and hide under desks. Now, what does any of that have to do with me having a love affair with dahlias? Well, it doesn't. I simply wanted to paint a picture of what school was like in my early years.

Now, here's how it all came about. There was one thing a lot of "brown nosers" would do back in those days: bring a gift to the teacher and place it on the the teacher's large oak desk, which was front and center in the classroom. Most would bring an apple, but in my class, there was one student who always brought a bouquet of flowers. It was the 4th grade, 1953 and at the time I had no idea they were dahlias, but for some reason, those flowers stuck in my mind for years and years and years and then it happened. Dalene and I moved to our present location in 1998 and our neighbor had his entire front yard covered with more dahlias than I knew existed.

I introduced myself to him, told him my story from the 4th grade. Told him my grandpa taught me the ins and outs of growing tomatoes and how much I enjoyed having fresh "toms" instead of those store-bought hot-house tomatoes. He showed me around his garden and said, "Here, let me give you a few tubers, but I warn you, they are very addictive." Nothing could be truer. Lonnie gave me 4 tubers 8 years ago and now I plant more than 200 of them. Yes, I still grow "a few" tomatoes, but nothing like I used to…

LIFE ON THE COLORADO

The "Rookie" aka...

If there's one good thing, and that's iffy, about cell phones it would have to be caller ID. I confess, there are times I ain't gonna answer; that's rare, but when it's family, I will always "lift the receiver".

It was mid-May. Dalene and I, along with my brother and his wife, Cindy, were spending a few days at Lake Tahoe. My cell phone rings; it's Doug.

"Doug. What's up?"
"Well, old man, you better get ready. You're gonna float the Grand Canyon with me, and you'll be rowin' the baggage boat. We shove off Aug 28th."

For the last five summers, Doug had been working for Moki Mac, a Colorado River outfitter, and he'd shared many exciting stories about the river. When Dalene and I returned home and knowing the Colorado was extremely challenging, physically and mentally, I immediately joined the YMCA. Not bein' in the best of condition, I started off slow, but after a couple weeks, it was 3 hrs. per day, 5 days a week. After three solid months of workin' out, I felt better than at the completion of Marine Corps boot camp. Ok, I was 63 years old vs. 21, and I guess memories can fool ya.

Moki Mac headquarters were located beneath the Vermillion Cliffs National Monument just south of the Utah state line. Dalene dropped me off on the 23rd, then continued on to a gal friend of hers in Phoenix. Douglas introduced me to the crew, all experienced boatmen, and we spent the next four days riggin' the rafts and packin' groceries. The provisions were outlandish: fresh fruits, apples, oranges, bananas, grapes, and more. Vegetables ~ lettuce, tomatoes, avocado ~ unbelievable. Then T-bone and rib-eye steaks ~ all this for a camping trip? Wow! Our trip was to last 13 days and cover 240 river miles, so nourishment was essential.

There were six boatmen and me. You can't be called a "boatman" until you've logged three or more trips... The crew had another title for me (I'm savin' that for later). Each of the boatmen would have four clients each in their raft. I wasn't licensed and would row the entire trip alone. Other than rowing, each of us had specific duties. All of us washed dishes, Doug and I cooked breakfast. Jay Healy and Dave Stinson were dinner cooks. They were awesome and even baked cookies and cakes. The entire crew would help with lunch, but that was mainly left up to Scotty.

The Grand Canyon is beautiful and totally free of trash. "What goes into the Grand Canyon, comes out of the Grand Canyon!" except for one thing... piddle. Yes. EVERYTHING!

I wasn't considered a boatman, but I did carry a title - not just rookie or baggage boat rower. Every time we stopped for lunch, and especially the final stop of the day, it was my job to set up the Porta-Potties. When we broke camp, I had to round up the toilets, which were lined with a plastic bag, and then store the "pooh" in ammo cans on my raft. 230 miles of "pooh". I was affectionately called "the shit monkey" ...enuff said.

Douglas cooking breakfast

That Ain't No Jet

We were about to shove off and our leader, Matt Herman, went over what to expect. The route through the Grand Canyon is considered one of the world's most exciting and technically challenging which a boater can experience. Matt discussed safety concerns.
I thought it a bit silly when he said, "If you get tossed from the raft, remember, don't try to breathe underwater." Well duh! More on that later.

I have rowed Mckenzie River drift boats on practically every Pacific Northwest river, but have never even stepped foot in a 19' rubber raft. The raft wasn't nearly as responsive as the dory-style boats I have rowed. I was cautioned to "Always keep at least one boat in front of ya, don't be last in line, and never, ever miss a pullout". Seemed simple enuff.

We left Lee's Ferry on a HOT August morning. The river was quite serene at the start. About four miles downstream, we entered Marble Canyon where I started hearing what sounded like a passenger jet passing overhead. I looked skyward, but never saw any planes. The noise got louder and louder, and when the raft, some 20 yards in front of me, dropped out of sight, I realized, "That ain't no jet." Here came my first test. Badger Creek rapid with a 15' drop. "Oh, baby. Point the bow in the tongue of the wave and be cool." I hit that standing wave so hard and got soaked, but I made it. The first of many challenges.

Our first day was one rapid after another: Soap Creek rapid with a drop of 16', Brown's Riffle and Sheer Wall Rapid with a mere 9' drop. The beauty of the canyon was not part of my experience. I was simply trying to get a feel for the water and my 19' rubber barge.

At our first campsite, Doug helped me set up the Porta Potties. Ok, Doug promised not to say anything, but I will confess. If it wasn't for Doug and his patient help with me and the potties, I would have had a lot of trouble. It was a lot of work for this rookie.

And as long as I'm being straightforward and open, one more confession, and this is the first time I've shared this part of the trip with anyone, even Dalene. At night the guests would get their tents from my raft and set up in a somewhat secluded location. The entire crew secured our boats to one another, sleeping on our own rig. After the first night, I was told (not so politely I might add) I had to anchor up away from the crew. It wasn't just the aroma of "pooh" wafting through the night air, but I tossed and turned so much, I rocked all the boats, keeping everyone awake.

Drinking, other than water, is an absolute No-No during the float, but when we had set up camp for the night and all chores were complete, we would down a few beers. During the day, the temperature in the canyon would approach triple digits and we would keep the cans "cold" in a drag bag.

The roar of the water falls was deafening

Flora and Fauna

Grand Canyon teems with flora and fauna and because of its many climatic environments, an extraordinary diversity of plants and animals live within it. The shrubs, cactus, and wildflowers are visible all along the river ~ ocotillo, mesquite, tamarisk, and barrel cactus. If you're lucky and happen to frequent the canyon when the cacti are in bloom, the colors seem to explode on the canyon walls. Brittlebush, dogweed, and snakeweed ~ don't let their names fool ya, they have brilliant yellow flowers.

One night, long after sunset, and let me say, when the sun goes down, the canyon is pitch black with no light pollution; it feels as if you're part of another galaxy. Anyhow, it was dark, and Scotty was leading a group of clients past my raft. "Come on, Mills, and watch the Datura open with us." I was so rummy, for a nanosecond I actually thought there might be a TV connection somewhere… true confession. I decided to tag along and see what was up, and it was a moment I will cherish forever.

The Sacred Datura and White Tufted Evening Primrose are both night-blooming plants. The Datura has large, showy white flowers and dangerous hallucinogenic properties, and the Evening Primrose has pretty white flowers that turn pink and wilt in the morning dew. It was spellbinding to watch the petals slowly open, and once full in their beauty, out of nowhere moths swept in to pollinate the flowers. God's glory in all its fullness.

We saw mule deer, desert bighorn sheep, ringtail cats, egrets, and blue wing teal. It is also home to lizards and rattlesnakes. Thank heaven I never encountered a snake. I hate snakes.

ABC

We were nearing the 98-mile mark of our trip and the treacherous Crystal Rapids. I breezed through Horn Creek Rapid with its 9' drop and Salt Creek Rapid, a mere 2 on the scale of difficulty. Next came the very difficult Granite Rapid with an 18' drop in elevation ~ one wrong move, and you'd end up on a flat rock in the middle of the river. I followed Doug through Granite and he made a technically beautiful run. Next came Hermit with its 15' drop in elevation and then Boucher Rapid. After Boucher, we pulled to shore about a hundred yards above Crystal, secured out rafts, and set out to scout the best route. As we walked along the shore, taking mental notes of every subtle eddy and current that could possibly suck you offline, the roar of Crystal got louder and louder and then nearly deafening.

In 1966 a tremendous flood unloaded tons of debris into the river. All the material acted as a dam, causing the river's width to narrow by 180'. The once minor rapid around Crystal Creek and the Colorado turned into one of the largest white-water obstacles in the canyon. As we stood to a wall of white water, you could see a deep pit on the backside of a massive wave, some 20' high. Miss your pre-determined line, and you'd be sucked into that hole, turning your 19' raft into a rubber taco. All of us knew the route; slide close to shore until you reach that first back eddy, then push hard toward a mossy rock with a deer fern growing from the top. Once past the rock, pull for all you're worth, away from the white water, but you're not home free quite yet. Just downstream from Crystal loomed Tuna Creek Rapid. With no shore access to scout a route, you had to rely on your own ability.

I navigated Crystal to perfection; after I was clear of the white water, my raft picked up significant speed. "Look for a tongue. Look for a tongue. Look for a good slot." My line was not quite what I had hoped for, but with a lot of pullin' on those 11' oars, I made a solid run. I was mentally shot and physically out of gas.

I barely had enough energy left to make it through dinner. After dishes, I stumbled back to my raft, stretched out, and crashed. I was about to nod off when the entire crew came by my raft led by Jay. "Come on, old man, we've got to take care of some business." I told Jay I was way too tired to go anywhere, but Doug piped up, "Dad, you will come, NOW!" As we walked up a narrow trail away from the river, I noticed one of the crew carrying a Frisbee full of cut-up lime wedges. Huh? We eventually stopped next to a sheer cliff dripping with saltwater.

Matt, our crew chief, summoned me forward, said a few words about how I ran Crystal, and then said words I will remember 'til the day I die. "Well, old man, you are now officially ABC ~ Alive Below Crystal, and its tradition to down a shot of tequila, lick salt from the wall, and suck on the lime. You're first. Go for it." The entire crew participated, welcoming me to ABC. Of course, you can't stop with one shot, and we all left that basalt ledge snockered. Doug led me back to my raft. I slept like a baby. No tossin' and turnin' that night.

Douglas scouting Crystal

*Doug and me on the Colorado.
Yes, even on dry land I felt (and looked)
nervous about the next set of rapids.*

Lava Falls

Lava Falls ~ you can hear the thunder for miles upstream. It's the biggest, most well-known rapid on the river and carries legendary status. Rivers around the US have a rapids scale rating between 1-10, but the Colorado has its own rating. A ten on most rivers would be a mere 5 in the canyon. Lava Falls is a full-blown 10 by Colorado River standards.

The night before running Lava, we had a Lava-Fest with singing and dancing. Jay and Stinny pulled out all the stops and prepared a fine meal. Rib-eye steaks, boiled potatoes, fresh broccoli mixed with cauliflower, and a thick, rich chocolate cake. I tried to enjoy the festivities, but I was haunted by Lava. In the morning, Doug and I prepared a great breakfast. Steak, eggs, bacon, baking powder biscuits, and of course, "cowboy coffee". My anxiety scale was a 12 out of a max 10, and I left my breakfast in some sagebrush. That is the one thing I DID leave in the canyon. As we shoved off, Doug was alongside and, with a wry smile on his face, said, "I'll bet you wish Lava was just around the corner, don't ya? Well, we've got 20 miles to go." That certainly made me feel warm and fuzzy. As we pushed downriver, the surrounding beauty was a blur. We passed Vulcan's Anvil and I knew we were getting close. When we were about a quarter-mile upstream from the falls, we pulled our rigs to shore, tied them to some sagebrush, and walked a narrow path to the falls.

"HOLY COW!!" It was magnificent, and to think I thought the hole in Crystal was deep. Lava made it look like a mere white cap on Hood Canal. We studied the line with a definitive tongue entering the falls to a standing wave about 15' tall. Matt told me, "Looks like an EZ set-up, but remember Upset? When you hit that white-water DUCK".

Matt's advice immediately shot me back to Upset Rapid. Not all that difficult if you set up on a correct line. Upset, at its hardest, is an 8 rating with a 15' drop. I entered the rapid slightly left of center, and a powerful current tossed me into and up a sheer wall that bordered the rapid. I was ok, but when the bow plowed into a 10' wall of water, and I didn't DUCK, I was tossed out of the raft like a twig. I was underwater for what felt like an eternity and remembered Matt's words on day one, "Don't breathe underwater." I bobbed up and down, my arms flailing for anything to grab, and I was lucky enough to find the "chicken wire," and I hung tight to that lifeline. The rest of the crew saw what happened and stalled out in a back eddy. As I approached, one of the guests jumped in the river, swam to my raft, and pulled me in. I coughed up Colorado River water for the next hour.

Now, I'm staring at a huge standing wave, rehearsing my every move. We walked back to our boats and got lined up for the run. The river was pretty soft for about 50 yds. above the falls, which made positioning pretty EZ. First Scotty, then Doug, now my turn. I lined up dead center on the tongue of the wave, giving four or five hard pushes downstream, and dropped into a giant hole. As I started up the backside, I buried my head between my knees and felt a powerful rush of water hit me on the back of my head and shoulders. It was incredible. Through Lava, then up and over a rock the size of my house, through Lower Lava, and pulled over some 200 yards downstream. I looked back and thought, "Eh, piece of cake." Ya right.

So many memories, I can't begin to put them all on paper. At 209 Mile rapid, I was tossed overboard. I put a death grip on one oar. The waves were slapping against my side, pinning me to one of the pontoons. But there's one defining moment on the trip that only a father and son can have.

Forever Eddy

An eddy is a section of a river near the bank that reverses course and flows upstream, usually found along a rapid. There is a legendary eddy in the Grand Canyon called "Forever Eddy" and borders Granite Rapid. Granite forced me to the right side of the rapid along a sheer cliff into some really big waves. I saw what could happen and tried to move toward the middle of the river through even bigger waves, but the tail waves kept pushing me deeper into the eddy and I was stuck. The force of the eddy shot me back upstream some 200 yds. Again and again and again, I tried to get out of the eddy, but failed. By this time, the crew was beached up well downstream, waiting for me. On my fifth attempt to free myself, I saw crew member Jay Healy walking up the shoreline in my direction. He was screaming at the top of his lungs, "ONE MORE STROKE! ONE MORE STROKE!" Over and over, he shouted, "ONE MORE STROKE!" I braced my legs against the front seat, stretched my body out, and gave it all I had. At the crucial moment, where it was "now or never" or get shot back to the top, I reached down deep and pulled with everything I had. SUCCESS! I blasted out of the eddy and joined the crew downstream. To say I was exhausted is a gross understatement. That final stroke was all I had, but I did it.

After dinner, I sat alone along the river, totally worn out and reflecting on the magnitude of what had happened. I looked up to see Doug heading my direction. Doug sat down, put his arm around me, and said, "I'm so proud that you're my father." I put my arms around him, and we both burst into tears. I found out later, when Jay had returned to the crew after encouraging me with his shouts, he went up to Doug and said, "Doug, your old man has guts!"

Thank-you Jay. I will forever be grateful.

Killer Fangs Falls Rapid

The day started out pretty much like every other day on the river. Doug and I prepared breakfast for the guests and crew, consisting of steak and eggs, bakin' powder biscuits, oatmeal, orange juice, and of course… cowboy coffee. Need I say, no white chocolate mocha mix?

Killer Fangs Falls Rapid was next on our journey. It is located at mile 232 downstream of the starting point at Lee's Ferry, and I was feelin' pretty cocky about my ability to navigate most sections of the Colorado. After all, what could go wrong after scouting the safest route through a particular stretch of water? And let's face it, Killer Fangs Falls Rapid is but a mere 4-7 on the Grand Canyon scale. This rapid has become famous, not so much for its degree of difficulty, as it is thought that Glen and Bessie Hyde met their demise in 1928 in this rapid. Glen and Bessie Hyde were newlyweds who disappeared while attempting to run rapids through the Grand Canyon in 1928. Had they succeeded, Bessie would have been the first woman known to navigate the river.

The name Killer Fang comes from 2 LARGE SHARP rocks at the bottom of the rapid that stick out of the water like fangs and can easily flip or puncture a raft. Standing on a rock as big as most houses, some 300 to 400 yards above the falls, Matt, our crew chief, pointed out the safest route. "Stay to the left, and a bit right of that pour-over, then lay heavy on the oars pulling away from the current that can suck you to the right. Ok?"

What is a pour-over? It's water flowing over a large rock, creating a vertical eddy with a hole at the bottom. It wasn't nearly as treacherous as Crystal, but you needed to stay dangerously close because it splits the current and forces most of the water toward the fangs. The crew stood in silence for a few moments, and I could sense a bit of anxiety; then each talked about how they had run the falls in past trips. The route was very technical. I paid attention to everyone's advice, and I studied the water's movement to the best of my limited ability. It wasn't going to be a piece of cake, but I felt oh-so-confident.

As we made our way back to our rafts, I tell myself, "You've run harder rapids, suck it up, pay attention to all the subtle currents, and you'll be fine. You made it through Lava (a class 10). You survived Upset. You rowed yer ass off in Forever Eddy and pulled out of that. SUCK IT UP MILLS." Oh ya, that's easy to say while standing on dry land.

We shove off, and I row hard, maintaining a safe distance from the raft in front of me. Oh my, the river looks nothing like what we had scouted, and I frantically look for my checkpoints. Where did they go? I look around for another crew member, thinking I can follow their raft, but none are to be found. There's the pour-over; I'm not close enough, and the current is sucking me closer and closer to the fangs. PULL! PULL! USE YOUR LEGS! USE YOUR LEGS! I pulled my oars harder than anywhere on the river, including Forever Eddy. Finally, I realize I have no time left to avoid the fangs. I'm now on a path directly toward Killer. I don't even have time to lose my breakfast, like I did before Lava. I know enough to "ship" my oars and I brace for the inevitable. One last look. I can't believe it. Miraculously, there's a sliver of a current shooting between the fangs and I'm sitting on top of it. I put a death grip on my oars and brace myself for the impact. I scraped one of the oars on a fang, and I felt both sides of my raft compress. That's it? I made it? Oh my!

I get my oars back in the water and pull with everything I have left toward the crew, now beached on the opposite shore. Jay Healy was the first to greet me and said, "Mills, you are the first one I have ever seen 'floss' the fangs, and I've got a great picture for you."

*My expression is only half the story.
I nearly met my fate at Killer Fang Falls.*

Summing It Up?

The Grand Canyon is one of the seven wonders of the world with 4.5 million visitors per year. I've been on the North rim and the South, but the true majesty of the Grand Canyon lies along the river.

So many memories:

Waterfalls tucked high in the crevice of sheer cliffs

A night sky with zero light pollution

The fern grotto

Floating on the Little Colorado with my life vest tucked between my legs

Big Dune campsite

Hieroglyphic writings next to ancient cave dwellings

The sound of a "locomotive" roaring down a small stream from a flash flood high in the hills

The entire trip was totally overwhelming, yet it taught me to accept more challenges in my life.

I do have one regret. I wish I was young enough to do it again, but at age 76, my time has come and gone.

I must say goodbye, but before I do, there were so many people that made my trip through the Grand Canyon an unforgettable experience. To Doug's wife, Susie, who told Doug, "Please take your dad on the Colorado before me. He deserves it." Susie, I love you. To Dalene, who prayed for my safety without ceasing; Dalene, my life would be empty without you. To the excellent boatmen who endured my shortcomings, our leader Matt Herman, Montana Jay Healy, Dave Stinson, and that guy with a rose tucked in his hat, Scotty, and of course, Douglas. Douglas, just remember, "What happens in the canyon STAYS in the canyon." And finally, a rare group of guests, the Nerd Pack, who gave me the nick-name, "Daddy Dave", and sang to me that final night of our trip. Vance Vaughn, Susie Mathews, Trudy Duffy, Jacquilyn Craig, Elaine Mariolle, and Bruce Lindsey, who participated in ABC.

I love you all.

MY 9 LIVES AND SAVING LIVES

My 9 Lives

Trust me when I tell you I'm on a first-name basis with most ER doctors at Harrison hospital. Now some of that came about with the number of times I took my parents to emergency when they were elderly, but I must confess, I haven't been the model of safe practices around our house. The top of my head feels like a sack full of doorknobs, what with all the stitches. Derek has told me more than once, "Hey old man, why don't you just rent a room. It would be cheaper."

Dahlia Shears

For example ~ my lack of anonymity became apparent in the Fall of 2018. One evening while in my garage, I was cleaning and dividing my dahlia tubers, and the shears I use are extremely sharp with a needle-like nose. I had been working several hours and now was no longer holding the tuber over my work table. My eyes were a bit tired, so I held the tuber near to my chest, and the shears fell from my hand straight down, penetrated my jeans, and I felt a sharp puncture in the top of my thigh. Could the shears have fallen side-ways? Nope! Could they have missed my leg at all? Nope! Directly into my thigh. It hurt a bit, but not bad, but I dropped my trousers to see what damage might have happened. Such a tiny hole with just an itty-bitty drop of blood. I went into the house to clean and bandage the puncture, and while sitting in the bathroom, that tiny, itty-bitty puncture started spurting blood. I shouted, "Dalene, I need some help." She tried a large band-aid, then first aid tape around the thigh, then lots of pressure and more tape, but it kept spurting mass quantities of red stuff. Dalene said, "We need to go to ER; I can't stop it."

We dashed to the ER and checked in. A nurse got the bleeding to stop using A LOT of pressure, took my vitals, and said told me the doctor would be in soon. We waited a few minutes, and when the doctor slid open the curtain and looked at me, he said, "David Mills? What have you done to yourself this time?" True story.

Gun Point at Fircrest

The year was 1971. I was the assistant manager and part-time bartender at Fircrest Golf and Country Club in Fircrest, Washington.

It was Wednesday, Men's Night. A "home and home" golf match with Tacoma Country Club was complete, and the lounge was packed. Women of the club were decorating the dining room in a cowboy theme for an upcoming party. The atmosphere was festive with western decorations throughout the club. The bar had settled down a bit. The backroom boys were heavy into their weekly poker game, which meant thousands of dollars on the table.

I had just filled a waitress' order, and while standing at the pour station, I looked up - directly down the barrel of a .45 cal. pistol, and the gunman said, "Empty the till!"

What with the cowboy theme in the club, my first thought was, "This is a joke.", but I wasn't sure. Then Mel Reimer, the General Manager, was sitting at the bar off to one side. Still not quite sure, I glanced in his direction with a look that spoke LOUD AND CLEAR, "Is this for real?" And he nodded his head, meaning "Yep". As I turned to get cash from the register, I saw another one collecting wallets from those sitting at the tables.

After handing the guy money from the till came the bone-chilling, knee-buckling words, "YOU, come with me." There was a pony wall between me and the gunman. As I was coming from behind the bar, my hand brushed against a whiskey bottle. I thought, "Grab it, and when you get the chance, coldcock the SOB." That thought passed as quickly as it came, "Nope, he's got a gun." I thought I was gonna be kidnapped as we marched to the clubhouse front door.

"Oh my!" Standing at the door was another gunman. He looked to be about 5 foot nothing, 200 plus pounds, and a nylon stocking covering his face. "I'm a dead man for sure." The 1st gunman took me to the office, "Open the door." I told him the keys were hanging in the bar. So, at gunpoint, we marched back to the bar, got the keys, and went back to the office. At this point, my knees had officially turned to jelly.

I opened the office door and the first gunman said, "Now, open the damn safe!"

It was a double safe, and I told him all I do at the end of my shift is put the receipts in the top.

Oh, did I forget to mention, the five-foot nothing crook was carrying a sawed-off double-barrel shotgun? Well, he was, and he pressed those barrels against my forehead and said, in no uncertain terms, mind you, "Open the mother 'effin safe NOW!!"

Oh Lord, help me! Oh Lord, help me! I barely choked out the words, "I can't; it's a double safe. I don't know the combination." Those words were still floating in the air when a waitress came into the bar, saw one of the holdup men, ran through the clubhouse screaming bloody murder, and hid in a broom closet. The holdup men panicked and made a mad dash for the exit.

The Tacoma police were called, and while interviewing me and others, one of the back-room poker players came into the bar, saw the police, and in utter amazement said, "What the hell is going on?" The boys in the backroom had no idea about the robbery, and the robbers had no idea there was a back room. Had they known, they could have made off with thousands of dollars and slipped out virtually un-detected.

I was summoned to a police line-up, but was unable to ID anyone.

Now, THAT'S the America I grew up in. WHEW!

Halibut Fishing with Howard

Another time Howard Kubli and I were halibut fishing near Port Angeles. We had launched our boat in Freshwater Bay. It was a rough launch and when the tide was out, you could not float your boat halfway up the trailer and winch in with ease. The tide was quite low, and to get the boat on a flat trailer made cranking difficult. Howard was at the stern pushing for all he was worth and I was on the winch. The handle slipped from my hand, blew right thru the winch brake, and smacked me in the back of the hand. Oh, baby, did it hurt. My hand was bleeding pretty good, and I jammed it under my armpit. Howard heard me yell, looked toward the bow, and saw blood coming from my wrist. He actually thought I severed my wrist and became ill to his stomach. I said, "I think I'm ok; it just smarts a bit." I pulled my hand from under my armpit and saw a bone sticking out of the skin. Then I got queasy.

We somehow managed to get the boat on the trailer, me with a broken hand and Howard sick to his stomach, and drove directly to ER.

The best part of the story was at the emergency room. After telling the admitting nurse what happened, she looked at me and said, "I certainly hope you caught some halibut, because you sure smell like fish." YUP, true story.

Ski Vacation Alta, Utah

There have been several near-death experiences where, by the grace of God, my life was spared. No question, God's hand has protected me and my family many times.

While on a ski vacation to Alta, Utah, we left our motel room and got on the freeway, headed for the slopes. Traffic was a "rolling slow down" due to icy conditions on the road. Dalene was in the cab with me and the boys in the back inside the camper. I had come to a complete stop when I noticed in the rear-view mirror a semi-truck, sideways in the road, bearing down on our tailgate... I'm sure you're feeling the same thing I did. I thought, "oh no" and shot up one of those "arrow prayers" of "Help, Lord!" and then the truck driver miraculously recovered, and the rig ended up in a field.

Upper Quinault River

For the sake of anonymity, names will be locked in my vault forever. We were steelhead fishing on the upper Quinault River. High water changes the main channel every year, and it's a must when coming to a blind corner to drop anchor and inspect what's ahead. Well, we didn't. As we rounded the corner, there was a "sweeper" - a fallen log stretched across the river – and there was nowhere to bail out of the way. We hit the log; the force of the river turned us broadside, and the boat filled with water in a flash, tossing us and all our gear in the river. I was swept away, ALONE. My feet were paddling like a duck, searching for bottom, anything to help push me toward shore. Finally, I touched bottom and was able to tip-toe to the bank. I reached out, grabbing twigs, brush, anything that would drag me from the freezing cold water. I made it up the bank, out of breath, wondering if the others made it. I yelled out. Nothing. Again. Nothing!

And then? Voices! They were calling out and looking for me. The three of us were together. We lost the boat and all our gear, but again, only by the grace of God, we were lifted out of the river.

Fall Off the Roof

It was January 3, 2015. Dalene and I had packed up the 5th-wheel and were ready to head south for the winter months, but one last job remained: take down the Christmas lights. The lights on the cedar tree in front stretched to the top; it was beautiful, and the icicle lights were hung from the eaves with care - ok, not funny.

I hesitate to describe what happened because I'm embarrassed 'bout my foolishness and extremely humbled how God saved my life. Yes, God saved my life AGAIN.

Dalene was in the house with Sophia and Davis, and I was on the roof removing the last of the lights. I had set the ladder on a slippery surface. I put one foot on the ladder, and when I raised the other the ladder gave way, and down I fell.

It was surreal. As I was falling, I had time to think to myself, "THIS IS NOT GOOD!" SPLAT. I landed flat on my back on the concrete patio slab. Dalene heard some noise, looked out the kitchen window and saw me falling. She explained that it was like in the cartoons, "He just floated horizontal past the window."

She ran to my aid and got me breathing. Sophia and Davis saw me lying there and thought I was dead. Davis ran and hid, but came back when he knew Popi needed prayer and held my hand. Sophia went to the street and hailed the aid car. I was rushed to the hospital with severe heart trauma.

I awoke from a coma and saw Derek, Mike Niemann, Fred Kegel, Big Larry Shurmard, and Wayne Edmonds wishing me well. That's the last thing I remember. For the next week, I was unconscious, and Dalene never left my side. I had many visitors and will never forget waking to a drawing Sophia made for me. Basic stick figures, but you could tell she was holding my hand, and in the center of the picture was a beautiful heart. Sophia, I love you.

I broke 7 ribs, my back in 5 places, and my pelvis in two places. I was in the hospital for 5 weeks and rehab for another two. I was so lucky not to require any surgery.

Need I say, only by the grace of my savior Jesus Christ was my life spared that January afternoon. God obviously kept me alive for a specific reason. I think of Ron Ayotte, holding his hand as he accepted Christ. The precious, quality time spent with my grandchildren, and yes, I believe He extended my life to complete this work. Some might be blessed, some might be amused, but I pray the Holy Spirit will work in the lives of those wherein the seed of truth was planted. Ephesians 2:10 is pretty clear, "For we are His workmanship, created in Christ Jesus unto good works, which God hath ordained, long ago, that we should walk in them."

Hospital Trips ~ By Request

Well, that was going to be the end of this section, but a couple of my oldest and longest friends (who shall be named below) have Pointedly Insisted I do this list, so here we go:

This adventure started in 1949. I was 5 years old, and the neighborhood gang was playin' cowboys and Indians in Sharon Noble's front yard. Did I forget to mention Sharon was the first girl I ever kissed? Well, let's put it this way. She was two years older, and SHE kissed me. Enough of that; let's continue.

I need to pause for a moment to recall all who were there... of course Sharon, she was dressed like an Indian princess. There was Phil Linden, who lived on the other side of Naval a couple houses down on 13th street, Brian Runnels, Shawn Bumpus, me, with my dual Lone Ranger pearl-handled cap shooters, and the war chief Denny Runnels.

Sharon's yard was the perfect setting with three large firs trees to hide behind, and the concrete path that led to the front door was the Rio Grande River. If you jumped across, you were in the fort and safe from attack, but if you touched any part of the stone, you were dead. We had been playing for some time and Denny threw his spear at the tree. I was safe, in the fort, some ten feet off to one side. Denny wasn't aiming at me, but that stinkin' spear hit the tree with a glancing blow and "in mid-air mind you, made a right turn" (anybody know where that comes from?) and struck me directly in my left eye.

There wasn't much blood, but I lay on the ground cryin' like a baby. Well? What would you have done? Come on now!

Denny ran up to my babysitter, Mrs. Bandy. She called the ambulance, and I was taken to Harrison Hospital, which at that time was on Marion Ave, just below Dad's fire station on top of Capitol Hill.

The rest of that day and the few that followed while in the hospital are quite blurry (no pun intended). What I can remember was in those days, hospitals had "visiting hours". Dad would see me during the day, and Mom would come up after work and stay 'til "closing" time. When the nurse made her rounds and came to my room, she would say, "Mrs. Mills, it's time to go". I would start crying, "Mom, Mom, please don't go. Please stay." After the nurse made several stops and I pleaded with Mom, "Please don't go." She would hold my hand and slip out the door. Nighttime all alone in a 1950's hospital was scary for a 5-year-old, let me tell ya.

Yes, that was the beginning of my hospital career. Some tell me, "Mills, you NEED to list all the times you've frequented a hospital and Emergency Room. Because I've never heard of so many visits." But two of my friends, Phil Linden and Jim Bennett, INSIST I list 'em all, and they WILL NOT let it go.

Not counting visits to the dentist ~ and let me tell ya, in the 1950's dentistry was still in the dark ages. The dentist would stuff your mouth full of cotton, use a jackhammer to remove cavities (we couldn't use fluoride, it was a communist plot... serious), not a high-speed drill. Then you had to spit out blood and stuff in a basin alongside your chair. I hated it.

Ok, back to my hospital visits. I never saw the inside of a hospital or emergency room after the Cowboy and Indian incident until 1969, when the onslaught began. Listing all my trips in the exact sequence is beyond my ability, but I'll give it my best shot; here goes:

+ 1969, 8 weeks in St "Joe's" after a car crash.

+ A month after release, I broke my tailbone... another 5 days in the "klink".

+ two separate hernia surgeries near the groin.

+ Surgery to repair a torn ligament in the right elbow, from rowing a drift boat.

+ Broken right hand with Howard when I lost grip of the winch handle on the boat trailer.

+ Drank a GULP of Clorox, thinking it was the water bottle, while duck hunting with Dad near Moses Lake. I could not breathe and spent a night in the hospital.

+ Torn rotator cuff surgery in the left shoulder. I suspect too much time spent on drift boat oars.

+ 4, count 'em FOUR, separate knee surgeries to remove the torn meniscus. Football and basketball officiating wear and tear.

+ Torn Achilles tendon during a football game. Surgery and two days in the "klink".

+ Two (2) separate surgeries to remove HUGE bunions, one on the left, one on the right foot. I lived with that pain since I was 14. Had to have my ski boot cut to fit.

+ Left hip prosthesis. I imagine just old age wear on the body.

+ two separate biopsies on the prostate. One was very painful; the other I was in La-La land.

+ Prostate cancer: Removal of prostate - definite game-changer.

+ Cataract surgery.

+ ER visit when I cut off the tip of a middle finger using a skill saw not so skillfully. The doctor knew my name on that one.

+ too many ER visits to mention, except the one when I stabbed myself dividing dahlia tubers and the doctor said, "David, what did you do to yourself this time?"

Point of order on ER visits. I became well known in the ER room while my parents were alive. I took THEM many a time and oft.

+ Frozen right toe. Outpatient surgery to extend ligament. Actually, that surgery was worthless because the toe is still frozen, and I'm leaving it that way.

+ Five weeks and two more in rehab after falling off the roof and breaking my back, 7 ribs, and 5 vertebrae, and the pelvis in two places. Angels had their hand on me during the fall because no "real" problems now.

+ But that was then, when I first wrote this section. Sometime after that, I began having severe headaches for over a year and in May of 2021 an MRI revealed a massive growth that was pushing against my spinal cord. In August of that year I had a cervical laminectomy which fused the top three vertebrae of my spine.
 {Editor's Note: David submitted an update for this book: surgery was successful. He reports the headaches which caused him to have surgery are gone, but the healing process will take over a year and his pain has remained extremely problematic. He is currently working with the amazing staff at Swedish Hospital on pain management. I have noticed that on the whole David is in good spirits, but this enforced change of lifestyle has been tough to adjust to. He has been surrounded by the prayers and support of family and friends, which sustain in his low moments.}

+ Now, let's get to my skull. I've developed a bad habit of walking with my head down, which can lead to gouging the top of the skull and boy oh boy does that bleed; tea bags will help, giving you time to get to the nearest Prompt Care facility. The need for staples and stitches in my bean are far too many to list. I've tried to count all the stitches up there, and I've come up with a conservative number of 70+ ish.

Posterior Cervical Laminectomy and fusion surgery. I won't go into any details, but yes, it's as painful as the name sounds.

But guess what? Guess what surgery I have never had? I still have my tonsils. Every kid around me in the '50s was having their tonsils removed. They got to eat nothing but ice cream for a week. I was so disappointed. Oh well.

Well, that should wrap it up. Phil? Jim? Are you satisfied?

Saving Lives

OK, I don't want to sound here like I'm bragging ~ believe me, that's the LAST thing on my mind with the following stories, but they happened, y'know? I guess they come under the heading and category of being maybe Part of the reason God's been saving my life…? They definitely come under the Ephesians 2:10 thing: For we are His workmanship, created in Christ Jesus for good works, which God prepared beforehand so that we would walk in them.

On the Bogy

One time while steelhead fishing on the Bogachiel River, I saw another fisherman hanging off the stern of his boat and his waders full of water. You could tell he could not hang on much longer, and his partner, downstream from the boat, could not hear his shouts for help. Derek quickly rowed to shore; I jumped out of our boat, ran down to the guy, who was now armpit deep in water. It took all my strength to pull him to shore and save him from sure drowning. I know God put me in that exact place for a reason.

Frog's Mayday Call

It was late August, and fishing had slowed down considerably. Freddy K, Fred Kegel, and I had taken time off from a long season, but decided to give a final push. Part of our mini fleet, Spring Skier, Bandito, Limb Lopper, and Frog were struggling to find fish close to home and set out on a long tack south, looking for fish, ending up in Ilwaco, which is at the mouth of the Columbia River. They left Westport in benign conditions: calm seas and no forecast of bad weather. That evening there was a bit of reveling, and the next morning they set sail for home. The Columbia River bar, which is one of the worst crossings in the world, was relatively calm, but once they turned north and got near Leadbetter, the ocean BLEW UP!

Fred and I had spent the morning fishing behind the south jetty, having marginal success, and monitored the boys' journey up the beach on our CB. The ocean was getting nastier by the minute; they had quit fishing and were making a B-line for home because word from the Coast Guard was that the bar was going to be closed to boats under 30' in length. Fred and I were in communication with each of them, but never heard from Frog. We gave Ralph Faulder the handle of "Frog" due to his distinctive, gravelly, raspy voice. As Skier, Bandito, and Limb Lopper passed by with no Frog in sight, we became very concerned. The boys made it over the bar as the Coast Guard was shutting it down, so Fred and I were stuck until the wind and tide settled down to make for a safe crossing.

Then it happened. A faint voice over the CB. It was Frog. We called back asking, "Where are you?" His reply? "I'm not sure, but I'm taking on water." Fred and I determined he must be behind the others and started motoring south. Nothing. No visual. No communication. Then came the chilling cry for help, "Mayday, Mayday"!" Fred and I got in touch with the Coast Guard. They asked for directions, but all we knew was "south beach somewhere".

More May Day cries.

"Frog, where are you?"

"I don't know, but my boat is full of water."

Frog had a wooden Dory, and the rough seas pounded a large crack in the bottom. The seas were getting rougher by the minute, with groundswells of 10 feet or more. It was a bright, sunny day and if we were on top of the swell, we could see a long way off - at the bottom, nothing but green water. We motored in toward the beach and back out, time after time all along the south beach, praying that the sun would bounce off Frog's bright blue boat. NOTHING. More Mayday calls. Come to find out, Frog had a couple friends with him and both, with 5-gallon buckets, were bailing for all they were worth.

After a couple-hour search and many distress calls, we were on top of a large swell. Frog had a bright blue boat and there he was, the sun shining off his hull like a beacon. We got hold of the Coast Guard, directed them to Frog's location. Once we saw the Coast Guard boat alongside, Fred and I turned for home. The bar was still a bit sloppy, but passable. We were mooring in Ocean Shores. Once back to the marina, the others knew what was happening, hooked up Frog's trailer, and had it at the ready. The Coast Guard led him into the harbor, and he ran his boat on the trailer.

All of us decided to have dinner at the local restaurant. Frog and his crewmates were drenched, went back to their cabin, and changed clothes. When Frog entered the restaurant, he came directly to my seat, wrapped his arms around me, and planted a kiss on my lips. I now understand why women want their men clean-shaven.

Who knows what might have happened, but I know God put Fred and me on the water that very day. We were there for Frog at the right time, and we were able to direct the Coast Guard to his exact location.

That's the America I grew up in.

Build A Wall, Save a Life

Another time while working at the church, building the concrete wall around the parking lot, I kept hearing someone from up the street screaming, "My baby! My baby!" At first, I thought there might be a domestic dispute occurring, and no way was I going to get in the middle of that. But the screams became more frantic, "My baby! My baby! My baby!" Something inside me said, "Drop what you're doing and get your ass up there." That did it.

I dropped my work apron, hopped over the concrete forms, and ran up the street. The mother was outside the duplex and said, "Please help, please!" Still somewhat leery, I carefully entered the house. The grandmother was holding the child in her lap, and it was not breathing.

"Oh my. I've only watched mouth-to-mouth resuscitation on television. What do I do?" A million other thoughts crept into my head, but I knelt down beside the grandma, pressed my lips gently on the child's mouth, and exhaled a few times. Nothing happened. I heard within, "Do it again." Once again, I pressed my lips on the child and gave a mighty exhale.

WHEW! The baby sputtered a bit and started to cry. The 911 medics arrived; I told them what happened and walked away. I know it was God's breath I breathed into that child.

Another Hospital Visit (not mine)

The year was 1954 when I first met Ron Ayotte. At the time, how could I possibly imagine the final outcome? Impossible.

Ron lived across the street from the Capitol Hill fire station and, like most kids, was fascinated by the big red fire trucks. Every time the trucks returned from a "call", neighborhood kids would show up and help the firemen wash, sometimes wax, and then wipe the rigs dry with a clean shammy. Ron was no exception, and he and my dad became instant friends when he took Ron into the station and showed him how to tie fishing flies.

I first met Ron on the basketball court in the Marion Avenue school gym playing for the West Bremerton PeeWee basketball team. Ron was a tremendous talent. Little did anyone know how phenomenal Ron would become in the world of track and field.

One day Dad invited Ron to go fishing with the two of us to Wildcat Lake. I don't remember too much about the day, but soon after, Ron disappeared.

Poof! Gone! Being a kid, I didn't give it too much thought. Let's face it, when you are 10 years old, there are a lot of distractions.

The next time Ron and I met was at CK high school. I believe I was 13, and we were waiting for a ride from local legendary track athlete Field Ryan. Let me pause here and introduce Field Ryan to those of you who may not know him with this bit from his obituary in the Bremerton Sun ~

"Field Ryan passed away in 2014 at the age of 82. Field had long been associated with distance running in Kitsap County and had the honor to compete on the US Masters Team internationally. Field graduated from Bremerton High School in 1950 and was a State long-distance track champion. He lettered all four years at the University of Washington in track and cross country. He used his math degree, touching many lives as a teacher at South Kitsap and West Brestmerton High Schools. He was the founder of the Kitsap Track Club and was a 2010 inductee into the Kitsap Sports Hall of Fame."

Mr. Ryan was attempting to establish a traveling summer league track team, and the first meet was in Shelton. I'm not exactly sure how I decided to join the squad because I had almost no interest in running. I guess it was because I was tired of pickin' strawberries, and I needed sumpthin' to do. Nonetheless, there I was riding to Shelton with Field Ryan, Ron Ayotte, and a couple other kids. The ride to Shelton was incredible. His car alone would have been the highlight of the trip ~ had I not ran in an event where you had to run under the grandstands at the Shelton track. I had never been in a car as big as Field's. It had every doo-dad on the market, and it was the epitome of a "lead sled". Don't ask me what make or model; it was just BIG.

Ron seemed to be entered in every event at the meet, from sprints to distance races, and I wandered around, having no idea what to do. After a bit, Field came to me and said, "Hey Mills, wanna run the half mile?"

"Sure, I'll give it a try." I have no idea the outcome of the race. Definitely not first, could have been last, not even sure if I finished. Not true on that part; no way would I quit. I don't remember the start, but I do remember the track running under the grandstands. As you came out of the far end of that tunnel, kids, high in the bleachers, were throwing tomatoes at the runners. I didn't get hit, probably because all tomatoes were gone by the time I emerged. HAH!

After that day in Shelton? Poof! Ron disappeared.

The next time Ron and I met was circa 1976. Dad wanted to take me to a newly opened fly shop in Silverdale, and lo and behold, who was working behind the counter? Yup. That's right, Ron Ayotte. My, how the "unexplainable encounters" keep occurring. Huh. Ron was a field rep for Abel fly reels and various fly rod manufacturers and was well on his way to becoming a world-class fly tyer. We visited for a while; I bought some fly line, and Ron sat with Dad at the fly-tying vise and taught him a few new techniques.

And just like that, Poof! Ron is gone again.

Another Chance Meeting?

Derek had recently opened a fishing and hunting store in Port Orchard, stocked with a little of this and a little of that. The store turned out to be a favorite hangout for many of the locals. Of course, Derek, who led quite a bit of river-guided steelhead trips, had the "old man" work behind the counter now and then. One day, guess who appeared in the store. Who else, but Ron Ayotte. Ron heard about the store and stopped in for a visit. Little did he know it was my son's store, and little did I know Ron lived just up the hill. Instantly Ron and I "hit it off". I would stop by his place just off Mile Hill and discuss fishing over a glass or two of Crown. Boy, did our paths cross over the ages. Ron knew each and every one of my "secret" sea run cutthroat beaches in Sinclair Inlet, and I swear we've stood on the same rock on the Madison River, Big Hole, and Henry's Fork of the Snake. It took a long time for me to ask why I lost sight of him during our high school years.

Ron opened up, some of which I will keep locked in the 'vault". Ron told me he had a very dysfunctional home life and was sent to Saint Martin's High School in Lacey, Washington, and would only return home for the summer. After our Shelton experience, I knew he was destined for good things in track, so I asked how all that worked out. He told me he won a couple state titles and was eventually recruited by Portland State University, where he ended up captain of the track team, won numerous NCAA distance events, and had the honor of passing the Olympic torch off to then-governor Mark Hatfield.

Ron was struggling with a few issues, and guess what, after a year of renewing our friendship, just like that. Poof! Ron disappears. I went to his house several times, looking for any clue of his whereabouts, but never could get a forwarding address.

The Plot Thickens

One evening in September of 2018, the home phone rings. On our television set, a caption appears indicating caller ID. "Un-identified caller". Normally, I would refuse to answer and put the call on Ignore, but lately we had been getting a lot of telemarketing calls, and I was plenty perturbed. I decided to answer and say, "TAKE US OFF YOUR CALL LIST", but for some "unknown" reason, I picked up the receiver and waited for a voice.

"David Mills? Is that you? David Mills?"

This was NOT a telemarketer. "Yup, this is Mills." "Hey, Mills, this is Ron Ayotte." My jaw nearly hit the floor. "Ron, is that really you? Where on earth have you been hiding?"

We had a lengthy conversation, and he told me that he couldn't afford to live at his place in Port Orchard financially. (There's more to that story, but it has found its way into the "vault".)

"So, where you living now?" He told me, and I said, "Oh my, you're not 5 minutes from here; I'll be right over." Re-united again.

Ron had led an adventurous life, traveling all over the world, fly fishing from Alaska to New Zealand. He waded just about every "blue ribbon" stream in between. Oh, how I wish he had kept a journal - some of the stories HE could tell about people, places, and things. Now, except for his former college roommate, who lived in Southern Cal, and Lynn, a very special gal friend, he had nobody. His three daughters, who lived in the area, had nothing to do with Dad. He was not only in poor health, but lonely.

Again, Ron and I were right back at sharing stories about fishing and fly tying. He talked about my father, "Had it not been for your dad, I probably would never have become a good fly tyer." Boy, did that make me feel proud.

I got to meet Lynn, and she and I became good friends. One evening Lynn called and said, "David, I've taken Ron to the hospital, and he's not doing too well."

"I'll be there in a few minutes."

For the next week, Lynn and I would take turns sitting with Ron. I invited my good friend, Jim Bennett, to come over with his keyboard and play for Ron. Jim, truly I believe that set the stage for what's next. During Ron's hospital stay, several times I asked him if he was a 'believer".

He told me, "Well, in school, the nuns told me there was a God, but I never could really make up my mind." One thing led to another, and on October 28th, 2018, Ron said, "Mills, come here and pray with me."

I knelt beside Ron's bed, held him in my arms, and with every ounce of energy he had left in his frail body, he said, "Jesus, I believe. I believe You died for my sins."

Lynn was on the other side of the bed, and with those words, Ron breathed his last.

And just like that, Poof, Ron was in the hands of the Lord.

Neither Lynn nor I could hold back the tears, and we wept like babes.

Now you tell me, were all those "chance" encounters over the years purely circumstantial, or was God's hand in each one? There's no question in my mind, how about you?

Ron Ayotte

JESUS IS MY LIFE

Christians, Hypocrisy, and Confession

After World War II, there was an intense rivalry between the United States and Russia, which led to the belief that communists and leftist sympathizers actively worked as spies inside the US, at the grassroots level, and even in Washington DC. As a result, a "red scare" swept across this nation. There was a saying, "I'd rather be dead than red." and quite naturally, a counter-revolution by those fearing nuclear expansion, who shot back, "I'd rather be red than dead."

Wouldn't you know, some things never change. The press, along with some senators, sensationalized the issue, and Hollywood jumped on the bandwagon as well. One popular TV show emerged in a weekly series, I Led Three Lives. It was based on the life of Herb Philbrick, an advertising executive who infiltrated a Brooklyn chapter of the communist party while working for the FBI.

The TV series loosely portrayed Philbrick's autobiography I Led 3 Lives. Over a 10-year period, he rose to become a top member of the New England chapter of the communist party, and he would feed the FBI info on the party's efforts in the US.

Philbrick was a family man, a spy, and an FBI informant.

Looking back at the series, I have been humbled by realizing I led three lives: a family man, an outdoorsman, and lastly, a Christian.

Dalene and I have had a wonderful life together. We raised two sons that have blossomed as husbands and fathers. I have no regrets.

I've spent countless hours in the field hunting, fishing, hiking, and camping and have made many long-lasting friendships. I have no regrets.

The day I accepted Christ as my personal savior is as real today as it was 68 years ago. If it wasn't for my church family, Grandma, Grandpa, Mom and Dad, all the friends and mentors alongside, I'm not sure where I would be today. I have no regrets.

Sharing my bio has been a lot of fun. Yes, many fond memories revisited, along with a few tears, but I've reached a crossroads.

I've spent hours in prayer. Hah! Actually, I've spent weeks wrestling with God, "Lord, do I 'hafta' share the shady side of my life?" I was truly hoping He would respond, "David, it's not that important. Just tell stories about hunting and fishing, and once in a while make reference to your faith in God."

Oh no. That DID NOT happen.

His message was clear. "David, you need to be true to yourself."

Growing up, there was a battle going on within my soul, and for that matter, the war continues to this very day.

There's a scene in the movie "Caddyshack" where Judge Smails (Elihu) confronts Danny Noonan. (Caddyshack has a relevant line for every one of life's situations, and this is no exception.)

Judge Smails: Danny, Danny, there's a lot of, uh, well, badness in the world today. I see it in court every day. I've sentenced boys younger than you to the gas chamber. Didn't wanna do it, but felt I owed it to them. The most important decision you can make right now is what you stand for, Goodness or Badness.

Danny Noonan: ……I wanna be Good.

And that's exactly what I WANT to be… Good.

But somehow, things don't always work out that way. Without a doubt, the biggest regrets in my life have been the times I felt the need to share my faith with others, especially close friends who have not made a commitment to Jesus Christ, but some of the known, sordid details in my life were a stumbling block.

When I've thought about sharing Jesus, I've stopped myself, expecting to hear:

"How can you talk to me about Jesus? I've been with you when…"

Mahatma Gandhi famously said, "I like your Christ; I do not like your Christians. Your Christians are so unlike your Christ."

The truth is, much as I despise this, my "walk" with Christ has not matched my talk. Do you think for one moment I would put a Christian fish symbol on my car? I speed. I can be impatient and blast my horn at others. I flash my lights if I was cut off. What would I say to someone who followed me into a parking lot, after noticing the fish symbol in the window, and asked, "You call yourself a Christian?"

And yet, I cannot - will not - deny the reality of what Christ has done in my life. I know I'm a sinner. ALL of us have sinned, as in every single one of us.

Romans 7:19 ~ For I do not do the good I want to do, but the evil I do not want to do, this I keep doing.

Let's take a look at that word "evil". I'm not a deep theologian, obviously, but it'd be good to understand what I mean here with this word. To me, in this verse, "evil" means wrong-doing, period. Bottom line ~ since the garden of Eden, we're all born with the knowledge of good and evil. Deep down, we all know what's right and what's wrong. In our society, we tend to make different levels of wrong, the worst kind being "evil". God doesn't look at it that way, but more on that later. For right now, let's just equate that biblical word "evil" with wrong-doing.

There is a never-ending battle in this lifetime between good intentions and actual actions.

I don't need to list all of my sordid past, but the 10 commandments have been ruptured; the least of which was digging too many razor clams or catching too many fish, and then lying to the game warden. Or drinking so much, when we stopped for more "refreshments", that mass quantities of cans rolled out of the truck onto the pavement. At the time, I perceived it as a badge of honor. Another story to tell the guys. Yet now I'm ashamed. Have I laughed at "dirty jokes"? Yes, and I've even told my share. Not proud of that either. I could go on and on, but I think you get the point.

When Sunday rolled around, there I was, back in church, teaching a Sunday school class and serving on the Deacon Board.

Sunday through Friday, I was the epitome of a solid Christian. A good father and husband. Prayer at family meals and week-night bible studies. I wasn't like Ward Clever from *Leave it to Beaver*, but the appearance of squeaky clean does come to mind, to those who didn't know all three of my lives that is.

When I accepted Christ, that was oh so easy. God spoke to me in such a real, compelling way, and I responded. As I got older, peer pressure and self-absorption crept into my being, and the "other" voice began lying to me: "How can it be wrong if no one knows? What's the harm?" Oh boy, does the flesh shout loud when it wants something, and it certainly can drown out the Holy Spirit.

I totally understand most people struggle with good vs. bad. Everyone has a conscience, but Christians can have an added measure of guilt feelings because we're supposed to be "good".

I am very much aware of letting many of my best friends down. I have not been the witness God intended.

This is where the rubber meets the road in leading the 3 lives. Christians are "supposed" to be different, to follow the Bible and the 10 commandments, and to not have 3 lives, but just 1 – a godly life. That's what most people think and suppose, and what I thought and supposed for most of my life. But I didn't live that way. I had my family life, and that merged with my church life. I had my outdoorsman life, and that merged with my family life. But mostly – except maybe on rare occasions – my Christian life and my outdoorsman life did NOT merge! And that's where, really, and honestly, and true-ly I've let down many of my best friends. That's where it can look like hypocrisy, and maybe in some ways was hypocritical, but hypocrisy was NEVER my intention. I was just living my life my way.

Part of the point of this whole book is to say now, plainly in black and white, that my life would have been better if I had NOT kept God and my Christian life in that box, separate, but actually let Him be God of my whole life. Some of your lives would likely have been better if I had done that. I can't fix the past now. I can't undo what was done, but my point here is this: PLEASE don't let my "failings" in that regard cause you to brush off or ignore what I want to share now about God with the excuse of "Dave's such a hypocrite!" I'm not. Wasn't ever my intention. Failed in some things, as we all have, and this is one of them, a big one. Again, don't let my failures keep you from hearing what I've learned, and what I want and need to share...

So, about Christianity, about God and you ~

Now some of you reading this are either gonna stop reading right here ~

but please don't, if our relationship matters at all, because this is important to me, Really Important, and I've never been able to get this out well in spoken words.

Or you're gonna say, "Now hang on here, Mills, I'm a good person!"

I'm not arguing with how you feel about yourself. It doesn't matter what we think or feel about ourselves.

There is a God – if you doubt that, read the section in this book about my "9 lives", which some of you were a witness to! Anyway, there Is a God, and at the end of all things, it's what He thinks about us that matters.

Here's the deal, as He says ~

... there is no one who does good, not even one... Romans Chapter 3:10

and

... for all have sinned... Romans 3:23

But!

Therefore, there is now no condemnation for those who are in Christ Jesus. Romans 8:1

Salvation is a gift. Only God can offer the gift of eternal life. I was called to proclaim the gospel, live it, share it, and pray for the salvation of others. Yes, I stumbled plenty along the way, but because of what Jesus has done, I am secure in the knowledge that God loves us all and has made a way for us to be not only clean in Him, but Loved!

John 3:16 For God so loved the world, that He gave His only begotten Son, that whosoever believes in Him shall not perish, but have everlasting life.

I know some of you feel you have reasons and causes to be mad at God, or that you've got good reasons for not believing Him or in Him. But just consider these 2 things:

If God loves us SO MUCH that He gave the life of His ONLY Son for our sakes, that's a powerful thing and at the very least shows that God is serious about meeting each and every one of us right where we are ~ angry with Him or disbelieving Him or whatever...

Also, even though things happen that we don't understand ~ even Really Hard things ~ God promises He'll make them all work out for good.

And we know that God causes all things to work together for good to those who love God, to those who are called according to His purpose. Romans 8:28

His ways aren't our ways... but it's impossible for God to lie ~ He really doesn't operate like we do...

Isaiah 55:8-9

For My thoughts are not your thoughts,
Nor are your ways My ways," declares the Lord.
For as the heavens are higher than the earth,
So are My ways higher than your ways
And My thoughts than your thoughts.

Even if we don't "get it" about what He's up to, we can be at peace because HE does.
(Notice I didn't say anywhere this is easy...)

And my most favorite two verses in all the bible, Ephesians 2:8-9 For by grace are ye saved through faith; and that not of yourselves: it is the gift of God, not of works, lest any man should boast.

God does it, not us.

And now the part that is hard:

Jesus says in John 14:6 ~ I am the Way, the Truth, and the Life, no one comes to the Father (God) except through Me.

It ain't popular, and it certainly isn't politically correct, but I'm really not doing right by any of you if I don't give you the whole truth. There's only one way to heaven, and that's God. There's only 1 way to God, and that's Jesus. We have so many voices telling us many different things... I'm asking you to simply believe that ALL your sins – past, present, and future - are forgiven through the blood of Jesus.

But remember this in closing, while you consider all this:

John 15:13 Greater love has no one than this, that one lay down his life for his friends.

That's what Jesus did for you because He loves you...

C. S. Lewis, in his book *Mere Christianity*, spoke to people in such a simple, easy-to-understand manner. "I am trying here to prevent anyone saying the really foolish thing that people often say about Him: I'm ready to accept Jesus as a great moral teacher, but I don't accept his claim to be God. That is the one thing we must not say. A man who was merely a man and said the sort of things Jesus said would not be a great moral teacher. He would either be a lunatic — on the level with the man who says he is a poached egg — or else he would be the Devil of Hell. You must make your choice. Either this man was, and is, the Son of God, or else a madman or something worse. You can shut him up for a fool, you can spit at him and kill him as a demon or you can fall at his feet and call him Lord and God, but let us not come with any patronizing nonsense about his being a great human teacher. He has not left that open to us. He did not intend to."

If you are struggling to commit to Christ, don't let those from your past who said you MUST do this or that to become a Christian stop you. Listen, there's only one requirement: Acts 16:31 spells it out so simply even I can understand it, "Believe in the Lord Jesus, and you will be saved, you and your household."

I'm not exactly sure where I read the following, but it meant a lot to me a few years ago, so I wrote it down; forgive me for not giving due credit*: "The devil has blinded the spiritual eyes of mankind to the simplicity of salvation and put it into the human heart that man must do something in order to be saved. And the stumbling stone? FAITH." To some, faith means countless things we have to do, and it even tinkers with man's efforts and emotions (feelings)." I've quoted it before because it is so powerful, so simple: Ephesians 2:8 "For by grace are ye saved through faith and that NOT OF YOURSELF, it is the GIFT of God... NOT of works." We are saved entirely by God's grace, a FREE gift, but we receive it by faith. All faith is, is BELIEVING! Faith in the word of God, not our feelings. Listen, Faith drives the engine, not our feelings, not our prayers, or anything we can do. TAKE HIM AT HIS WORD. YOU DO NOT NEED PROOF. GOD CANNOT LIE. WHEN HE SAID, "For God so loved the world He gave his only begotten son that whosoever believeth in Him shall not perish, but have everlasting life." (John 3:16) BELIEVE IT! BELIEVE HIM!!

{*Editor's note: From "What does it mean to believe on the Lord Jesus Christ?"
 ~ Mrs. Oliver B. Greene via www.cookfamilyhome.com/saved.htm}

EPILOGUE

In the final analysis, I've lived a life intensely personal yet fearful of projecting myself.

I lived a life of paranoia and self-doubt, yet with a hunger to be relevant.

It has been a pleasure to write about and relive some of my adventures, but I'm now starting a new chapter in my life. I find joy in watching my boys become devoted husbands and loving fathers.

The grandchildren? That is indescribable.

Hmmmm...

I leave you with a faith in Jesus Christ. Please keep it, use it, cherish it, and pass it on. My favorite song from Sunday school was, "This little light of mine, I'm gonna let it shine… Hide it under a bushel? NO!"

Tears? Yes. Laughter? Yes. Could I have done more? Certainly. Can't we all? But it was a great time in which to live, the best of all times for me.

What a life it has been, and guess what, it ain't over, and "it ain't over 'til I say it's over". For those of you old enough to remember the famous actor, comedian, singer, and pianist Jimmy Durante, "I've got a million of 'em". I haven't got another 76 years left to enjoy the life of those that surround me, but I'm gonna give it my best shot. I thought the hardest part of getting older was dealing with all my personal aches 'n' pains, but that pales in comparison to watching my friends pass away. Maybe that's a bit selfish? I'm not sure, but a void exists where once was a warm heart and fine fellowship.

Douglas, Derek, Mikey, Sophia, Davis, Conrad, Harrison, Jennifer, Susie, Tauna, you guys have the world at your fingertips. Embrace it, cling for all you are worth to the values that have made this country the greatest nation on earth.

Listen, freedom as I grew up with is utterly impossible without values from the Bible. Christianity is under attack. Churches have been forced to close as a matter of "public health". Come on, give me a break! That's simply a ruse, in my opinion. I'll leave it at that.

My life story never was intended to force anyone to believe in God. It didn't start out that way, but as I told these stories, it became obvious, Christ was with me all the way, all the time. He was there in every situation. I have no regrets, NONE, but I often wonder what would have happened had I been listening to the Holy Spirit. I'm sure you've heard it said a hundred times, "Oh how I wish I could go back to high school, knowing what I know now." Well, you can't. We can't. None of us can. So, give up on that idea.

Life's lessons are staring each of us in the face, learn from our past, and focus on what lies ahead. For most of us, and especially all you old-timers, remember the 1946 movie, "It's a Wonderful Life"? George Bailey, Jimmy Stewart, thought about ending it all on Christmas Eve, but Clarence Oddbody, an angel trying to gain his wings, showed George all the lives he has touched and how different life would be had he not been born.

Ok, I have never thought about jumping off a bridge or ending it all, but I've been given a GREAT gift also. With this writing, I've had an opportunity to see many lives I have touched. In some lives, the touch was not so good, and I apologize for that. Some were touched in a positive way, but I take no credit for that. God had His hand there. And then there are some for whom I still have a "vested" interest. I will never give up on the power of prayer. Listen, I pray you will come to realize the power Christ can have in YOUR life.

To all those that have contributed to my life and passed away, oh how I wish you were here so I could put my arms around you and say, "I love you!"

ACKNOWLEDGMENTS

In 2020 while the Covid-19 coronavirus spread around the world and really impacted the citizenry here in the United States, Dalene and I have spent most of our evenings at home playing games and watching movies. Before, we loved having friends over for dinner or a BBQ. Then we would finish the evening playing Mexican Train, Cribbage, Pinochle, or other such games. Being alone, we also found time (heaven forbid) to just have conversation. Well, one night, I asked Dalene, "Say, when do you think I actually started writing my bio?" It took us a while, but we figured, at the very least 4 years, then Dalene said, "Actually, the idea for your book came from Howard and Betty years and years ago." Howard has since passed away, but I will be eternally grateful to them, especially Betty, for her constant encouragement to write my life story. "David, you've got so many stories to tell; you need to write a book." How many times did I hear that one? A LOT!

A Christmas-time tradition: Betty Kubli and I making Swedish hardtack

Betty, Betty Kubli, we have been friends forever. Thank you, and I love you.

There comes a time when telling a story once just ain't enough, and I know I told this before, but it is so important.

There was a period when I just could not put "pen to paper". Actually, those "dry" moments happened several times over the course of four years, but this time I really was stuck in the mud. No matter how hard I tried, I was unable to write anything. Then one Sunday, while at church, I approached Pastor Grant Christensen for help. Pastor Grant and I had become close friends; he majored in English at Evergreen State College prior to seminary, and I knew he would be able to get me going. I could tell he was honored at being asked, but something deep within had him direct me to Jacquie Wagner. I thought it appropriate to ask Jacquie's husband Dean for permission. I started to describe my project and Dean said, "Oh, you need to talk to Jacs on this – she's a really good editor." Jacquie was busy at the time, so I stopped to talk with Dean and Jacquie's daughters, Naphtali and Allie, to see if they would help me get started. Funny how the Lord works, because all paths were leading to Jacquie, but I wasn't listening. Allie said, "Mom has a gift for writing. You should talk to her." I finally approached Jacquie and she asked me to print a sample of what I had accomplished so far and bring it to church for her to read, which by the way didn't take ANY persuasion. The next Sunday, after she had read what I had given her, she said with those inspiring words, "David, you have such a marvelous writing style." Jacquie lit a fire within me, and it has yet to burn out. She kept me going. She would not let me stagnate. Ok, I tried making excuses for not continuing, but she would say, "David, if nothing else works... write an outline!" and that worked, many times. I put my pen down time and again, asking the Lord to let me wrap this up, and He says, "Keep writing."

Jacquie, you and I know this hasn't been easy, but we have become a great team. JQ, we have become close friends and are truly brother and sister in Christ.

I love you. I also would like to thank the entire Wagner family for allowing me to steal Jacquie from y'all. Husband Dean for being patient with my lack of computer knowledge, son Deej, daughter Naphtali, and daughter Allie.

Thanks, guys.

Jacquie helping me with my autobiography

Well, that pretty much sums up those that helped and encouraged, or does it?

Dalene, I didn't forget you, and you know it. How could I have ever accomplished ANYTHING without your love? Would not have happened, and it's been that way ever since we met in Geology class at Olympic College in 1964, and it will be that way 'til the day I die.

Dalene, I love you. CHEERS!

ADDENDUM

Sharing my life story has truly been a joyful experience. Oh, there were plenty of challenges, and I wrestled with the Lord along the way about what I should or should not say. I battled tooth 'n' nail on some things and caved in on others. In the process, I LISTENED, I WAS LED, I FOLLOWED, and here we are.

I closed the story of my life on what I thought was a high note, expressing gratitude to those that helped me along the way, but now, January 6th, 2021, I find myself saddened to the very core of my being, torn between "Aw, David, leave it alone, let it be, just keep silent, it will be forgotten." and "NO! David, you NEED to speak out. This is such an historic moment in the United States of America, you CANNOT keep your mouth shut."

The question "What Happened to the America I Grew Up In..." cannot be more relevant. As Congress prepared to affirm President-Elect Joe Biden as the 46th president of the United States, thousands upon thousands of President Donald Trump supporters converged on Washington DC to protest the election results on claims of fraud.

People rallied in DC because Georgia, Michigan, Pennsylvania, and Wisconsin compromised the security and integrity of the election. Those states violated statutes enacted by their duly elected legislatures, thereby violating the constitution. Now, did President Trump receive enough votes to overturn the results in those states? That is NOT the issue! Those four states violated the United States constitution and "cumulatively preclude knowing who legitimately won the 2020 election and threaten to cloud all future elections." (Mark Levin)

Hundreds of people stormed and vandalized the capitol building, a US Capitol police officer died. One woman was fatally shot by police, and three people died of apparent medical emergencies. Several DC Metropolitan police officers were also injured during the violence. One officer had significant facial injuries after being struck by a projectile, and another was hospitalized after being pepper-sprayed.

Do I condone the violent action of a few that vandalized the capitol building on January 6th, 2021… NO I DO NOT!! And those people should be punished to the fullest extent of the law. I believe all rational Americans will agree with that.

I broke down in tears because blood was shed. I broke down in tears because I felt betrayed by the actions of a few. Let's be clear, it was a mere handful of idiots that caused the damage, but all Trump supporters will forever be painted with that broad brush of criminality.

I thought back to when I was a child - always standing and saluting our American Flag. I broke down in tears.

I reflected on my military service in the Marine Corps. How I raised my hand and took an oath to support the US constitution. I broke down in tears.

I saw a rioter enter the Senate Chamber waving a Christian flag. I saw another waving a banner saying "Jesus Saves". Others displayed banners that said, "Jesus is my savior, Trump is my President". Another said, "Proud American Christian". That is not the Christianity I embrace. I broke down in tears.

Let me be clear, what I saw was Un-American and had nothing to do with Christianity. It was a form of what has been labeled "Christian nationalism," which is a dangerous ideology that is starting to take root. It distorts the gospel of Jesus Christ and should be a wake-up call to all believers.

Personally, I need to adjust my set of values and put Christ first in my life, not patriotism, not love of flag. I admit it, guilty as charged! Yes, I still love this country; I will be an American Patriot 'til the day I die, that will never change, but I have placed far too much value on nationalism. Remember, this world is not my home. Jesus, in His sermon on the mount, said, "…lay not up for yourselves treasures upon earth, where moth and rust doth corrupt and where thieves break through and steal; but lay up for yourselves treasures in heaven…" (Matthew 6) That doesn't mean as a Christian I shouldn't give gifts, buy homes or save for retirement. So many misquote the bible and say, "money is the root of all evil" - NOT TRUE… it's the LOVE of money that corrupts. When a person experiences a "new birth" - a new life through believing in Jesus - their gift-giving is out of love, not duty, not guilt, but a love that came by the grace of God.

Our nation's Capitol building will be restored, Federal tax dollars will accomplish that, and "business as usual" will continue. What happened on January 6th, 2021, was sickening, but let us not have a case of amnesia over the unrest that occurred in major cities across this country during the summer of 2020. Families had loved ones murdered; their lives will never be the same. Who will restore the livelihoods of people whose businesses in Seattle, Portland, Atlanta, Minneapolis, and Philadelphia were destroyed due to arson and vandalism? There has been a constant barrage of pointing and outrage over the events of January 6th, 2021, but where is the outrage over the destruction of once-proud American cities brought to their knees because governors and mayors ordered police to "stand down"?

It's staggering to think my Triune God (God the Father, God the Son, God the Holy Spirit), maker of this universe, sent the Holy Spirit - which resides in me and is standing at the ready, willing to talk to me. A. W. Tozer wrote in *The Pursuit of God*, "He is omniscient, which means He knows in one free and effortless act, all matter, all spirit, all relationships, all events." God already sees the end result; all I need to do is back away from "self" and LISTEN. God is NOT dead. His words are ALIVE, and He leads us individually step by step. God is a personal God. I challenge you to surrender your life to Him and watch Him work.

As Christians in the United States of America, we have had it too easy and too good for too long. Now is the time to get a clear focus on what it means to be a "believer". Christians in the United States are being attacked by a disfunctional political system; therefore, do Christians have a moral and biblical obligation to participate in the democratic process? Some people say, why risk compromising our witness by getting involved in something so divisive? They continue with the notion politics is inherently corrupt and inappropriate for anyone serious about the gospel. Others say Christians need to be heavily involved because politics is so important; it is worth investing time and energy to educate the uninformed.

In my feeble attempt to put this issue in context, what does the bible say? In Romans 13:1-7, Paul describes the governing authorities as "ministers of God". He says they are responsible for administering civil justice and God, being sovereign, chooses human governments to carry out His will in the civil sphere.

Here's where I believe "we the people" are losing our footing in a republic like the United States. The government, which derives its authority from the people, has contaminated the ballot box. They have contaminated the media and our public school system.

While visiting the Ronald Reagan Presidential Library and Museum, I read newly-elected President Reagan's January 5th, 1981 inaugural address, and a portion of that speech is more important today than ever before:

"...This continuing fact that the people, by democratic process, can delegate power, and yet retain the custody of it. Perhaps you and I have lived too long with this miracle to properly be appreciative.

FREEDOM IS A FRAGILE THING, AND IT'S NEVER MORE THAN ONE GENERATION AWAY FROM EXTINCTION. IT IS NOT OURS BY WAY OF INHERITANCE; IT MUST BE FOUGHT FOR AND DEFENDED CONSTANTLY BY EACH GENERATION, FOR IT COMES ONLY ONCE TO A PEOPLE. AND THOSE IN WORLD HISTORY WHO HAVE KNOWN FREEDOM AND THEN LOST IT HAVE NEVER KNOWN IT AGAIN."

I fervently ask you to read that speech in its entirety. It will "rock your world."

Listen, stick with it; the tide will turn, and remember where our focus needs to rest. And don't forget to vote, and when you do, think biblically about moral issues, candidates, and party platforms.

APPENDIX

The Simple, Good Life

Cooking Life

I really enjoy cooking, yet I HATE baking. By now, does that surprise you? When I cook, it's a dash of this and a pinch of that, a touch of salt and a little pepper. I can simply "wing it". But when you bake, all ingredients have to be precise, no "wingin' it", and that ain't for me.

As noted in the Family Life – Grandparents section, my grandfather, Conrad George Mills, was a longtime fry cook in Bremerton and noted for his feats of strength. Every 4th of July, Grandpa would attach a rope to a city fire truck, grab the rope with his teeth, and pull it down Pacific Ave. He bent RR spikes in his bare hands and once, for his weight class, held the unofficial world record in the deadlift. I believe the cooking portion of his DNA was passed on to me. Hey, 1 outta 2 ain't bad.

Here are some of my favorite things to cook. I hope you try a few.

Smoked Salmon (Dry Brine)

¼ cup non-iodized salt
2 cups dark brown sugar
1 Tablespoon pepper
1 Tablespoon onion powder
1 Tablespoon celery salt

Mix all ingredients together. Cut salmon into fillet-sized pieces, leaving the skin on (I always de-scale a fish prior to brining). Rinse fillets in cold water. Pat dry and completely cover the fish with the brine mixture. Place in an aluminum tray, cover with saran wrap and chill in the fridge for 24 hours. Remove fish from tray, rinse under cold - water removing all of the brine, pat dry, and let it air dry for 2-3 hours. Bring smoker to 200 degrees and cook for approx. 2 to 3 hours. The smoke time really depends on the thickness of the fillets, so be careful not to over-cook. I prefer Alder or Apple wood chips and typically use no more than 2 pans' worth.

Wintertime is excellent for a pot roast, and for years I needed to use catsup on the meat, until I discovered the following:

Uncooked Ripe Tomato Relish (Much Better than catsup)

8 qts. fully ripe chopped tomatoes
1 Cup salt
2 cups chopped onions
1 cup chopped fresh celery
3 large green peppers, seeded and chopped (optional)
2 cups white sugar
1 cup mustard seed
3 cups pure white vinegar
2 tsp cinnamon
2 tsp ground clove

Mix tomatoes and salt. Drain for 12 hours. Add remaining ingredients. Seal cold, without cooking, in hot sterilized jars.

I have frozen the finished relish, and it turns out just fine. I use this relish just about everywhere in lieu of catsup.

Braised Oxtail

When Dalene and I were first married, all we could afford from the meat dept was hamburger. That was it. We lived next to the Food King on Bridgeport Way in Tacoma, WA and became good friends with the butcher. He took a likin' to us and said, "Why don't you kids try oxtail? They ain't bad!" Oxtail? Neither of us had even heard of oxtail, but we decided to give it a shot. I dredged them in seasoned flour, browned them, and then simmered them in beef stock for an hour or so. We thought it was great.

Oxtail was a cheaper cut of meat than burger and wasn't 'til years later I found out why. Oxtail was considered "soul food," and most people turned up their noses. Oh, how foolish! When oxtail was "discovered" by the white community, the cost per pound sky-rocketed. Now it's approximately $12/lb., if you're even lucky enough to find it.

Dalene and I ate oxtail for years and loved it, but then… my oh my, we "discovered" how the Spanish prepared oxtail. We were sittin' along a sidewalk café in Seville, Spain and about to order lunch. Dalene said, "David, check this out. They have oxtail on the menu; let's give it a try!" So, we did, and it was AWESOME. I mean mouth-watering delicious. Oh, so tender. Such flavor. After we ate, I asked the waiter if I could get the chef's recipe. His English was worse than my Spanish, so he left and returned with the manager, whose English was not much better, but we did manage to communicate, and he took me into the kitchen. What a beautiful kitchen. Spotless. The chef knew absolutely no English, but guess what, the dishwasher, who spoke perfect Spanish and English, said he would translate. Well, the chef told the dishwasher the recipe and asked for my e-mail account, would write it down, and send it to me. I thought to myself, "What-ever, I'll never see that recipe, but what an experience anyhow."

Well, lo and behold, three days later I got a text from the dishwasher with the recipe. When we returned home, I sent a thank you gift to the dishwasher.

Oxtail requires a lot of TLC, but it's worth it. I hope you enjoy it as much as we.

Steam the oxtail in equal portions of water, beef stock, and a cup of avocado oil (enough to cover) for about an hour. Remove oxtail and simmer in a mixture of:

½ cup sugar
1/8th cup salt
4 cups water
½ bottle Pedro Ximenez port wine (save remaining half for sippin› during the meal)

Simmer for approx. 3 hrs. When complete, you might desire to add a touch of sugar for taste... I do.

Serve with Yukon Gold potatoes or rice (we drizzle the reduced mixture over the spuds/rice).

NOTE: Pedro Ximenez is a velvety smooth sherry from the 180-year-old Gonzales-Byass family in Jerez, Spain. If unable to find Ximenez, pick a quality sherry.

Pickled Salmon

I got this recipe from a good friend I met while commercial salmon fishing at Westport, Washington. His mother would pickle Ken's left-over herring, which never quite worked for me, so I tried pickling salmon, and oh boy, is it yummy. Again, this recipe requires considerable TLC, but if you have a touch of Norwegian in ya, you'll love it.

Fillet the salmon and remove the skin. Cut into 1-2" wide strips.

Brine:
4 cups Water
1 cup Salt (non-iodized)

Pickling Mixture:
2 cups White Vinegar
1 cup water
1 cup granulate white sugar
3 Tablespoons Pickling spices.

Cover fillets with brine mixture and soak in the fridge for 24 hours. Remove from fridge, drain, and thoroughly rinse in cold water. Pour pure white vinegar over the fillets and soak for 24 in the fridge. Remove from fridge, drain, and thoroughly rinse in cold water.

Simmer pickling mix 10 to 15 minutes and allow to cool completely, then add fillets and as many sliced onions as possible to the pot. Place in fridge and will be ready to eat in 12 hours.

Keep this a secret from your Swedish friends because once they find out, it won't last long.

Wild Mushroom Soup

During the Fall, I pick a lot of wild mushrooms. I use quite a few in spaghetti sauce and in scrambled eggs. Then our daughter-in-law Jennifer gave me this soup recipe and it's wonderful. Please, give it a try.

2 pkgs long grain wild rice
2 tablespoons butter
2 small garlic gloves (minced)
4 large shallots (minced)
1 tsp thyme
2 bay leaves
3 tablespoons flour
10 cups chicken stock
2 cups heavy cream
Salt/pepper to taste
Sherry
Lemon Juice

In a 4 qt. saucepan melt the butter, add the garlic, shallots and sauté 'til translucent. Fill pan with mushrooms (dice if needed), thyme, and bay leaf. Continue to sauté 'til mushrooms have released liquid and some has evaporated. Gradually add flour, whisking to make smooth, and cook a couple minutes without boiling. Add rice, chicken stock, and bring to a full boil, then simmer. When rice is done, add cream, remove bay leaves, salt 'n' pepper to taste, and add a few drops of lemon juice. Slow boil for 5 minutes max. Serve with French bread and sherry.

Here's a bit of trivia regarding the seemingly lowly bay leaf. The bay leaf, a perennial shrub with spearheaded leaves, is indigenous to the Mediterranean region. Early Greeks and Romans associated the bay laurel with Apollo. It was a symbol of victory. Heroes were crowned with wreaths of laurel. That's why people are advised not to "rest on their laurels. Ok, enjoy the soup.

BBQ Salmon

Let me finish with BBQ'd salmon.

It just wouldn't be a summer-time BBQ at the Mills' home and not have salmon on the grill. Growing up in the '40s, '50s, and early '60s people over-cooked everything, and I was no exception. It wasn't until the early '80s I found out how to cook fish and boy, what a difference that made ~ from dry and requiring a lot of tartar sauce to moist and full of flavor. The secret? Remove the fish ~ cod, salmon, halibut ~ makes no difference. Hot, fast, and get that fish off the grill when it's still a touch raw in the middle. When it arrives at the table and on the plate, it will be perfect.

BBQ salmon is not all that tricky, but timing is everything, and keep it simple. Some people prefer Chinook for grillin', but I lean toward Coho. Here are couple options ~

Foil-Wrapped:
Preheat the grill to 400–450 degrees. Place the fillet on a long sheet of heavy-duty foil, enough to fold over the top creating a tent. Drizzle olive oil over the full length of the fish using a light brush. Sprinkle with Johnny's seasoning salt, garlic powder, freshly chopped basil, parsley, and lemon zest. Lay lemon slices on top, then wrap it up. Cook 10 – 15 minutes. THAT'S IT! The amount of seasoning is your individual taste and time can vary based on the size of the fish.

Cedar Plank:
Grilling salmon on the plank became a game-changer for me. I'll buy an 8' long x ¾" thick x 6" wide plank from Home Depot and cut to suit. Soak the plank under a mixture of 50% water and apple cider for several hours. Preheat the grill to 400–450 degrees. Place the water-logged plank on the grill; when it begins to smoke and lightly char, flip it over, remove from the grill, and place the seasoned fillet, skin side down, on the non-charred side, then cook on medium to high heat for 10-12 minutes. Season like the foil-wrapped fish, and remember ~ timing is everything.

Final Thoughts on Food

I always cook crab fresh, whole, and in seawater.

I love oysters: raw, fried, or off the BarB. No bacon, no butter, just plain.

Red wine with seafood is just fine; it doesn't have to be white.

My favorite breakfast cereal? Bite-size Frosted Mini-wheats with wild huckleberries.

While hunting or fishing, my favorite drink is … Hot Tomato Soup.

I'm not much for booze, but I enjoy a cold beer on a hot summer day.

Reading Life

Great Reads (In No Particular Order)

Nonfiction

Unbroken, Laura Hillenbrand

Boys in the Boat, Daniel James Brown

In His Grip, Jim Sheard & Wally Armstrong, intro by Billy Graham

The Devil's Delusion, David Berlinski

Wasa Wasa, Harry MacFie

Wild at Heart, John Eldredge

A Torch Kept Lit, William F Buckley, Jr.

My Utmost for His Highest, Oswald Chambers

Dupes, Paul Kengor

The Jesus I Never Knew, Philip Yancey

Oh, There Are a Couple Fiction Books I've Read

I read the first book of the Harry Potter series only because I was held captive on an airplane to Hawaii.

The Da Vinci Code, Dan Brown

The Adventures of Huckleberry Finn, Mark Twain

The Old Man and the Sea, Ernest Hemmingway

The Lion, The Witch, and The Wardrobe, C. S. Lewis

Some quotes I love, 'though I can't remember where they're from (but my editor looked them up):

"Age is a high price to pay for maturity." ~ Tom Stoppard

"I can remember when the air was clean and sex was dirty." ~ George Burns

"The hardest thing in life is knowing which bridge to cross and which to burn." ~ David Russell

My Bucket List

It has been one heck of a wet, cold, miserable winter, with very little time to enjoy the outdoors. I've even caught myself turning around, going back to my recliner because the few steps from the laundry room to do some woodworking in the garage would have required far too much rain gear. So here I sit, watching flyfishing adventures in New Zealand, Norway, and far corners of the world on... YOUTUBE.

So, I sat in my easy chair thinking, "Am I really ready to cash in my chips? Lean back and 'drool' the rest of my life away?" No way! Ain't gonna happen! "But why should all these young guys, on YouTube, have all the fun and Literally rub it in my face. I need to put together a bucket list."

It was then I realized I may have one foot in the grave, but God is not finished with me. The Holy Spirit told me, "Go ahead, Mills, enjoy more of the outdoors, but I've got a few more doors that will open to you, just keep your eyes and ears open."

Now the phrase "bucket list" is a relatively new one. It comes from "kick the bucket" (to die). Then you add the word "List" (things to do before you die). It was really popularized by a movie of the same name starring Jack Nicholson and Morgan Freeman. Billionaire Edward Cole (Jack Nicholson) and car mechanic Carter Chambers (Morgan Freeman), complete strangers, find themselves in the same hospital room and find out they have two things in common: a need to come to terms with who they are and what they have done with their lives.

Come to terms with who THEY are? What they have done with THEIR lives? OH MY! If you don't think that didn't hit me square in the kisser, you better think again, because it certainly did.

I must confess, probably for the umpteenth time, my "bio" was just gonna be stories about hunting, fishing, and a few tidbits here and there, but boy-oh-boy did the Lord have other plans and would not let go. Writing my autobiography truly brought ME to "grips" with how God dealt with me all my life, but I didn't know it.

The bucket list was to be about MY dreams, but He told me, "David, there's something much bigger you need to share."

In the back of, ok, in the forefront of my mind, I've always had a bit of a list, and sometimes it appeared that Christians were not having as much fun as their secular counterparts, which is really a strange way of looking at things, because I've been handed the most beautiful list anyone could ever hope for. Jesus has completely secured my life in the hands of Almighty God.

Listen, I know what it's like being raised under a critical eye. My early church experience was like walking on eggshells, but boy-oh-boy am I thankful for being introduced to "grace"! I'm no longer going to waste time hoping to check off everything on my list, but live thanking God daily for the rich, full life I have been given.

Now, all that being said, and it truly came from my heart, let's enjoy the moment, shall we?

Do you have a bucket list? I know my wife, Dalene, has one. She wants to travel. She REALLY wants to go on a riverboat cruise.

Here's my "wish" list:

1. A Notre Dame or Michigan home football game.

2. Flyfish New Zealand or Norway.

3. Return to Alaska. Of course, go fishing.

4. Float the Kamchatka River in Russia

5. Visit Santorini in Greece

6. Tour Niagara Falls and the Statue of Liberty

7. And Finally. More than importantly than anything, I always want to be there for my grandchildren.

Now, that wasn't so bad. Was it?